RED ROONEY

A Tale of Eskimo (Innuit) Life in Greenland at the end of the Eighteenth Century.

R. M. BALLANTYNE

1ˢᵗ WORLD
LIBRARY
Literary Society

Red Rooney

R. M. Ballantyne

© 1st World Library, 2007
PO Box 2211
Fairfield, IA 52556
www.1stworldlibrary.com
First Edition

LCCN: 2007934200

Softcover ISBN: 978-1-4218-9672-4
Hardcover ISBN: 978-1-4218-9772-1
eBook ISBN: 978-1-4218-9572-7

Purchase *"Red Rooney"*
as a traditional bound book at:
www.1stWorldLibrary.com/purchase.asp?ISBN=978-1-4218-9672-4

1st World Library is a literary, educational organization
dedicated to:

- Creating a free internet library of downloadable ebooks

- Hosting writing competitions and offering book publishing
scholarships.

Interested in more 1st World Library books? contact:
literacy@1stworldlibrary.com
Check us out at: www.1stworldlibrary.com

1ˢᵗ World Library Literary Society

Giving Back to the World

"If you want to work on the core problem, it's early school literacy."

- James Barksdale, former CEO of Netscape

"No skill is more crucial to the future of a child, or to a democratic and prosperous society, than literacy."

- Los Angeles Times

"Literacy... means far more than learning how to read and write... The aim is to transmit... knowledge and promote social participation."

- UNESCO

"Literacy is not a luxury, it is a right and a responsibility. If our world is to meet the challenges of the twenty-first century we must harness the energy and creativity of all our citizens."

- President Bill Clinton

"Parents should be encouraged to read to their children, and teachers should be equipped with all available techniques for teaching literacy, so the varying needs and capacities of individual kids can be taken into account."

- Hugh Mackay

CHAPTER ONE

THE LAST OF THE CREW

LOST AND FOUND

There is a particular spot in those wild regions which lie somewhere near the northern parts of Baffin's Bay, where Nature seems to have set up her workshop for the manufacture of icebergs, where Polar bears, in company with seals and Greenland whales, are wont to gambol, and where the family of Jack Frost may be said to have taken permanent possession of the land.

One winter day, in the early part of the eighteenth century, a solitary man might have been seen in that neighbourhood, travelling on foot over the frozen sea in a staggering, stumbling, hurried manner, as if his powers, though not his will, were exhausted.

The man's hairy garb of grey sealskin might have suggested that he was a denizen of those northern wilds, had not the colour of his face, his brown locks, and his bushy beard, betokened him a native of a very different region.

Although possessing a broad and stalwart frame, his movements indicated, as we have said, excessive weakness.

A morsel of ice in his path, that would have been no impediment even to a child, caused him to stumble. Recovering himself, with an evidently painful effort, he continued to advance with quick, yet wavering steps. There was, however, a strange mixture of determination with his feebleness. Energy and despair seemed to be conjoined in his look and action—and no wonder, for Red Rooney, although brave and resolute by nature, was alone in that Arctic wilderness, and reduced to nearly the last extremity by fatigue and famine. For some days—how many he scarcely remembered—he had maintained life by chewing a bit of raw sealskin as he travelled over the frozen waste; but this source of strength had at last been consumed, and he was now sinking from absolute want.

The indomitable spirit of the man, however, kept his weakened body moving, even after the mind had begun to sink into that dreamy, lethargic state which is said to indicate the immediate approach of death, and there was still a red spot in each of his pale and hollow cheeks, as well as an eager gleam of hope in his sunken eyes; for the purpose that Red Rooney had in view was to reach the land.

It was indeed a miserably faint hope that urged the poor fellow on, for the desolate shore of Western Greenland offered little better prospect of shelter than did the ice-clad sea; but, as in the case of the drowning man, he clutched at this miserable straw of hope, and held on for life. There was the bare possibility that some of the migratory Eskimos might be there, or, if not, that some scraps of their food— some bits of refuse, even a few bones—might be found. Death, he felt, was quickly closing with him on the sea. The great enemy might, perhaps, be fought with and kept at bay for a time if he could only reach the land.

Encouraging himself with such thoughts, he pushed on, but

again stumbled and fell—this time at full length. He lay quiet for a few seconds. It was so inexpressibly sweet to *rest*, and feel the worn-out senses floating away, as it were, into dreamland! But the strong will burst the tightening bands of death, and, rising once more, with the exclamation, "God help me!" he resumed his weary march.

All around him the great ocean was covered with its coat of solid, unbroken ice; for although winter was past, and the sun of early spring was at the time gleaming on bergs that raised their battlements and pinnacles into a bright blue sky, the hoary king of the far north refused as yet to resign his sceptre and submit to the interregnum of the genial sun.

A large hummock or ridge of ice lay in front of the man, blocking his view of the horizon in that direction. It had probably been heaved up by one of the convulsions of the previous autumn, and was broken into a chaotic mass. Here he stopped and looked up, with a sigh. But the sinking of the heart was momentary. Deep snow had so filled up the crevices of the shattered blocks that it was possible to advance slowly by winding in and out among them. As the ascent grew steeper the forlorn man dropped on all-fours and crawled upwards until he reached the top.

The view that burst upon him would have roused enthusiasm if his situation had been less critical. Even as it was, an exclamation of surprise broke from him, for there, not five miles distant, was the coast of Greenland; desolate, indeed, and ice-bound—he had expected that—but inexpressibly grand even in its desolation. A mighty tongue of a great glacier protruded itself into the frozen sea. The tip of this tongue had been broken off, and the edge presented a gigantic wall of crystal several hundred feet high, on which the sun glittered in blinding rays.

This tongue—a mere offshoot of the great glacier itself—filled a valley full ten miles in length, measuring from its tip in the ocean to its root on the mountain brow, where the snow-line was seen to cut sharply against the sky.

For some minutes Red Rooney sat on one of the ice-blocks, gazing with intense eagerness along the shore, in the hope of discerning smoke or some other evidence of man's presence. But nothing met his disappointed gaze save the same uniform, interminable waste of white and grey, with here and there a few dark frowning patches where the cliffs were too precipitous to sustain the snow.

Another despairing sigh rose to the man's lips, but these refused to give it passage. With stern resolve he arose and stumbled hurriedly forward. The strain, however, proved too great. On reaching the level ice on the other side of the ridge he fell, apparently for the last time, and lay perfectly still. Ah! how many must have fallen thus, to rise no more, since men first began to search out the secrets of that grand mysterious region!

But Red Rooney was not doomed to be among those who have perished there. Not far from the spot where he fell, one of the short but muscular and hairy-robed denizens of that country was busily engaged in removing the skin from a Polar bear which he had just succeeded in spearing, after a combat which very nearly cost him his life. During the heat of the battle the brave little man's foot had slipped, and the desperately wounded monster, making a rush at the moment, overturned him into a crevice between two ice-blocks, fortunately the impetus of the rush caused the animal to shoot into another crevice beyond, and the man, proving more active than the bear, sprang out of his hole in time to meet his foe with a spear-thrust so deadly that it killed him on the spot. Immediately he began to skin the animal,

R. M. Ballantyne

intending to go home with the skin, and return with a team of dogs for the meat and the carcass of a recently-caught seal.

Meanwhile, having removed and packed up the bear-skin, he swung it on his broad shoulders, and made for the shore as fast as his short legs would carry him. On the way he came to the spot where the fallen traveller lay.

His first act was to open his eyes to the uttermost, and, considering the small, twinkling appearance of those eyes just a minute before, the change was marvellous.

"Hoi!" then burst from him with tremendous emphasis, after which he dropped his bundle, turned poor Rooney over on his back, and looked at his face with an expression of awe.

"Dead!" said the Eskimo, under his breath—in his own tongue, of course, not in English, of which, we need scarcely add, he knew nothing.

After feeling the man's breast, under his coat, for a few seconds, he murmured the word "Kablunet" (foreigner), and shook his head mournfully.

It was not so much grief for the man's fate that agitated this child of the northern wilderness, as regret at his own bad fortune. Marvellous were the reports which from the south of Greenland had reached him, in his far northern home, of the strange Kablunets or foreigners who had arrived there to trade with the Eskimos—men who, so the reports went, wore smooth coats without hair, little round things on their heads instead of hoods, and flapping things on their legs instead of sealskin boots—men who had come in monster kayaks (canoes), as big as icebergs; men who seemed to possess everything, had the power to do anything, and feared nothing. No fabrications in the *Arabian Nights*, or *Gulliver*, or *Baron Munchausen*, ever transcended the stories about those Kablunets which had reached this broad, short, sturdy Eskimo—stories which no doubt began in the south of Greenland with a substratum of truth, but which, in travelling several hundreds of miles northward, had grown, as a snowball might have grown if rolled the same distance over the Arctic wastes; with this difference—that whereas the snowball would have retained its original shape, though not its size, the tales lost not only their pristine form and size, but became so amazingly distorted that the original reporters would probably have failed to recognise them. And now, at last, here was actually a Kablunet—a *real* foreigner in the body; but not alive! It was extremely disappointing!

Our sturdy Eskimo, however, was not a good judge of Kablunet vitality. He was yet rubbing the man's broad chest, with a sort of pathetic pity, when a flutter of the heart startled him. He rubbed with more vigour. He became excited, and, seizing Red Rooney by the arms, shook him with considerable violence, the result being that the foreigner opened his eyes and looked at him inquiringly.

"Hallo, my lad," said Rooney, in a faint voice; "not quite so hard. I'm all right. Just help me up, like a good fellow."

He spoke in English, which was, of course, a waste of breath in the circumstances. In proof of his being "all right," he fell back again, and fainted away.

The Eskimo leaped up. He was one of those energetic beings who seem to know in all emergencies what is best to be done, and do it promptly. Unrolling the bear-skin, which yet retained a little of its first owner's warmth, he wrapped the Kablunet in it from head to foot, leaving an opening in front of his mouth for breathing purposes. With his knife—a stone one—he cut off a little lump of blubber from the seal, and placed that in the opening, so that the stranger might eat on reviving, if so inclined, or let it alone, if so disposed. Then, turning his face towards the land, he scurried away over the ice like a hunted partridge, or a hairy ball driven before an Arctic breeze.

He made such good use of his short legs that in less than an hour he reached a little hut, which seemed to nestle under the wing of a great cliff in order to avoid destruction by the glittering walls of an impending glacier. The hut had no proper doorway, but a tunnel-shaped entrance, about three feet high and several feet long. Falling on his knees, the Eskimo crept into the tunnel and disappeared. Gaining the inner end of it, he stood up and glared, speechless, at his astonished wife.

She had cause for surprise, for never since their wedding-day had Nuna beheld such an expression on the fat face of her amiable husband.

"Okiok," she said, "have you seen an evil spirit?"

"No," he replied.

"Why, then, do you glare?"

Of course Nuna spoke in choice Eskimo, which we render into English with as much fidelity to the native idiom as seems consistent with the agreeable narration of our tale.

"Hoi!" exclaimed Okiok, in reply to her question, but without ceasing to glare and breathe hard.

"Has my husband become a walrus, that he can only shout and snort?" inquired Nuna, with the slightest possible twinkle in her eyes, as she raised herself out of the lamp-smoke, and laid down the stick with which she had been stirring the contents of a stone pot.

Instead of answering the question, Okiok turned to two chubby and staring youths, of about fifteen and sixteen respectively, who were mending spears, and said sharply, "Norrak, Ermigit, go, harness the dogs."

Norrak rose with a bound, and dived into the tunnel. Ermigit, although willing enough, was not quite so sharp. As he crawled into the tunnel and was disappearing, his father sent his foot in the same direction, and, having thus intimated the necessity for urgent haste, he turned again to his wife with a somewhat softened expression.

"Give me food, Nuna. Little food has passed into me since yesterday at sunrise. I starve. When I have eaten, you shall hear words that will make you dream for a moon. I have seen,"—he became solemn at this point, and lowered his voice to a whisper as he advanced his head and glared again—"I have seen a—a—Kablunet!"

He drew back and gazed at his wife as connoisseurs are wont to do when examining a picture. And truly Nuna's countenance *was* a picture-round, fat, comely, oily, also open-mouthed and eyed, with unbounded astonishment depicted thereon; for she thoroughly believed her husband, knowing that he was upright and never told lies.

Her mental condition did not, however, interfere with her duties. A wooden slab or plate, laden with a mess of broiled meat, soon smoked before her lord. He quickly seated himself on a raised platform, and had done some justice to it before Nuna recovered the use of her tongue.

"A Kablunet!" she exclaimed, almost solemnly. "Is he dead?"

Okiok paused, with a lump of blubber in his fingers close to his mouth.

"No; he is alive. At least he was alive when I left him. If he has not died since, he is alive still."

Having uttered this truism, he thrust the blubber well home, and continued his meal.

Nuna's curiosity, having been aroused, was not easily allayed. She sat down beside her spouse, and plied him with numerous questions, to which Okiok gave her brief and very tantalising replies until he was gorged, when, throwing down the platter, he turned abruptly to his wife, and said impressively—

"Open your ears, Nuna. Okiok is no longer what he was. He has been born only to-day. He has at last seen with his two eyes—a Kablunet!"

He paused to restrain his excitement. His wife clasped her hands and looked at him excitedly, waiting for more.

"This Kablunet," he continued, "is very white, and not so ruddy as we have been told they are. His hair is brown, and twists in little circles. He wears it on the top of his head, and on the bottom of his head also—all round. He is not small or short. No; he is long and broad,—but he is thin, very thin, like the young ice at the beginning of winter. His eyes are the colour of the summer sky. His nose is like the eagle's beak, but not so long. His mouth—I know not what his mouth is like; it is hid in a nest of hair. His words I understand not. They seem to me nonsense, but his voice is soft and deep."

"And his dress—how does he dress?" asked Nuna, with natural feminine curiosity.

"Like ourselves," replied Okiok, with a touch of disappointment in his tone. "The men who said the Kablunets wear strange things on their heads and long flapping things on their legs told lies."

"Why did you not bring him here?" asked Nuna, after a few moments' meditation on these marvels.

"Because he is too heavy to lift, and too weak to walk. He has been starving. I wrapped him in the skin of a bear, and left him with a piece of blubber at his nose. When he wakes up he will smell; then he will eat. Perhaps he will live; perhaps he will die. Who can tell? I go to fetch him."

As the Eskimo spoke, the yelping of dogs outside told that his sons had obeyed his commands, and got ready the sledge. Without another word he crept out of the hut and jumped on the sledge, which was covered with two or three warm bearskins. Ermigit restrained the dogs, of which there were about eight, each fastened to the vehicle by a single line. Norrak handed his father the short-handled but heavy, long-lashed whip.

Okiok looked at Norrak as he grasped the instrument of punishment.

"Jump on," he said.

Norrak did so with evident good-will. The whip flashed in the air with a serpentine swing, and went off like a pistol. The dogs yelled in alarm, and, springing away at full speed, were soon lost among the hummocks of the Arctic sea.

CHAPTER TWO

DESCRIBES A RESCUE AND A HAPPY FAMILY

While the Eskimos were thus rushing to his rescue, poor Red Rooney—whose shipmates, we may explain at once, had thus contracted his Christian name of Reginald—began to recover from his swoon, and to wonder in a listless fashion where he was. Feeling comparatively comfortable in his bear-skin, he did not at first care to press the inquiry; but, as Okiok had anticipated, the peculiar smell near his nose tended to arouse him. Drawing his hand gently up, he touched the object in front of his mouth. It felt very like blubber, with which substance he was familiar. Extending his tongue, he found that it also tasted like blubber. To a starving man this was enough. He pulled the end of the raw morsel into his mouth and began to chew.

Ah, reader, turn not up your refined nose! When you have been for several months on short allowance, when you have scraped every shred of meat off the very last bones of your provisions, and sucked out the last drop of marrow, and then roasted and eaten your spare boots, you may perhaps be in a position to estimate and enjoy a morsel of raw blubber.

Regardless of time, place, and circumstance, our poor wanderer continued to chew until in his great weakness he fell into a sort of half slumber, and dreamed—dreamed of feasting on viands more delightful than the waking imagination of man has ever conceived.

From this state of bliss he was rudely awakened by a roughish poke in the back. The poke was accompanied by a snuffing sound which caused the blood of the poor man to curdle. Could it be a bear?

He was not left long in doubt. After giving him another poke on the shoulder, the creature walked round him, snuffing as it went, and, on reaching the air-hole already referred to, thrust its snout in and snorted. Rooney turned his face aside to avoid the blast, but otherwise lay quite still, knowing well that whatever animal his visitor might be, his only hope lay in absolute inaction. Venturing in a few seconds to turn his face round and peep through the opening, he found that the animal was in very deed a large white bear, which, having found and abstracted the remains of the blubber he had been chewing, was at that moment licking its lips after swallowing it. Of course, finding the morsel satisfactory, the bear returned to the hole for more.

It is easier to conceive than to describe the poor man's feelings at that moment, therefore we leave the reader to conceive them. The natural and desperate tendency to spring up and defend himself had to be combated by the certain knowledge that, encased as he was, he could not spring up, and had nothing wherewith to defend himself except his fingers, which were no match for the claws of a Polar bear.

The blood which a moment before had begun apparently to curdle, now seemed turned into liquid fire; and when the snout again entered and touched his own, he could contain himself no longer, but gave vent to a yell, which caused the startled bear to draw sharply back in alarm. Probably it had

R. M. Ballantyne

never heard a yell through the medium of its nose before, and every one must know how strong is the influence of a new sensation. For some minutes the monster stood in silent contemplation of the mysterious hole. Rooney of course lay perfectly still. The success of his involuntary explosion encouraged hope.

What the bear might have done next we cannot tell, for at that moment a shout was heard. It was followed by what seemed a succession of pistol shots and the howling of dogs. It was the arrival of Okiok on the scene with his sledge and team.

Never was an arrival more opportune. The bear looked round with a distinct expression of indignation on his countenance. Possibly the voice of Okiok was familiar to him. It may be that relations or friends of that bear had mysteriously disappeared after the sounding of that voice. Perhaps the animal in whose skin Rooney was encased had been a brother. At all events, the increasing hullabaloo of the approaching Eskimo had the effect of intimidating the animal, for it retired quickly, though with evident sulkiness, from the scene.

A few seconds more, and Okiok dashed up, leaped from his vehicle, left the panting team to the control of Norrak, and ran eagerly to the prostrate figure. Unwrapping the head so as to set it free, the Eskimo saw with intense satisfaction that the Kablunet was still alive. He called at once to Norrak, who fetched from the sledge a platter made of a seal's shoulder-blade, on which was a mass of cooked food. This he presented to the starving man, who, with a look of intense gratitude, but with no words, eagerly ate it up. The Eskimo and his son meanwhile stood looking at him with an expression of mingled interest, awe, and surprise on their round faces.

When the meal was ended, Red Rooney, heaving a deep sigh of satisfaction, said, "Thank God, and thank *you*, my friends!"

There was reason for the increase of surprise with which this was received by the two natives, for this time the foreigner spoke to them in their own language.

"Is the Kablunet a messenger from heaven," asked Okiok, with increased solemnity, "that he speaks with the tongue of the Innuit?"

"No, my friend," replied Rooney, with a faint smile; "I bring no message either from heaven or anywhere else. I'm only a wrecked seaman. But, after a fashion, you are messengers from heaven to *me*, and the message you bring is that I'm not to die just yet. If it had not been for you, my friends, it strikes me I should have been dead by this time. As to my speaking your lingo, it's no mystery. I've learned it by livin' a long time wi' the traders in the south of Greenland, and I suppose I've got a sort o' talent that way; d'ye see?"

Red Rooney delivered these remarks fluently in a curious sort of Eskimo language; but we have rendered it into that kind of English which the wrecked seaman was in the habit of using—chiefly because by so doing we shall give the reader a more correct idea of the character of the man.

"We are very glad to see you," returned Okiok. "We have heard of you for many moons. We have wished for you very hard. Now you have come, we will treat you well."

"Are your huts far off?" asked the seaman anxiously.

"Not far. They are close to the ice-mountain—on the land."

"Take me to them, then, like a good fellow, for I'm dead-beat, and stand much in need of rest."

The poor man was so helpless that he could not walk to the sledge when they unrolled him. It seemed as if his power of will and energy had collapsed at the very moment of his rescue. Up to that time the fear of death had urged him on, but now, feeling that he was, comparatively speaking, safe, he gave way to the languor which had so long oppressed him, and thus, the impulse of the will being removed, he suddenly became as helpless as an infant.

Seeing his condition, the father and son lifted him on the sledge, wrapped him in skins, and drove back to the huts at full speed.

Nuna was awaiting them outside, with eager eyes and beating heart, for the discovery of a real live Kablunet was to her an object of as solemn and anxious curiosity as the finding of a veritable living ghost might be to a civilised man. But Nuna was not alone. There were two other members of the household present, who had been absent when Okiok first arrived, and whom we will now introduce to the reader.

One was Nuna's only daughter, an exceedingly pretty girl—according to Eskimo notions of female beauty. She was seventeen years of age, black-eyed, healthily-complexioned, round-faced, sweet-expressioned, comfortably stout, and unusually graceful—for an Eskimo. Among her other charms, modesty and good-nature shone conspicuous. She was in all respects a superior counterpart of her mother, and her name was Nunaga. Nuna was small, Nunaga was smaller. Nuna was comparatively young, Nunaga was necessarily younger. The former was kind, the latter was kinder. The mother was graceful and pretty, the daughter was more graceful and prettier. Nuna wore her hair gathered on the top of her head into a high top-knot, Nunaga wore a higher top-knot. In regard to costume, Nuna wore sealskin boots the whole length of her legs—which were not long—and a frock or skirt reaching nearly to her knees, with a short tail in front and a long tail behind; Nunaga, being similarly clothed, had a shorter tail in front and a longer tail behind.

It may be interesting to note here that Eskimos are sometimes named because of qualities possessed, or appearance, or peculiar circumstances connected with them. The word Nuna signifies "land" in Eskimo. We cannot tell why this particular lady was named Land, unless it were that she was born on the land, and not on the ice; or perhaps because she was so nice that when any man came into her company he might have thought that he had reached the land of his hopes, and was disposed to settle down there and remain. Certainly many of the Eskimo young men seemed to be of that mind until Okiok carried her off in triumph. And let us tell you, reader, that a good and pretty woman is as much esteemed among the Eskimos as among ourselves. We do not say that she is better treated; neither do we hint that she is sometimes treated worse.

The Eskimo word Nunaga signifies "*my* land," and was bestowed by Okiok on his eldest-born in a flood of tenderness at her birth.

Apologising for this philological digression, we proceed. Besides Nuna and Nunaga there was a baby boy—a fat, oily, contented boy—without a name at that time, and without a particle of clothing of any sort, his proper condition of heat being maintained when out of doors chiefly by being carried between his mother's dress and her shoulders; also by being stuffed to repletion with blubber.

R. M. Ballantyne

The whole family cried out vigorously with delight, in various keys, when the team came yelping home with the Kablunet. Even the baby gave a joyous crow—in Eskimo.

But the exclamations were changed to pity when the Kablunet was assisted to rise, and staggered feebly towards the hut, even when supported by Okiok and his sons. The sailor was not ignorant of Eskimo ways. His residence in South Greenland had taught him many things. He dropped, therefore, quite naturally—indeed gladly—on his hands and knees on coming to the mouth of the tunnel, and crept slowly into the hut, followed by the whole family, except Ermigit, who was left to unfasten the dogs.

The weather at the time was by no means cold, for spring was rapidly advancing; nevertheless, to one who had been so reduced in strength, the warmth of the Eskimo hut was inexpressibly grateful. With a great sigh of relief the rescued man flung himself on the raised part of the floor on which Eskimos are wont to sit and sleep.

"Thank God, and again I thank *you*, my friends!" he said, repeating the phrase which he had already used, for the sudden change from despair to hope, from all but death to restored life, had filled his heart with gratitude.

"You are weary?" said Okiok.

"Ay, ay—very weary; well-nigh to death," he replied.

"Will the Kablunet sleep?" asked Nuna, pointing to a couch of skins close behind the seaman.

Rooney looked round.

"Thankee; yes, I will."

He crept to the couch, and dropped upon it, with his head resting on an eider-down pillow. Like a tired infant, his eyes closed, and he was asleep almost instantaneously.

Seeing this, the Eskimos began to move about with care, and to speak in whispers, though it was needless caution, for in his condition the man would probably have continued to sleep through the wildest thunderstorm. Even when baby, tumbling headlong off the elevated floor, narrowly missed spiking himself on a walrus spear, and set up a yell that might have startled the stone deaf, the wearied Kablunet did not move. Okiok did, however. He moved smartly towards the infant, caught him by the throat, and almost strangled him in a fierce attempt to keep him quiet.

"Stupid tumbler!" he growled—referring to the child's general and awkward habit of falling—"Can't you shut your mouth?"

Curious similarity between the thoughts and words of civilised and savage man in similar circumstances! And it is interesting to note the truth of what the song says:—

"We little know what great things from little things may rise."

From that slight incident the Eskimo child derived his future name of "Tumbler"! We forget what the precise Eskimo term is, but the English equivalent will do as well.

When supper-time arrived that night, Okiok and Nuna consulted as to whether they should waken their guest, or let him lie still—for, from the instant he lay down, he had remained without the slightest motion, save the slow, regular heaving of his broad chest.

"Let him sleep. He is tired," said Okiok.

"But he must be hungry, and he is weak," said Nuna.

"He can feed when he wakens," returned the man, admiring his guest as a collector might admire a foreign curiosity which he had just found.

"Kablunets sleep sounder than Eskimos," remarked the woman.

"Stupid one! Your head is thick, like the skull of the walrus," said the man. "Don't you see that it is because he is worn-out?"

Eskimos are singularly simple and straightforward in their speech. They express their opinions with the utmost candour, and without the slightest intention of hurting each other's feelings. Nuna took no offence at her husband's plain speaking, but continued to gaze with a gratified expression at the stranger.

And sooth to say Reginald Rooney was a pleasant object for contemplation, as well as a striking contrast to the men with whom Nuna had been hitherto associated. His brow was broad; the nose, which had been compared to the eagle's beak, was in reality a fine aquiline; the mouth, although partially concealed by a brown drooping moustache, was well formed, large, and firm; the beard bushy, and the hair voluminous as well as curly. Altogether, this poor castaway was as fine a specimen of a British tar as one could wish to see, despite his wasted condition and his un-British garb.

It was finally decided to leave him undisturbed, and the Eskimo family took care while supping to eat their food in comparative silence. Usually the evening meal was a noisy, hilarious festival, at which Okiok and Norrak and Ermigit were wont to relate the various incidents of the day's hunt, with more or less of exaggeration, not unmingled with fun, and only a little of that shameless boasting which is too strong a characteristic of the North American Indian. The women of the household were excellent listeners; also splendid laughers, and Tumbler was unrivalled in the matter of crowing, so that noise as well as feasting was usually the order of the night. But on this great occasion that was all changed. The feasting was done in dead silence; and another very striking peculiarity of the occasion was that, while the six pairs of jaws kept moving with unflagging pertinacity, the twelve wide-open eyes kept glaring with unwinking intensity at the sleeping man.

Indeed this unwavering glare continued long after supper was over, for each member of the family lay down to rest with his or her face towards the stranger, and kept up the glare until irresistible Nature closed the lids and thus put out the eyes, like the stars of morning, one by one; perhaps it would be more strictly correct to say two by two.

Okiok and his wife were the last to succumb. Long after the others were buried in slumber, these two sat up by the lamp-light, solacing themselves with little scraps and tit-bits of walrus during the intervals of whispered conversation.

"What shall we do with him?" asked Okiok, after a brief silence.

"Keep him," replied Nuna, with decision.

"But we cannot force him to stay."

"He cannot travel alone," said Nuna, "and we will not help him to go."

R. M. Ballantyne

"We are not the only Innuits in all the land. Others will help him if we refuse."

This was so obvious that the woman could not reply, but gazed for some time in perplexity at the lamp-smoke. And really there was much inspiration to be derived from the lamp-smoke, for the wick being a mass of moss steeped in an open cup of seal-oil, the smoke of it rose in varied convolutions that afforded almost as much scope for suggestive contemplation as our familiar coal-fires.

Suddenly the little woman glanced at her slumbering household, cast a meaning look at her husband, and laughed— silently of course.

"Has Nuna become a fool that she laughs at nothing?" demanded Okiok simply.

Instead of replying to the well-meant though impolite question, Nuna laughed again, and looked into the dark corner where the pretty little round face of Nunaga was dimly visible, with the eyes shut, and the little mouth wide-open.

"We will marry him to Nunaga," she said, suddenly becoming grave.

"Pooh!" exclaimed Okiok—or some expression equivalent to that—"Marry Nunaga to a Kablunet? Never! Do you not know that Angut wants her?"

It was evident from the look of surprise with which Nuna received this piece of information that she was *not* aware of Angut's aspirations, and it was equally evident from the perplexed expression that followed that her hastily-conceived little matrimonial speculation had been knocked on the head.

After this their thoughts either strayed into other channels, or became too deep for utterance, for they conversed no more, but soon joined the rest of the family in the realms of oblivion.

CHAPTER THREE

OUR HERO AND HIS FRIENDS BECOME FAMILIAR

It was a fine balmy brilliant morning when Red Rooney awoke from the most refreshing sleep he had enjoyed for many a day, gazed thoughtfully up at the blackened roof of the Eskimo hut, and wondered where he was.

There was nothing that met his eyes to recall his scattered senses, for all the members of the family had gone out to their various avocations, and one of them having thrust a sealskin into the hole in the wall which served for a window the sun found admittance only through crevices, and but faintly illumined the interior.

The poor man felt intensely weak, yet delightfully restful— so much so that mere curiosity seemed to have died within him, and he was content to lie still and think of whatever his wayward mind chose to fasten on, or not to think at all, if his mind saw fit to adopt that course in its vagaries. In short, he felt as if he had no more control over his thoughts than a man in a dream, and was quite satisfied that it should be so.

As his eyes became accustomed to the dim light, however, he began slowly to perceive that the walls around him were made of rough unhewn stone, that the rafters were of drift timber, and the roof of moss, or something like it; but the whole was so thickly coated with soot as to present a uniform appearance of blackness. He also saw, from the position in which he lay, a stone vessel, like a primitive classical lamp, with a wick projecting from its lip, but no flame. Several skulls of large animals lay on the floor within the range of his vision, and some sealskin and other garments hung on pegs of bone driven into the wall. Just opposite to him was the entrance to the tunnel, which formed the passage or corridor of the mansion, and within it gleamed a subdued light which entered from the outer end.

Rooney knew that he saw these things, and took note of them, yet if you had asked him what he had seen it is probable that he would have been unable to tell—so near had he approached to the confines of that land from which no traveller returns.

Heaving a deep sigh, the man uttered the words, "Thank God!" for the third time within the last four-and-twenty hours. It was an appropriate prelude to his sinking into that mysterious region of oblivion in which the mind of worn-out man finds rest, and out of which it can be so familiarly yet mysteriously summoned—sometimes by his own pre-determination, but more frequently by a fellow-mortal.

He had not lain long thus when the tunnel was suddenly darkened by an advancing body, which proved to be the mistress of the mansion.

Nuna, on thrusting her head into the interior, looked inquiringly up before venturing to rise. After a good stare at the slumbering Kablunet, she went cautiously towards the window and removed the obstruction. A flood of light was let in, which illumined, but did not awaken, the sleeper.

Cautiously and on tip-toe the considerate little woman went about her household duties, but with her eyes fixed, as if in fascination, on her interesting guest.

It is at all times an awkward as well as a dangerous mode of proceeding, to walk in one direction and look in another. In crossing the hut, Nuna fell over a walrus skull, upset the lamp, and sent several other articles of furniture against the opposite wall with a startling crash. The poor creature did not rise. She was too much overwhelmed with shame. She merely turned her head as she lay, and cast a horrified gaze at the sleeper.

To her great joy she saw that Red Rooney had not been disturbed. He slept through it all with the placidity of an infant. Much relieved, the little woman got up, and moved about more freely. She replenished the lamp with oil, and kindled it. Then she proceeded to roast and fry and grill bear ribs, seal chops, and walrus steaks with a dexterity that was quite marvellous, considering the rude culinary implements with which she had to deal. In a short time breakfast was prepared, and Nuna went out to announce the fact. Slowly and with the utmost caution each member of the family crept in, and, before rising, cast the same admiring, inquiring, partially awe-stricken gaze at the unconscious Kablunet. Okiok, Nunaga, Norrak, Ermigit, and Tumbler all filed in, and sat down in solemn silence.

Okiok took Tumbler on his knee, so as to be ready to throttle him on the shortest notice if he should venture to cry, or even crow.

But as the best of human arrangements often fail through unforeseen circumstances, so the quietude was broken a second time that morning unexpectedly. One of the hungry dogs outside, rendered desperate by the delicious fumes that issued from the hut, took heart, dashed in, caught up a mass of blubber, and attempted to make off. A walrus rib, however, from Norrak's unerring hand, caught him on the haunch as he entered the tunnel, and caused him to utter such a piercing howl that Red Rooney not only awoke, but sat bolt upright, and gazed at the horrified Eskimos inquiringly.

Evidently the seaman was touched with a sense of the ludicrous, for he merely smiled and lay down again. But he did not try to sleep. Having been by that time thoroughly refreshed, he began to sniff the scent of savoury food as the war-horse is said to scent the battle from afar—that is, with an intense longing to "go at it." Okiok, guessing the state of his feelings, brought him a walrus rib.

Red Rooney accepted it, and began to eat at once without the use of knife or fork.

"Thankee, friend. It's the same I'll do for yourself if you ever come to starvation point when I've got a crust to spare."

Charmed beyond measure at hearing their native tongue from the mouth of a foreigner, the stare of the whole party became more intense, and for a few moments they actually ceased to chew—a sure sign that they were, so to speak, transfixed with interest.

"My man," said Rooney, after a few minutes' intense application to the rib, "what is your name?"

"Okiok," replied the Eskimo.

"Okiok," muttered the seaman to himself in English; "why, that's the Eskimo word for winter." Then, after a few minutes' further attention to the rib, "Why did they name you after the cold season o' the year?"

R. M. Ballantyne

"I know not," said Okiok. "When my father named me I was very small, and could not ask his reason. He never told any one. Before I was old enough to ask, a bear killed him. My mother thought it was because the winter when I was born was very cold and long."

Again the hungry man applied himself to the rib, and nothing more was said till it was finished. Feeling still somewhat fatigued, Rooney settled himself among his furs in a more upright position, and gave his attention to the natives, who instantly removed their eyes from him, and resumed eating with a will. Of course they could not restrain furtive glances, but they had ceased to stare.

In a few minutes Okiok paused, and in turn became the questioner.

"No Kablunet ever came here before," he said. "We are glad to see you; but why do you come, and why alone, and why starving?"

"Not very easy to answer these questions off-hand to the likes of you," said Rooney. "However, I'll try. You've heard of the settlements—the traders—no doubt, in the far-off land over *there*?"

Rooney pointed to the southward, the direction of which he knew from the position of the sun and the time of day, which latter he guessed roughly.

The Eskimo nodded. From the special character of the nod it was evident that he meant it to express intelligence. And it did!

"Well," continued Rooney, "you may have heard that big, big—tremendous big—kayaks, or rather oomiaks, have come to that country, an' landed men and women, who have built houses—igloos—and have settled there to trade?"

At this his host nodded with such decision, and so frequently, as to show that he not only knew of the Kablunet settlements, but was deeply interested in them, and would be glad to know something more.

"Well, then," continued the sailor, "I came out from a great and rich country, called England, in one o' these big tradin' canoes, which was wrecked close to the settlements, and there I stayed with my mates, waiting for another big kayak to come an' take us off; but no kayak came for two winters— so that's the way I came to understand an' speak the Eskimo—"

At this point, as if it could endure the stranger's voice no longer, Tumbler set up a sudden and tremendous howl. He was instantly seized, half strangled, metaphorically sat upon, and reduced to sobbing silence, when the sailor resumed his narrative.

"All that time I was workin' off and on for the—"

He stopped abruptly, not having any words in the native language by which to name the Moravian Missionaries. The Eskimos waited with eager looks for the next word.

"Well, well," resumed Rooney, with a pathetic smile, "it *is* a pity the whole world don't speak one language. I was workin' for, for—these Kablunets who have come to Greenland, (that's the name we've given to your country, you must know)—who have come to Greenland, not to trade, but to teach men about God—about Torngarsuk, the Good Spirit— who made all the world, and men, and beasts."

At this point the interest of Okiok became, if possible, more intense.

"Do the Kablunets know God, the Good Spirit? Have they seen him?" he asked.

"They haven't exactly seen Him," replied the sailor; "but they have got a book, a writing, which tells about Him, and they know something of His nature and His wishes."

Of course this reference to a book and a writing—which Rooney had learned to speak of from the Moravians—was quite incomprehensible to the Eskimo. He understood enough of what was said, however, to see the drift of his visitor's meaning.

"Huk!" he exclaimed, with a look of satisfaction; "Angut will be glad to hear this."

"Who is Angut?" asked the sailor.

The whole party looked peculiarly solemn at this question.

"Angut is a great angekok," answered Okiok, in a low voice.

"Oh! he is one of your wise men, is he?" returned Rooney, with an involuntary shrug of his shoulders, for he had heard and seen enough during his residence at the settlements to convince him that the angekoks, or sorcerers, or wise men of the Eskimos, were mostly a set of clever charlatans, like the medicine-men of the North American Indians, who practised on the credulity and superstition of their fellow-men in order to gain their own ends. Some of these angekoks, no doubt, were partly self-deceivers, believing to some extent the deceptions which they practised, and desiring more or less the welfare of their dupes; but others were thorough, as well as clever, rogues, whose sole object was self-interest.

"Well, then," continued Rooney, "after I'd been two winters with these Kablunets, another big kayak came to the settlement, not to trade, nor to teach about God, but to go as far as they could into the ice, and try to discover new lands."

"Poor men!" remarked Okiok pitifully; "had they no lands of their own?"

"O, yes; they had lands at home," replied the sailor, laughing.

"Huk!" exclaimed several of the natives, glancing at each other with quite a pleased expression. It was evident that they were relieved as well as glad to find that their visitor could laugh, for his worn and woe-begone expression, which was just beginning to disappear under the influence of rest and food, had induced the belief that he could only go the length of smiling.

"Yes," continued the sailor; "they had lands, more or less— some of them, at least—and some of them had money; but you must know, Okiok, that however much a Kablunet may have, he always wants more."

"Is he *never* content?" asked the Eskimo.

"Never; at least not often."

"Wonderful!" exclaimed Okiok; "when I am stuffed with seal-blubber as full as I can hold, I want nothing more."

Again the sailor laughed, and there was something so hearty and jovial in the sound that it became infectious, and the natives joined him, though quite ignorant of the exciting cause. Even Tumbler took advantage of the occasion to give

R. M. Ballantyne

vent to another howl, which, having something of the risible in it, was tolerated. When silence was restored, the visitor resumed—

"I joined these searchers, as they wanted an interpreter, and we came away north here. Nothing particular happened at first. We had a deal of squeezing an' bumping in the ice of course, but got little damage, till about six days back I think, or thereabouts, when we got a nip that seemed to me to cut the bottom clean out o' the big kayak, for when the ice eased off again it went straight to the bottom. We had only time to throw some provisions on the ice and jump out before it went down. As our provisions were not sufficient to last more than a few days, I was sent off with some men over the floe to hunt for seals. We only saw one, asleep near its hole. Bein' afraid that the sailors might waken it, I told them to wait, and I would go after it alone. They agreed, but I failed. The seal was lively. He saw me before I got near enough, and dived into his hole. On returnin' to where I had left the men I found a great split in the ice, which cut me off from them. The space widened. I had no small kayak to take me across. It was too cold to swim. The floe on which my comrades stood was driftin', along wi' the big floe, where the rest of them were. The ice on which I stood was fast. A breeze was blowin' at the time, which soon carried the pack away. In an hour they were out of sight, and I saw them no more. I knew that it was land-ice on which I stood, and also that the coast could not be far off; but the hummocks and the snow-drift prevented me from seein' far in any direction. I knew also that death would be my portion if I remained where I was, so I set off straight for land as fast as I could go. How long I've been on the way I can't tell, for I don't feel quite sure, and latterly my brain has got into a confused state. I had a small piece of seal meat in my pouch when I started. When it was done I cut a strip off my sealskin coat an' sucked that. It just kept body and soul together. At last I saw the land, but fell, and should have died there if the Good Spirit had not sent you to save me, Okiok—so give us a shake of your hand, old boy!"

To this narrative the natives listened with breathless attention, but at the conclusion Okiok looked at the extended hand in surprise, not knowing what was expected of him. Seeing this, Rooney leaned forward, grasped the man's right hand, shook it warmly, patted it on the back, then, raising it to his lips, kissed it.

Stupid indeed would the man have been, and unusually savage, who could have failed to understand that friendship and good-will lay in these actions. But Okiok was not stupid. On the contrary, he was brightly intelligent, and, being somewhat humorous in addition, he seized Rooney's hand instantly after, and repeated the operation, with a broad smile on his beaming face. Then, turning suddenly to Tumbler, he grasped and shook that naked infant's hand, as it sat on the floor in a pool of oil from a lamp which it had overturned.

An explosion of laughter from everybody showed that the little joke was appreciated; but Okiok became suddenly grave, and sobered his family instantly, as he turned to Rooney and said—

"I wish that Angut had been there. He would have saved your big oomiak and all the men."

"Indeed. Is he then such a powerful angekok?"

"Yes; very, very powerful. There never was an angekok like him."

"I suppose not," returned Rooney, with a feeling of doubt, which, however, he took care to hide. "What like is this great wise man—very big, I suppose?"

"No, he is not big, but he is not small. He is middling, and very strong, like the bear; very active and supple, like the seal or the white fox; and very swift, like the deer—and very different from other angekoks."

"He must be a fine man," said the sailor, becoming interested in this angekok; "tell me wherein he differs from others."

"He is not only strong and wise, but he is good; and he cares nothing for our customs, or for the ways of other angekoks. He says that they are all lies and nonsense. Yes, he even says that he is not an angekok at all; but we know better, for he is. Everybody can see that he is. He knows everything; he can do anything. Do I not speak what is true?"

He turned to his wife and daughter as he spoke. Thus appealed to, Nuna said it was all true, and Nunaga said it was all *very* true, and blushed—and, really, for an Eskimo, she looked quite pretty.

Don't laugh, good reader, at the idea of an Eskimo blushing. Depend upon it, that that is one of those touches of nature which prove the kinship of the world everywhere.

While they were talking a step was heard outside, and the Eskimos looked intelligently at each other. They knew that the comer must be a friend, because, had he been a stranger, the dogs would have given notice of his approach. Besides, these animals were heard fawning round him as he spoke to them.

"Ujarak!" exclaimed Okiok, in a low voice.

"Is Ujarak a friend?" asked the sailor.

"He is an angekok," said the Eskimo evasively—"a great angekok, but not so great as Angut."

Another moment, and a man was seen to creep into the tunnel. Standing up when inside, he proved to be a tall, powerful Eskimo, with a not unhandsome but stern countenance, which was somewhat marred by a deep scar over the left eye.

CHAPTER FOUR

OKIOK BECOMES SIMPLE BUT DEEP, AND THE WIZARD TRIES TO MAKE CAPITAL OUT OF EVENTS

Of course Ujarak, wise man though he was esteemed to be, could not help being struck dumb by the unexpected sight of the gaunt foreigner. Indeed, having so long held supposed intercourse with familiar spirits, it is not improbable that he imagined that one of them had at last come, without waiting for a summons, to punish him because of his deceptive practices, for he turned pale—or rather faintly green—and breathed hard.

Perceiving his state, it suddenly occurred to the sailor to say—"Don't be afraid. I won't hurt you." He inadvertently said it in English, however, so that Ujarak was none the wiser.

"Who is he?" demanded the angekok—perhaps it were more correct to call him wizard.

Okiok, expecting Rooney to reply, looked at him, but a spirit of silence seemed to have come over the stranger, for he made no reply, but shut his eyes, as if he had dropped asleep.

"He is a Kablunet," said Okiok.

"I could see that, even if I had not the double sight of the angekok," replied the other, with a touch of sarcasm, for Eskimos, although by no means addicted to quarrelling, are very fond of satire. They are also prone to go straight to the point in conversation, and although fond of similes and figurative language, they seldom indulge in bombast.

With much solemnity Okiok rejoined that he had no doubt of Ujarak's being aware that the man was a Kablunet.

"And I am glad you have come," he added, "for of course you can also tell me where the Kablunet has come from, and whither he is going?"

The angekok glanced at his host quickly, for he knew—at least he strongly suspected—that he was one of that uncomfortable class of sceptics who refuse to swallow without question all that self-constituted "wise men" choose to tell them. Okiok was gazing at him, however, with an air of the most infantine simplicity and deference.

"I cannot tell you that," replied the wizard, "because I have not consulted my torngak about him."

It must be explained here that each angekok has a private spirit, or familiar, whose business it is to enlighten him on all points, and conduct him on his occasional visits to the land of spirits. This familiar is styled his "torngak."

"Did your torngak tell you that he was a Kablunet?" asked Okiok simply—so simply that there was no room for Ujarak to take offence.

"No; my eyes told me that."

R. M. Ballantyne

"I did not know that you had ever seen a Kablunet," returned the other, with a look of surprise.

"Nor have I. But have I not often heard them described by the men of the south? and has not my torngak showed them to me in dreams?"

The wizard said this somewhat tartly, and Okiok, feeling that he had gone far enough, turned away his sharp little eyes, and gazed at the lamp-smoke with an air of profound humility.

"You have got seal-flesh?" said Ujarak, glad to change the subject.

"Yes; I killed it yesterday. You are hungry? Nuna will give you some."

"No; I am not hungry. Nevertheless I will eat. It is good to eat at all times."

"Except when we are stuffed quite full," murmured Okiok, casting at Nunaga a sly glance, which threw that Eskimo maiden into what strongly resembled a suppressed giggle. It was catching, for her brothers Norrak and Ermigit were thrown into a similar condition, and even the baby crowed out of sympathy. Indeed Red Rooney himself, who only simulated sleep, found it difficult to restrain his feelings, for he began to understand Okiok's character, and to perceive that he was more than a match for the wizard with all his wisdom.

Whatever Ujarak may have felt, he revealed nothing, for he possessed that well-known quality of the Eskimo—the power to restrain and conceal his feelings—in a high degree. With a quiet patronising smile, he bent down in quite a lover-like way, and asked Nunaga if the seal-flesh was good.

"Yes, it is good; *very* good," answered the maiden, looking modestly down, and toying with the end of her tail. You see she had no scent-bottle or fan to toy with. To be sure she had gloves—thick sealskin mittens—but these were not available at the moment.

"I knew you had a seal," said the angekok, pausing between bites, after the edge of his appetite had been taken off; "my torngak told me you had found one at last."

"Did he tell you that I had also found a bear?" asked Okiok, with deeper simplicity than ever.

The wizard, without raising his head, and stuffing his mouth full to prevent the power of speech, glanced keenly about the floor. Observing the fresh skin in a corner, and one or two ribs, he bolted the bite, and said—

"O yes. My torngak is kind; he tells me many things without being asked. He said to me two days ago, 'Okiok is a clever man. Though all the people are starving just now, he has killed a seal and a bear.'"

"Can torngaks make mistakes?" asked Okiok, with a puzzled look. "It was *yesterday* that I killed the seal and the bear."

"Torngaks *never* make mistakes," was the wizard's prompt and solemn reply; "but they see and know the future as well as the past, and they sometimes speak of both as the present."

"How puzzling!" returned the other meekly. "He meant you, then, to understand that I was *going* to kill a seal and a bear. Glad am I that I am not an angekok, for it would be very difficult work for a stupid man,—enough almost to kill him!"

R. M. Ballantyne

"You are right. It is difficult and hard work. So you see the torngak told me go feast with Okiok, and at his bidding of course I have come, on purpose to do so."

"That's a lie. You came to see my Nunaga, and you hope to get her; but you never will!" said Okiok. He said it only to himself, however, being far too polite to say it to his guest, to whom he replied deferentially—

"If they are starving at your village, why did you not bring your mother and your father? They would have been welcome, for a seal and a bear would be enough to stuff us all quite full, and leave something to send to the rest."

For some minutes the wizard did not reply. Perhaps he was meditating, perchance inventing.

"I brought no one," he said at last, "because I want you and your family to return with me to the village. You know it is only two days distant, and we can take the seal and the bear with us. We are going to have a great feast and games."

"Did you not say the people were starving?" asked Okiok, with a look of gentle surprise.

"They *were* starving," returned Ujarak quickly; "but two walruses and four seals were brought in yesterday and my torngak has told me that he will point out where many more are to be found if I consult him on the night of the feast. Will you come back with me?"

Okiok glanced at the Kablunet.

"I cannot leave my guest," he said.

"True, but we can take him with us."

"Impossible. Do you not see he is only bones in a bag of skin? He must rest and feed."

"That will be no difficulty," returned the wizard, "for the feast is not to be held for twice seven days. By that time the Kablunet will be well, and getting strong. Of course he must rest and be well stuffed just now. So I will go back, and say that you are coming, and tell them also what you have found—a Kablunet. Huk!"

"Yes; and he speaks our language," said Okiok.

"That was not our language which he spoke when I came in."

"No; yet he speaks it."

"I should like to hear him speak."

"You must not wake him," said Okiok, with an assumed look of horror. "He would be sure to kill you with a look or a breath if you did. See; he moves!"

Rooney certainly did move at the moment, for the conversation had tickled him a good deal, and the last remark was almost too much for him. Not wishing, however, to let the angekok go without some conversation, he conveniently awoke, yawned, and stretched himself. In the act he displayed an amount of bone and sinew, if not flesh, which made a very favourable impression on the Eskimos, for physical strength and capacity is always, and naturally, rated highly among savages.

Our shipwrecked hero had now heard and seen enough to understand something of the character of the men with whom he had to deal. He went therefore direct to the point, without introduction or ceremony, by asking the angekok who he was and where he came from. After catechising him closely, he then sought to establish a kind of superiority over him by voluntarily relating his own story, as we have already given it, and thus preventing his being questioned in return by the wizard.

"Now," said Red Rooney in conclusion, "when you go home to your village, tell the people that the Kablunet, having been nearly starved, must have some days to get well. He will stay with his friend Okiok, and rest till he is strong. Then he will go to your village with his friends, and join in the feast and games."

There was a quiet matter-of-course tone of command about the seaman, which completely overawed the poor angekok, inducing him to submit at once to the implied superiority, though hitherto accustomed to carry matters with a high hand among his compatriots. His self-esteem, however, was somewhat compensated by the fact that he should be the bearer of such wonderful news to his people, and by the consideration that he could say his torngak had told him of the arrival of the Kablunet—an assertion which they would believe all the more readily that he had left home with some mysterious statements that something wonderful was likely to be discovered. In truth, this astute wizard never failed to leave some such prediction behind him every time he quitted home, so as to prepare the people for whatever might occur; and, should nothing occur, he could generally manage to colour some event or incident with sufficient importance to make it fulfil the prediction, at least in some degree.

When at last he rose to depart, Ujarak turned to Nunaga. As her father had rightly guessed, the wizard, who was quite a young man, had come there on matrimonial views intent; and he was not the man to leave the main purpose of his journey unattempted.

"Nunaga," he said, in a comparatively low yet sufficiently audible voice, "my sledge is large. It is too large for one—"

He was interrupted suddenly at this point by Rooney, who saw at once what was coming.

"Okiok," he said, "I want Nunaga to mend and patch my torn garments for the next few days. Her mother has enough to do with cooking and looking after the house. Can you spare her for that work?"

Yes, Okiok could spare her; and was very glad to do all that he could to accommodate the foreigner.

"Will Ujarak carry a message from the Kablunet to his village?" asked Rooney, turning to the wizard.

"He will," replied the latter somewhat sulkily.

"Does he know the angekok named Angut?"

It is doubtful whether anger or surprise was most strongly expressed in the countenance of the Eskimo as he replied sternly, "Yes."

"Then tell him that the Kablunet will stay in his hut when he visits your village."

Having delivered this message, he turned his face to the wall, and, without awaiting a reply, coolly went to sleep, or appeared to do so, while Ujarak went off, with a storm of very mingled feelings harrowing his savage breast.

When he was gone Red Rooney raised himself on one elbow, and looked over his shoulder at Okiok with a broad grin. Okiok, who felt grave enough at the moment, and somewhat perplexed, opened his eyes gradually, and reciprocated the smile with interest. By degrees he closed the eyes, and allowed the smile to develop into a high falsetto chuckle which convulsed his broad hairy shoulders for full five minutes.

From that hour Okiok and the Kablunet were united! They understood each other. The chords of sympathetic humour had vibrated within them in harmony. They were thenceforward *en rapport*, and felt towards each other like brothers, or rather like father and son, for Okiok was forty-five years of age at least, while Rooney was not yet thirty.

"He's a very bad man, is he not?" asked the seaman, when the heaving of the shoulders had subsided.

"Ho! yes. Bad, bad! *very* bad! He lies, and steals, and cheats, and talks nonsense, and wants Nunaga for a wife."

"And you don't want him for a son?"

"No!"—very decidedly.

Rooney laughed, and, turning away with a wink and a nod, lay down to sleep—this time in earnest. Okiok responded with a falsetto chuckle, after which he proceeded to solace himself with a mass of half-cooked blubber. Observing that Tumbler was regarding him with longing looks, he good-naturedly cut off part of the savoury morsel, and handed it to the child. It is well-known that the force of example is strong—stronger than that of precept. In a few minutes the entire family set to work again on the viands with as much gusto as though they had eaten little or nothing for a week.

Leaving them thus pleasantly and profitably occupied, let us follow Ujarak to his village.

Every man and woman of superior intelligence in this world has probably one blind worshipper, if not more—some weak brother who admires, believes in, perhaps envies, but always bows to the demigod. Such a worshipper had Ujarak in Ippegoo, a tall young man, of weak physical frame, and still weaker mental capacity.

Ippegoo was not malevolent, like his master, but he was sufficiently wicked to laugh at his evil doings, and to assist him in his various plans, in the implicit belief that he was aiding a great and wise man. He did so all the more readily that he himself aimed at the high and dignified office of an angekok, an aspiration which had at first been planted in him, and afterwards been carefully encouraged by his deceiver, because it made his dupe, if possible, a blinder and more willing tool.

"Ippegoo," said Ujarak, on drawing near to the outskirts of his village, and coming unexpectedly on his satellite, who was in the act of dragging home a seal which he had just killed, "I meet you in the nick of time—but that is no wonder, for did not my torngak tell me he would cause you to meet me near the village? I want your assistance just now."

"I am glad, then, that we have met," said Ippegoo, with a cringing motion not unlike a bow—though of the ceremonial bow the Eskimos have no knowledge.

"Yes, strange things have happened," continued the angekok, rolling his eyes impressively. "Did I not tell you before I started to visit Okiok that strange things would happen?"

Ippegoo, who had a good deal of straightforward simplicity in his nature, looked puzzled, and tried hard to recollect what Ujarak had told him.

"You will never make an angekok," said Ujarak, with a look of displeasure, "if you do not rouse up your memory more. Do you not remember when I whispered to you in a dream last night that strange things were going to happen?"

"O ye-e-es,—in a dream; yes, I remember now," returned the satellite in some confusion, yet with a good deal of faith, for he was a heavy feeder, and subject to nightmares, so that it was not difficult to imagine the "whisper" which had been suggested to him.

"Yes, you remember now, stupid walrus! Well, then, what was the strange thing like?" Ujarak looked awfully solemn while he put this question.

"What was it like?" repeated the poor youth with hesitation, and an uneasy glance at the sky, as if for inspiration. "What—was—it—oh, I remember; it was big—big; very big—so high," (holding his hand up about seven feet from the ice).

"No, Ippegoo, not *so* big. He was about my size. Don't you remember? and he was pale, with hair twisted into little rings all over his head, and—"

"Yes, yes; and a nose as long as my leg," interrupted the eager pupil.

"Not at all, stupid puffin! A nose no longer than your own, and much better-shaped."

The angekok said this so sternly that the too willing Ippegoo collapsed, and looked, as he felt, superlatively humble.

"Now go," resumed Ujarak, with an unrelaxed brow; "go tell your story to the people assembled in the big hut. They feast there to-night, I know. Tell them what your dream has revealed. Tell them how I spoke to you before I left the village—but don't be too particular in your description. Let that be—like your own mind—confused, and then it will be true to nature. Tell them also that you expect me soon, but say not that you have met me to-day, for that might displease my torngak, whom I go to consult."

Without giving his pupil time to reply, the wizard strode off, and disappeared among the ice hummocks, as a bad actor might strut behind the side scenes.

Deeply impressed with the solemnity of the whole affair, and with the importance of his mission, the young Eskimo went off to the village, dragging his seal behind him, and wondering what new discovery had been made by his mysterious patron.

That something of unusual import had occurred he never doubted, for although he had often seen Ujarak, with unbounded admiration, wriggle out of unfulfilled prophecy like an eel, he had never seen him give way to demonstrations such as we have described without something real and surprising turning up ere long.

Strong in this faith, he ran into the large hut where a considerable party of his tribe were feasting on a recently captured walrus, and told them that something tremendous, something marrow-thrilling, had occurred to the great angekok Ujarak, who, before leaving the village, had told him that he was going off to find a—a—something—he knew not exactly what—with rings of hair all over its body, pale as the ice-floe, more wonderful than the streaming lights —incomprehensible!—immense!

At this point he glared, and became dumb. Not knowing well

R. M. Ballantyne

what to say next, he judiciously remained silent, then sat down and gasped, while the united company exclaimed "Huk!" with unusual emphasis.

The consultation which Ujarak had with his torngak was somewhat peculiar. It consisted chiefly in a wild run at full speed out upon the floes. Having pretty well exhausted himself by this device, and brought on profuse perspiration, he turned homewards. Drawing near to the village, he flung back his hood, ran his fingers through his long black hair until it was wildly dishevelled, then, springing suddenly into the midst of the festive party, he overturned feasters right and left, as he made his way to the part of the edifice furthest from the door.

A close observer might have noted, however, that there was method in his madness, for he overturned only women and children, and kept carefully clear of men—at least of such men as he knew would resent his roughness.

Wheeling suddenly round, and facing the solemnised assembly, he addressed it, as if with difficulty, in a low-toned, awesome voice.

CHAPTER FIVE

PLOTS AND COUNTER-PLOTS ALREADY

It is not necessary, neither would it be profitable, to give in full detail what Ujarak said to the gaping crowd. Enough to know that, like other statesmen, he made the most of his subject, and fully impressed his audience with the belief that this first of Kablunets who had ever visited these ice-bound regions had been mysteriously, yet irresistibly, drawn there through his, Ujarak's, influence, with the assistance of his torngak or familiar spirit.

One man there was in that assembly, however, who seemed to be not very deeply touched by the wizard's eloquence. Yet he did not express unbelief by his looks, but received all that was said with profound gravity. This was Angut, the reputed angekok, to whom reference has been made in a previous chapter.

Although a thorough Eskimo in dress and in cast of feature, there was a refinement, a gravity, a kindliness, and a *something* quite indescribable about this man, which marked him out as an exceptional character among his fellows. As we have said elsewhere, he was not unusually large, though he was unusually strong, for his power lay rather in a well-knit and splendidly proportioned than a bulky frame. Ujarak was

R. M. Ballantyne

taller and broader, yet did not possess half his muscular strength. Ujarak knew this, and had hitherto avoided coming into collision with him. But there was also a moral strength and enthusiasm in Angut, which placed him on a platform high above not only Ujarak, but all the other men of his time and country. In short, he was one of those far-seeing and thoughtful characters, who exist in all countries, in all ranks and conditions of life, civilised and savage, and who are sometimes styled "Nature's gentlemen."

Despite his surroundings, temptations, examples, trials, and worries, Angut was at all times unvaryingly urbane, kind, sedate, equable, obliging, honest, and self-sacrificing. It mattered not that other men spoke freely—sometimes even a little boastfully—of their exploits. Angut never did so of his, although no other man could hold a candle—perhaps we should say a lamp—to him in the matter of daring. It signified not that Eskimos in general were in the habit of treating friendless widows and orphans ill, even robbing as well as neglecting them, Angut always treated well those with whom he had to do. Other men might neglect people in distress, but he helped and defended them; and it was a matter of absolute indifference to him what "people" thought of his conduct. There is a modified "Mrs Grundy" even in Eskimo land, but Angut despised her. Indeed she was the only creature or thing in his limited world that this good man did despise. He puzzled his countrymen very much, for they could not understand him. Other men they could put to shame, or laugh out of their ideas and plans, or frighten into submission—at least into conformity. Not so Angut. He was immovable, like an ancient iceberg; proof against threats, wheedling, cajoling, terrifying, sarcasm—proof against everything but kindness. He could not stand before that. He went down before it as bergs go down before the summer sun.

Angut was shrewd also and profound of thought, insomuch

that, mentally, he stood high above his kinsfolk. He seemed to see through his fellows as if their bosoms and brains had been made of glass, and all their thoughts visible. Ujarak knew this also, and did not like it. But no one suffered because of Angut's superior penetration, for he was too amiable to hurt the feelings of a mosquito.

After all that we have said, the reader will perhaps be prepared to expect that Angut never opened his mouth save to drop words of love and wisdom. Not so. Angut was modest to excess. He doubted his own wisdom; he suspected his own feelings; he felt a strong tendency to defer to the opinion of others, and was prone rather to listen than to speak. He was fond of a joke too, but seldom perpetrated one, and was seldom severe.

While Ujarak was speaking, Angut listened with that look of unmoved gravity with which he always met a new thing or idea, and which effectually concealed his real feelings, though the concealment was unintentional. But when at last the wizard came to the most distasteful part of his discourse, namely the message from Reginald Rooney, that, on the occasion of his visit to the camp, he would take up his abode with Angut, that hero's countenance lighted up with surprise, not unmingled with pleasure.

"Is Ujarak sure that the Kablunet said this?" asked Angut.

"Quite sure," replied the wizard.

"Huk!" exclaimed Angut, by which exclamation you may be sure that he meant to express much satisfaction.

"But," continued the wizard, "the Kablunet is ill. He is thin; he is weak. He wants rest. I have consulted with my torngak, who tells me he will get better soon if we do not trouble him."

At this point Ujarak glanced at Angut, but that worthy's countenance had resumed its look of impenetrable gravity.

"We must not worry him or go near him for some days," continued the wizard. "We must let him alone. And this will not try our patience, for my torngak tells me that seals have come. Yesterday I went to the house of the great Fury under the sea, and wrestled with her; and my torngak and I overcame her, and set many of the seals and other animals free."

"Huk!" exclaimed the assembly, in gratified surprise.

Lest the reader should feel some surprise also, we may as well explain what the Greenlanders believed in former times. They held, (perhaps they still hold), that there were two great spirits—the one was good, named Torngarsuk; the other was bad, and a female—a Fury—without a name. This malevolent woman was supposed to live in a great house under the ocean, in which by the power of her spells she enthralled and imprisoned many of the sea monsters and birds, thus causing scarcity of food among the Eskimos. The angekoks claimed to have the power of remedying this state of things by paying a visit to the abode of the Fury.

When an angekok has sufficient courage to undertake this journey, his torngak, after giving him minute instructions how to act, conducts him under the earth or sea, passing on the way through the kingdom of those good souls who spend their lives in felicity and ease. Soon they come to a frightful vacuity—a sort of vasty deep—over which is suspended a narrow wheel, which whirls round with great rapidity. This awful abyss is bridged by a rope, and guarded by seal sentinels. Taking the angekok by the hand, his torngak leads him on the rope over the chasm and past the sentinels into the palace of the Fury.

No sooner does the wicked creature spy the unwelcome visitors than, trembling and foaming with rage, she immediately sets on fire the wing of a sea-fowl, with the stench of which she hopes to suffocate angekok and torngak together, and make both of them captives. The heroes, however, are prepared for this. They seize the Fury before she has succeeded in setting fire to the wing, pull her down, and strip her of those amulets by the occult powers of which she has enslaved the inhabitants of ocean. Thus the spell is broken, for the time at least, and the creatures, being set free, ascend to their proper abodes at the surface of the sea!

After this explanation the reader will easily understand the flutter of excitement that passed through the assembly, for, although feasting at that moment on a walrus, they had suffered much during the latter part of that winter from the scarcity of animals of all kinds.

But Angut did not flutter. That peculiar man was an incorrigible sceptic. He merely smiled, and, chucking a rotund little boy beside him under the chin, said, "What think ye of that, my little ball of fat?" or some Eskimo equivalent for that question. Our intelligent wizard had not, however, ventured on these statements without some ground to go on. The fact is, that, being a close observer and good judge of the weather, he had perceived a change of some sort coming on. While on his way to the hut of Okiok he had also observed that a few seals were playing about on the margin of some ice-floes, and from other symptoms, recognisable only by angekoks, he had come to the conclusion that it would be safe as well as wise at that time to prophesy a period of plenty.

"Now I would advise," he said, in concluding his discourse, "that we should send off a hunting party to the south, for I can tell you that seals will be found there—if the young men do not put off time on the way."

This last proviso was a judicious back-door of escape. Slight delays, he knew, were almost inevitable, so that, if the hunt should prove a failure, he would have little difficulty in accounting for it, and saving his credit. The most of his credulous and simple-minded hearers did not reflect on the significance of the back-door remark, but Angut did, and grinned a peculiar grin at the little fat boy, whom he chucked a second time under the chin. Ujarak noted the grin, and did not like it.

Among the people there who gave strongest expression to their joy at the prospect of the good living in store for them, were several young and middle-aged females who sat in a corner grouped together, and conveyed their approval of what was said to each other by sundry smirks and smiles and nods of the head, which went far to prove that they constituted a little coterie or clique.

One of these was the wife of Simek, the best hunter of the tribe. Her name was Pussimek. She was round and short, comely and young, and given to giggling. She had a baby—a female baby—named after her, but more briefly, Pussi, which resembled her in all respects except size. Beside her sat the mother of Ippegoo. We know not her maiden name, but as her dead husband had been called by the same name as the son, we will style her Mrs Ippegoo. There was also the mother of Arbalik, a youth who was celebrated as a wonderful killer of birds on the wing—a sort of Eskimo Robin Hood—with the small spear or dart. The mother of Arbalik was elderly, and stern—for an Eskimo. She was sister to the great hunter Simek. Kannoa, a very old dried-up but lively woman with sparkling black eyes, also formed one of the group.

"Won't we be happy!" whispered Pussimek, when Ujarak spoke in glowing terms of the abundance that was in prospect. She followed up the whisper by hugging the baby.

"Yes, a good time is coming," said the mother of Ippegoo, with a pleasant nod. "We will keep the cooking-lamps blazing night and—"

"And stuff," rejoined Pussimek, with a giggle, "till we can hold no more."

"Do you want to grow fatter?" asked the mother of Arbalik in a sharp tone, which drew forth a smothered laugh all round, for Pussimek had reached that condition of *embonpoint* which rendered an increase undesirable.

"I would not object to be fatter," replied the wife of Simek, with perfect good-humour, for Eskimos, as a rule, do not take offence easily.

"Stuff, stuff," murmured Kannoa, nodding her old head contemplatively; "that's what I'm fond of; stuff—stuff—stuff."

"All your stuffing will never make *you* fat," said the stern and rather cynical mother of Arbalik.

She paid no attention to Kannoa's reply—which, to do her justice, was very mild—for, at the moment, Arbalik himself rose to address the assembly. He was a fine specimen of an Eskimo—a good-looking young savage; slim and wiry, with a nose not too flat, and only a little turned up; a mouth that was well shaped and pleasant to look at, though very large, and absolutely cavernous when in the act of yawning; and his eyes looked sharp and eager, as if always on the outlook for some passing bird, with a view to transfixion.

R. M. Ballantyne

"The words of Ujarak are wise," he said. "I was down at the high bluffs yesterday, and saw that what he says is true, for many seals are coming up already, and birds too. Let us go out to the hunt."

"We would like much to see this wonderful Kablunet," remarked the jovial big hunter Simek, with a bland look at the company, "but Ujarak knows best. If the Kablunet needs rest, he must have it. If he needs sleep, he must have it. If he wants food, he must have it. By all means let him have it. We will not disturb him. What the torngak of Ujarak advises we will do."

Several of the other leading men also spoke on this occasion—some inclining to accept the wizard's advice; others, who were intolerably anxious to see the Kablunet, rather inclining to the opinion that they should remain where they were till he recovered strength enough to be able to pay his contemplated visit.

Ippegoo spoke last. Indeed, it was not usual for him to raise his voice in council, but as he had been the first to carry the important news, and was known to be an ardent admirer and pupil of Ujarak, he felt that he was bound to back his patron; and his arguments, though not cogent, prevailed.

"Let us not doubt the wisdom of the angekok," he said. "His torngak speaks. It is our business to obey. We have starved much for some moons; let us now feast, and grow fat and strong."

"Huk!" exclaimed the auditors, who had been touched on their weakest point.

"But Angut has not yet uttered his mind," said the jovial Simek, turning with a bland expression to the man in question; "he is an angekok, though he will not admit it. Has not his familiar spirit said anything to him?"

Angut looked gravely at the speaker for a moment or two, and shook his head. Dead silence prevailed. Then in a voice that was unusually soft and deep he said: "I am no angekok. No torngak ever speaks to me. The winds that whistle round the icebergs and rush among the hummocks on the frozen sea speak to me sometimes; the crashing ice-cliffs that thunder down the glens speak to me; the noisy rivulets, the rising sun and moon and winking stars all speak to me, though it is difficult to understand what they say; but no familiar spirit ever speaks to me."

The man said this quietly, and in a tone of regret, but without the slightest intention of expressing poetical ideas, or laying claim to originality of thought. Yet his distinct denial of being an angekok or wise man, and his sentiments regarding the voices of Nature, only confirmed his countrymen in their belief that he was the greatest angekok they had ever seen or heard of.

"But surely," urged Simek, "if so many spirits speak to you, they must tell you *something*?"

"They tell me much," replied Angut in a contemplative tone, "but nothing about hunting."

"Have you no opinion, then, on that subject?"

"Yes, I have an opinion, and it is strong. Let all the hunters go south after seals without delay; but I will not go. I shall go among the icebergs—alone."

"He will go to hold converse with his numerous torngaks," whispered old Kannoa to Pussimek.

"He will go to visit Okiok, and see the Kablunet, and court Nunaga," thought the jealous and suspicious Ujarak.

And Ujarak was right; yet he dared not follow, for he feared the grave, thoughtful man, in spite of his determination to regard and treat him with lofty disdain.

Utterly ignorant of the wizard's feelings towards him—for he was slow to observe or believe in ill-will towards himself when he felt none to any one else—Angut set off alone next morning in the direction that led to the great glacier, while his countrymen harnessed their dogs, loaded their sledges with lines and weapons, and went away southward on a hunting expedition. Wishing the latter all success, we will follow the fortunes of Angut, the eccentric angekok.

Had you and I, reader, been obliged to follow him in the body, we should soon have been left far behind; fortunately, spirit is more powerful and fleet than matter!

Without rest or halt, the stalwart Eskimo journeyed over the ice until he reached the residence of Okiok.

The dogs knew his step well, and gave no noisy sign of his approach, though they rose to welcome him with wagging tails, and rubbed their noses against his fur coat as he patted their heads.

Creeping into the hut, he presented himself unexpectedly. Okiok bade him silent welcome, with a broad grin of satisfaction. Nunaga did the same, with a pleased smile and a decided blush. The other inmates of the hut showed similar friendship, and Tumbler, trying to look up, fell over into an oil-puddle, with a loud crow of joy. They all then gazed suddenly and simultaneously, with mysterious meaning, at Red Rooney, who lay coiled up, and apparently sound asleep, in the innermost corner.

Angut also gazed with intense interest, though nothing of the sleeping man was visible save the point of his nose and a mass of curling brown hair protruding from his deerskin coverings.

Seating himself quietly between Nunaga and Nuna, and taking the oily Tumbler on his knee, the visitor entered into a low-toned conversation respecting this great event of their lives—the arrival of a real live Kablunet! They also talked of Kablunets in general, and their reported ways and manners. It is to be noted here that they did not talk in whispers. Okiok and Nuna had indeed begun the conversation thus, but had been immediately checked by Angut, whose intelligence had long ago taught him that no sound is so apt to awaken a sleeper as the hiss of a whisper; and that a steady, low-toned hum of conversation is more fitted to deepen than interrupt slumber.

"Is he *very* thin?" asked Angut, who had been somewhat impressed by Ujarak's description of the stranger, and his evident desire that no one should go near him.

"He is not fat," answered Okiok, "but he has not been starving long; sleeping and stuffing will soon make him strong. Don't you think so, Norrak? You saw him at his worst, when we found him on the ice."

Thus appealed to, Okiok's eldest son laid down the piece of blubber with which he had been engaged, nodded his head several times, and said, "Yes, he will be able to run, and jump soon."

"And he speaks our language *well*," said Okiok, with a look of great interest.

"I know it," returned his friend; "Ujarak told us about that. It is because of that, that I have come at once to see him." Nunaga winced here, for she had timidly hoped that Angut had come to see *her*! "I would not," continued the visitor, "that Ujarak should be the first to speak to him, for he will poison his ears."

"Yes, Ujarak is a dreadful liar," said Okiok solemnly, but without the slightest touch of ill feeling.

"An awful liar," remarked Nuna softly.

Nunaga smiled, as though acquiescing in the sentiment, but said nothing.

Just as they gave utterance to this decided opinion as to the character of the wizard, Red Rooney turned round, stretched himself, yawned, and sat up.

CHAPTER SIX

ANGUT AND ROONEY HOLD
CONVERSE ON MANY THINGS

At first Rooney did not observe that there was a visitor in the hut, but, when his eyes alighted on him, he rose at once, for he felt that he was in the presence of a man possessed of intelligence vastly superior to that of the ordinary natives. It was not so much that Angut's presence was commanding or noble, as that his grave expression, broad forehead, and earnest gaze suggested the idea of a man of profound thought.

The angekok who had been so graphically described to him by Okiok at once recurred to Rooney's mind. Turning to his host, he said, with a bland expression—

"I suppose this is your friend Angut, the angekok?"

"Yes," replied Okiok.

While the mysterious foreigner was speaking, Angut gazed at him with looks and feelings of awe, but when he stepped forward, and frankly held out his hand, the Eskimo looked puzzled. A whispered word from his host, however, sufficed to explain. Falling in at once with the idea, he grasped the

R. M. Ballantyne

offered hand, and gave it a squeeze of good-will that almost caused the seaman to wince.

"I am glad to meet you," said Rooney.

"I am more than glad," exclaimed the Eskimo with enthusiasm; "I have not language to tell of what is in my mind. I have heard of Kablunets, dreamed of them, thought of them. *Now* my longings are gratified—I behold one! I have been told that Kablunets know nearly everything; *I* know next to nothing. We will talk much. It seems to me as if I had been born only to-day. Come; let us begin!"

"My friend, you expect too much," replied Rooney, with a laugh, as he sat down to devote himself to the bear-steak which Nunaga had placed before him. "I am but an average sort of sailor, and can't boast of very much education, though I have a smattering; but we have men in my country who do seem to know 'most everything—wise men they are. We call them philosophers; you call 'em angekoks. Here, won't you go in for a steak or a rib? If you were as hungry as I am, you'd be only too glad and thankful to have the chance."

Angut accepted a rib, evidently under the impression that the Kablunet would think it impolite were he to refuse. He began to eat, however, in a languid manner, being far too deeply engaged with mental food just then to care for grosser forms of nourishment.

"Tell me," said the Eskimo, who was impatient to begin his catechising, "do your countrymen all dress like this?" He touched the sealskin coat worn by the sailor.

"O no," said Rooney, laughing; "I only dress this way because I am in Eskimo land, and it is well suited to the country; but the men in my land—Ireland we call it—dress in all sorts of fine cloth, made from the hair of small animals—Why, what do you stare at, Angut? Oh, I see—my knife! I forgot that you are not used to such things, though you have knives—stone ones, at least. This one, you see, is made of steel, or iron—the stuff, you know, that the southern Eskimos bring sometimes to barter with you northern men for the horns of the narwhal an' other things."

"Yes, I have seen iron, but never had any," said Angut, with a little sigh; "they bring very little of it here. The Innuits of the South catch nearly the whole of it on its journey north, and they keep it."

"Greedy fellows!" said Rooney. "Well, this knife is called a clasp-knife, because it shuts and opens, as you see, and it has three blades—a big one for cuttin' up your victuals with, as you see me doin'; and two little ones for parin' your nails and pickin' your teeth, an' mendin' pens an' pencils—though of course you don't know what that means. Then here, you see, there are two little things stuck into the handle. One is called tweezers, an' is of no earthly use that I know of except to pull the hairs out o' your nose, which no man in his senses ever wants to do; and the other thing is, I suppose, for borin' small holes in things—it's almost as useless. This thing on the back is for pickin' stones out of horses' hoofs—but I forgot you never saw horses or hoofs! Well, no matter; it's for pickin' things out of things, when—when you want to pick 'em out! But below this is an uncommon useful thing—a screw—a thing for drawin' corks out of bottles—there, again, I'm forgettin'. You never saw corks or bottles. Happy people—as the people who don't drink spirits would call you—and, to say truth, I think they are right. Indeed, I've been one of them myself ever since I came to this region. Give us another steak, Nunaga, my dear—no, not a bear one; I like the walrus better. It's like yourself—tender."

R. M. Ballantyne

The fair Nunaga fell into a tremendous giggle at this joke, for although our hero's Eskimo was not very perfect, he possessed all an Irishman's capacity for making his meaning understood, more or less; and truly it was a sight to behold the varied expressions of face—the childlike surprise, admiration, curiosity, and something approaching to awe—with which those unsophisticated natives received the explanation of the different parts of that clasp-knife!

"But what did we begin our talk about?" he continued, as he tackled the walrus. "O yes; it was about our garments. Well, besides using different kinds of cloths, our coats are of many different shapes: we have short coats called jackets, and long coats, and coats with tails behind—"

"Do your men wear tails behind?" asked Angut, in surprise.

"Yes; two tails," replied Rooney, "and two buttons above them."

"Strange," remarked Angut; "it is only our women who have tails; and they have only one tail each, with one button in front—not behind—to fasten the end of the tail to when on a journey."

"Women with tails look very well," remarked Okiok, "especially when they swing them about in a neat way that I know well but cannot describe. But men with tails must look very funny."

Here Mrs Okiok ventured to ask how the Kablunet women dressed.

"Well, it's not easy to describe that to folk who have never seen them," said the sailor, with a slight grin. "In the first place, they don't wear boots the whole length of their legs like you, Nuna."

"Surely, then," remarked the hostess, "their legs must be cold?"

"By no means, for they cover 'em well up with loose flapping garments, extending from the waist all the way down to the feet. Then they don't wear hoods like you, but stick queer things on their heads, of all shapes and sizes—sometimes of no shape at all and very small size—which they cover over with feathers, an' flowers, an' fluttering things of all colours, besides lots of other gimcracks."

How Rooney rendered "gimcracks" into Eskimo we are not prepared to say, but the whole description sent Nunaga and her mother into fits of giggling, for those simple-minded creatures of the icy north—unlike sedate Europeans—are easily made to laugh.

At this point Angut struck in again, for he felt that the conversation was becoming frivolous.

"Tell me, Kablunet," he began; but Rooney interrupted him.

"Don't call me Kablunet. Call me Red Rooney. It will be more friendly-like, and will remind me of my poor shipmates."

"Then tell me, Ridroonee," said Angut, "is it true what I have heard, that your countrymen can make marks on flat white stuff, like the thin skin of the duck, which will tell men far away what they are thinking about?"

"Ay, that's true enough," replied the sailor, with an easy smile of patronage; "we call it writing."

A look of grave perplexity rested on the visage of the Eskimo.

"It's quite easy when you understand it, and know how to do it," continued Rooney; "nothing easier."

A humorous look chased away the Eskimo's perplexity as he replied—

"Everything is easy when you understand it."

"Ha! you have me there, Angut," laughed the sailor; "you're a 'cute fellow, as the Yankees say. But come, I'll try to show you how easy it is. See here." He pulled a small note-book from his pocket, and drew thereon the picture of a walrus. "Now, you understand that, don't you?"

"Yes; *we* draw like that, and understand each other."

"Well, then, we put down for that w-a-l-r-u-s; and there you have it—walrus; nothing simpler!"

The perplexed look returned, and Angut said—

"That is not very easy to understand. Yet I see something— always the same marks for the same beast; other marks for other beasts?"

"Just so. You've hit it!" exclaimed Rooney, quite pleased with the intelligence of his pupil.

"But how if it is not a beast?" asked the Eskimo. "How if you cannot see him at all, yet want to tell of him in—in—what did you say—writing? I want to send marks to my mother to say that I have talked with my torngak. How do you mark torngak? I never saw him. No man ever saw a torngak. And how do you make marks for cold, for wind, for all our thoughts, and for the light?"

It was now Red Rooney's turn to look perplexed. He knew that writing was easy enough to him who understands it, and he felt that there must be some method of explaining the matter, but how to go about the explanation to one so utterly ignorant did not at once occur to him. We have seen, however, that Rooney was a resolute man, not to be easily baffled. After a few moments' thought he said—

"Look here now, Angut. Your people can count?"

"Yes; they can go up to twenty. I can go a little further, but most of the Innuits get confused in mind beyond twenty, because they have only ten fingers and ten toes to look at."

"Well now," continued Rooney, holding up his left hand, with the fingers extended, "that's five."

Yes, Angut understood that well.

"Well, then," resumed Rooney, jotting down the figure 5, "there you have it—five. Any boy at school could tell you what that is."

The Eskimo pondered deeply and stared. The other Eskimos did the same.

"But what," asked Okiok, "if a boy should say that it was six, and not five?"

"Why, then we'd whack him, and he'd never say that again."

There was an explosion of laughter at this, for Eskimos are tender and indulgent to their children, and seldom or never

R. M. Ballantyne

whack them.

It would be tedious to go further into this subject, or to describe the ingenious methods by which the seaman sought to break up the fallow ground of Angut's eminently receptive mind. Suffice it to say that Rooney made the discovery that the possession of knowledge is one thing, and the power to communicate it another and a very different thing. Angut also came to the conclusion that, ignorant as he had thought himself to be, his first talk with the Kablunet had proved him to be immeasurably more ignorant than he had supposed.

The sailor marked the depression which was caused by this piece of knowledge, and set himself good-naturedly to counteract the evil by displaying his watch, at sight of which there was a wild exclamation of surprise and delight from all except Angut, who, however deep his feelings might be, always kept them bridled. The expansion of his nostrils and glitter of his eyes, however, told their tale, though no exclamation passed his lips.

Once or twice, when Rooney attempted to explain the use of the instrument, the inquisitive man was almost irresistibly led to put some leading questions as to the nature of Time; but whenever he observed this tendency, the sailor, thinking that he had given him quite enough of philosophy for one evening, adroitly turned him off the scent by drawing particular attention to some other portion of the timepiece.

The watch and the knife, to which they reverted later on, kept the lecturer and audience going till late in the evening, by which time our sailor had completely won the hearts of the Eskimos, and they had all become again so hungry that Okiok gave a hint to his wife to stir up the lamp and prepare supper. Then, with a sigh of relief, they all allowed their strained minds to relax, and the conversation took a more general turn. It is but fair to add that, as the sailor had won the hearts of the natives, so his heart had been effectually enthralled by them. For Angut, in particular, Rooney felt that powerful attraction which is the result of similar tastes, mutual sympathies, and diversity of character. Rooney had a strong tendency to explain and teach; Angut a stronger tendency to listen and learn. The former was impulsive and hasty; the latter meditative and patient. Rooney was humorously disposed and jovial, while his Eskimo friend, though by no means devoid of humour, was naturally grave and sedate. Thus their dispositions formed a pleasing contrast, and their tastes an agreeable harmony.

"What did you say was the name of your country?" asked Angut, during a brief pause in the consumption of the meal.

"England," said Rooney.

"That was not the name you told me before."

"True; I suppose I said Ireland before, but the fact is, I can scarcely claim it as my own, for you see my father was Irish and my mother was Scotch. I was born in Wales, an' I've lived a good bit o' my life in England. So you see I can't claim to be anything in particular."

As this was utterly incomprehensible to the Eskimo, he resumed his bit of blubber without saying a word. After a brief silence, he looked at the Kablunet again, and said—

"Have they houses in your land?"

"Houses? O yes; plenty of 'em—made of stone."

"Like the summer-houses of the Innuit, I suppose?" said Angut. "Are they as big?"

Rooney laughed at this, and said, Yes; they were much bigger—as big as the cliffs alongside.

"Huk!" exclaimed the Eskimos in various tones. Okiok's tone, indeed, was one of doubt; but Angut did not doubt his new friend for a moment, though his credulity was severely tested when the seaman told him that one of the villages of his countrymen covered a space as big as they could see— away to the very horizon, and beyond it.

"But, Angut," said Rooney, growing somewhat weary at last, "you've asked me many questions; will you answer a few now?"

"I will answer."

"I have heard it said," began the sailor, "that Angut is a wise man—an angekok—among his people, but that he denies the fact. Why does he deny it?"

The Eskimo exchanged solemn glances with his host, then looked round the circle, and said that some things could not be explained easily. He would think first, and afterwards he would talk.

"That is well said," returned Rooney. "'Think well before you speak' is a saying among my own people."

He remained silent for a few moments after that, and observed that Okiok made a signal to his two boys. They rose immediately, and left the hut.

"Now," said Okiok, "Angut may speak. There are none but safe tongues here. My boys are good, but their tongues wag too freely."

"Yes, they wag too freely," echoed Mrs Okiok, with a nod.

Thus freed from the danger of being misreported, Angut turned to the seaman, and said—

"I deny that I am an angekok, because angekoks are deceivers. They deceive foolish men and women. Some of them are wicked, and only people-deceivers. They do not believe what they teach. Some of them are self-deceivers. They are good enough men, and believe what they teach, though it is false. These men puzzle me. I cannot understand them."

The Eskimo became meditative at this point, as if his mind were running on the abstract idea of self-delusion. Indeed he said as much. Rooney admitted that it *was* somewhat puzzling.

"I suppose," resumed the Eskimo, "that Kablunets never deceive themselves or others; they are too wise. Is it so?"

"Well, now you put the question," said Rooney, "I rather fear that some of us do, occasionally; an' there's not a few who have a decided tendency to deceive others. And so that is the reason you won't be an angekok, is it? Well, it does you credit. But what sort o' things do they believe, in these northern regions, that you can't go in with? Much the same, I fancy, that the southern Eskimos believe?"

"I know not what the southern Eskimos believe, for I have met them seldom. But our angekoks believe in torngaks, familiar spirits, which they say meet and talk with them. There is no torngak. It is a lie."

"But you believe in one great and good Spirit, don't you?" asked the seaman, with a serious look.

R. M. Ballantyne

"Yes; I believe in One," returned the Eskimo in a low voice, "One who made me, and all things, and who *must* be good."

"There are people in my land who deny that there is One, because they never saw, or felt, or heard Him—so they say they cannot know," said Rooney. Angut looked surprised.

"They must be fools," he said. "I see a sledge, and I know that some man made it—for who ever heard of a sledge making itself? I see a world, and I know that the Great Spirit made it, because a world cannot make itself. The greatest Spirit must be One, because two greatests are impossible, and He is good—because good is better than evil, and the Greatest includes the Best."

The seaman stared, as well he might, while the Eskimo spoke these words, gazing dreamily at the lamp-flame, as if he were communing with his own spirit rather than with his companion. Evidently Okiok had a glimmering of what he meant, for he looked pleased as well as solemn.

It might be tedious to continue the conversation. Leaving them therefore to their profound discussions, we will turn to another and very different social group.

CHAPTER SEVEN

TREATS OF CROSS-PURPOSES
AND DIFFICULTIES

Partially concealed in a cavern at the base of a stupendous, almost perpendicular, cliff, stood the wizard Ujarak and his pupil Ippegoo. The former silently watched the latter as he fitted a slender spear, or rather giant arrow, to a short handle, and prepared to discharge it at a flock of sea-birds which were flying about in front of them within what we would call easy gunshot.

The handle referred to acted as a short lever, by means of which the spear could be launched not only with more precision but with much greater force than if thrown simply by hand like a javelin.

"There, dart it now!" cried Ujarak, as a bird swept close to the cave's mouth. "Boh! you are too slow. Here is another; quick! dart!"

Ippegoo let fly hastily, and missed.

"Poo! you are of no more use than the rotten ice of spring. There; try again," said Ujarak, pointing to a flock of birds which came sweeping towards them.

R. M. Ballantyne

The crestfallen youth fitted another spear to the handle—for he carried several—and launched it in desperation into the middle of the flock. It ruffled the wings of one bird, and sent it screaming up the cliffs, but brought down none.

"Boo!" exclaimed the wizard, varying the expression of his contempt. "It is well that your mother has only a small family."

Ippegoo was accustomed to severe backhanders from his patron; he was not offended, but smiled in a pathetic manner as he went out in silence to pick up his weapons.

Just as he was returning, Arbalik, nephew to the jovial Simek, appeared upon the scene, and joined them. The wizard appeared to be slightly annoyed, but had completely dissembled his feelings when the young man walked up.

"Have the hunters found no seals?" asked Ujarak.

"Yes, plenty," answered Arbalik cheerily, for he had a good deal of his old uncle's spirit in him, "but you know variety is agreeable. Birds are good at a feast. They enable you to go on eating when you can hold no more seal or walrus blubber."

"That is true," returned the wizard, with a grave nod of appreciation. "Show Ippegoo how to dart the spear. He is yet a baby!"

Arbalik laughed lightly as he let fly a spear with a jaunty, almost careless, air, and transfixed a bird on the wing.

"Well done!" cried the wizard, with a burst of genuine admiration; "your wife will never know hunger."

"Not after I get her," returned the youth, with a laugh, as he flung another spear, and transfixed a second bird.

Ippegoo looked on with slightly envious but not malevolent feelings, for he was a harmless lad.

"Try again," cried Arbalik, turning to him with a broad grin, as he offered him one of his own spears.

Ippegoo took the weapon, launched it, and, to his own great surprise and delight, sent it straight through the heart of a bird, which fell like a stone.

A shout of pleasure burst from Arbalik, who was far too good a shot to entertain mean feelings of jealousy at the success of others.

"It is the luck of the spear," said Ujarak, "not the skill of the hunter."

This would have been an unkind cut to ordinary mortals, but it fell as harmless on Ippegoo as water on the back of the eider-duck. A snub from the wizard he took almost as a compliment, and the mere success of his shot afforded him unbounded pleasure.

The good-natured Arbalik offered him another spear, but Ujarak interposed.

"No; Ippegoo must come with me," he said. "I have work for him to do. One who would be an angekok must leave bird-spearing to boys." Then turning to Arbalik—"Did you not say that the hunters have found plenty of game?"

"Yes, plenty."

"I told you so," said the wizard, using a phrase not unfamiliar to civilised ears. "Remain here, and spear plenty of birds; or go where you will."

Having thus graciously given the youth free permission to do as he pleased—which Arbalik received with inward scorn, though outward respect—he left the cave, followed meekly by his satellite.

After walking in silence till well out of earshot of the expert young hunter, the wizard said in solemn tones—

"Ippegoo, I have work of more importance for you to do than spearing birds—work that requires the wisdom of a young angekok."

All Ujarak's backhanders vanished before this confidential remark, and the poor tool began to feel as if he were growing taller and broader even as he walked.

"You know the hut of Okiok?" continued the wizard.

"Yes; under the ice-topped cliff."

"Well, Angut is there. I hate Angut!"

"So do I," said Ippegoo, with emphasis quite equal to that of his master.

"And Nunaga is there," continued Ujarak. "I—I love Nunaga!"

"So do I," exclaimed Ippegoo fervently, but seeing by the wizard's majestic frown that he had been precipitate, he took refuge in the hasty explanation—"Of course I mean that—that—I love her because *you* love her. I do not love her for herself. If *you* did not love her, I would hate her. To me she is not of so much value as the snout of a seal."

The wizard seemed pacified, for his frown relaxed, and after a few moments' thought he went on savagely—

"Angut also loves Nunaga."

"The madman! the insolent! the fool!" exclaimed Ippegoo; "what can he expect but death?"

"Nothing else, and nothing less," growled the wizard, clenching his teeth—"*if* he gets her! But he shall never get her! I will stop that; and that is why I ask you to listen—for you must be ready to act, and in haste."

As Ippegoo began to entertain uncomfortable suspicions that the wizard was about to use him as an instrument of vengeance, he made no response whatever to the last remark.

"Now," continued his master, "you will go to the hut of Okiok. Enter it hurriedly, and say to Nunaga that her father's grandmother, Kannoa, is ill—ill in her mind—and will not rest till she comes to see her. Take a small sledge that will only hold her and yourself; and if Okiok or Angut offer to go with you, say that old Kannoa wants to see the girl alone, that there is a spell upon her, that she is bewitched, and will see no one else. They will trust you, for they know that your mind is weak and your heart good."

"If my mind is weak," said Ippegoo somewhat sadly, "how can I ever become an angekok?"

With much affectation of confidence, the wizard replied that there were two kinds of men who were fit to be angekoks— men with weak minds and warm hearts, or men with strong minds and cold hearts.

"And have you the strong mind?" asked Ippegoo.

"Yes, of course, very strong—and also the cold heart," replied Ujarak.

"But how can that be," returned the pupil, with a puzzled look, "when your heart is warmed by Nunaga?"

"Because—because," rejoined the wizard slowly, with some hesitation and a look of profound wisdom, "because men of strong mind do not love as other men. They are quite different—so different that you cannot understand them."

Ippegoo felt the reproof, and was silent.

"So, when you have got Nunaga on the sledge," resumed Ujarak, "you will drive her towards the village; but you will turn off at the Cliff of Seals, and drive at full speed to the spot where I speared the white bear last moon. You know it?"

"Yes; near Walrus Bay?"

"Just so. There you will find me with two sledges. On one I will drive Nunaga away to the far-south, where the Innuit who have much iron dwell. On the other you will follow. We will live there for ever. They will be glad to receive us."

"But—but—" said Ippegoo hesitatingly, and with some anxiety, for he did not like to differ on any point from his master—"I cannot leave my—my mother!"

"Why not?"

"I suppose it is because I love her. You know you told me

that the weak minds have warm hearts—and my mind must be very, very weak indeed, for my heart is *very* warm—quite hot—for my mother."

The wizard perceived that incipient rebellion was in the air, so, like a wise man, a true angekok, he trimmed his sails accordingly.

"Bring your mother with you," he said abruptly.

"But she won't come."

"Command her to come."

"Command my *mother*!" exclaimed Ippegoo, in amazement.

Again the wizard was obliged to have recourse to his wisdom in order to subdue this weak mind.

"Yes, of course," he replied; "tell your mother that your torngak—no, you haven't got one yet—that Ujarak's torngak—told him in a vision that a visit to the lands of the far-south would do her good, would remove the pains that sometimes stiffen her joints, and the cough that has troubled her so much. So you will incline her to obey. Go, tell her to prepare for a journey; but say nothing more, except that I will call for her soon, and take her on my sledge. Away!"

The peremptory tone of the last word decided the poor youth's wavering mind. Without a word more he ran to the place where his dogs were fastened, harnessed them to his sledge, and was soon driving furiously back to the Eskimo village over the frozen sea, while the wizard returned to the place where the hunters of his tribe were still busy hauling in the carcases of seals and other game, which they had succeeded in killing in considerable numbers.

Approaching one of the band of hunters, which was headed by the jovial Simek, and had halted for the purpose of refreshment, Ujarak accosted them with—

"Have the young men become impatient women, that they cannot wait to have their food cooked?"

"Ha! *ha*!" laughed Simek, holding up a strip of raw and bloody seal's flesh, with which he had already besmeared the region of his mouth and nose; "Yes, we have become like women; we know what is good for us, and take it when we need it, not caring much about the cooking. My young men are hungry. Must they wait till the lamps are lighted before they eat? Come, Ujarak, join us. Even an angekok may find a bit of good fat seal worth swallowing. Did you not set them free? You deserve a bit!"

There was a spice of chaff as well as jollity in the big Eskimo's tone and manner; but he was such a gushing fellow, and withal so powerful, that the wizard deemed it wise not to take offence.

"It is not long since I fed," he replied, with a grim smile; "I have other work on hand just now."

"I also have work—plenty of it; and I work best when stuffed full."

So saying, Simek put a full stop, as it were, to the sentence with a mass of blubber, while the wizard went off, as he said, to consult his torngak as to state affairs of importance.

Meanwhile Ippegoo went careering over the ice, plying his long-lashed whip with the energy of a man who had pressing business on hand.

Arrived at the village, he sought his mother's hut. Kunelik, as his mother was named, was seated therein, not exactly darning his socks, but engaged in the Eskimo equivalent—mending his waterproof boots. These were made of undressed sealskin, with soles of walrus hide; and the pleasant-faced little woman was stitching together the sides of a rent in the upper leather, using a fine sharp fish-bone as a needle and a delicate shred of sinew as a thread, when her son entered.

"Mother," he said in a somewhat excited tone, as he sat down beside his maternal parent, "I go to the hut of Okiok."

Kunelik bestowed an inquiring glance upon her boy.

"Ippe," she said, (for Eskimos sometimes use endearing abbreviations), "has Nunaga turned you upside down?"

The lad protested fervently that his head was yet in its proper position. "But," he added, "the mother of Oki—no, the grandmother of Okiok—is sick—very sick—and I am to go and fetch the mother of—no, I mean the daughter of—of Okiok, to see her, because—because—"

"Take time, Ippe," interrupted Kunelik; "I see that your head is down, and your boots are in the air."

Again Ippegoo protested earnestly that he was in the reverse position, and that Nunaga was no more to him than the snout of a seal; but he protested in vain, for his pleasant little mother believed that she understood the language of symptoms, and nodded her disbelief smilingly.

"But why do you say that Kannoa is very ill, Ippe?" she asked; "I have just come from her hut where she was seemingly quite well. Moreover, she has agreed to sup this very night with the mother of Arbalik, and she could not do that if she was ill, for that means much stuffing, because the mother of Arbalik has plenty of food and cooks it very fast."

"Oh, but it is not Kannoa's body that is ill," said Ippegoo quickly; "it is her mind that is ill—very ill; and nothing will make it better but a sight of Nunaga. It was Ujarak that told me so; and you know, mother, that whatever he says *must* be true somehow, whether it be true or not."

"Ujarak is a fool," said Kunelik quietly; "and you are another, my son."

We must again remind the reader here that the Eskimos are a simple as well as straightforward folk. They say what they mean and mean what they say, without the smallest intention of hurting each other's feelings.

"And, mother," continued the son, scarce noticing her remark, "I want you to prepare for a journey."

Kunelik looked surprised.

"Where to, my son?"

"It matters not just now. You shall know in time. Will you get ready?"

"No, my son, I won't."

"But Ujarak says you are to get ready."

"Still, my son, I won't."

"Mother!" exclaimed Ippegoo, with that look and tone which usually follows the saying of something very wicked; but the pleasant little woman went on with her work with an air of such calm good-natured resolution that her son felt helpless.

"Then, mother, I know not what to do."

"What did he tell you to do?" asked Kunelik abruptly.

The youth gave as much of his conversation with the wizard as sufficed to utterly perplex his mother's mind without enlightening it much. When he had finished, or rather had come to an abrupt stop, she looked at him calmly, and said—

"My son, whatever he told you to do, go and do it. Leave the rest to me."

From infancy Ippegoo had rejoiced in his wise little mother's decisions. To be saved the trouble of thinking; to have a straight and simple course clearly pointed out to him, so that he should have nothing to do but shut his eyes and walk therein—or, if need be, run—was the height of Ippegoo's ambition—next to solid feeding. But be not hard on him, good reader. Remember that he was an ignorant savage, and that you could not expect him to be as absolutely and entirely free from this low type of spirit as civilised people are!

Without another word, therefore, the youth leaped on to his sledge, cracked his whip, and set off on his delicate mission. Poor lad! disappointment was in store for him. But compensation was in store also.

While he was galloping along under the ice-cliffs on the east side of a great berg, not far from the end of his journey, Okiok, with his wife and daughter on a sledge, chanced to be galloping with equal speed in the opposite direction on the west side of the same berg. It was a mighty berg—an ice-mountain of nearly half a mile in length—so that no sound of

R. M. Ballantyne

cracking lash or yelping dogs passed from the one party to the other. Thus when Ippegoo arrived at his destination he found his fair bird flown. But he found a much more interesting personage in the Kablunet, who had been left under the care of Angut and Ermigit. This great sight effectually banished disappointment and every other feeling from his breast.

He first caught a glimpse of the wonderful man when half-way through the tunnel-lobby, and the sight rooted him to the spot, for Red Rooney had just finished making a full-dress suit of clothes for little Tumbler, and was in the act of fitting them on when the young Eskimo arrived.

That day Ermigit had managed to spear a huge raven. Rooney, being something of a naturalist, had skinned it, and it was while little Tumbler was gazing at him in open-eyed admiration that the thought struck him—Tumbler being very small and the raven very large.

"Come," said he, seizing the child—with whom he was by that time on the most intimate terms of affection—"Come, I'll dress you up."

Tumbler was naked at the moment, and willingly consented. A few stitches with needle and thread, which the sailor always carried in his pocket, soon converted the wings of the bird into sleeves, a button at the chest formed the skin into a rude cut-away coat, the head, with the beak in front, formed a convenient cap, and the tail hung most naturally down behind. A better full-dress coat was never more quickly manufactured.

Ermigit went into convulsions of laughter over it, and the sailor, charmed with his work, kept up a running commentary in mingled English and Eskimo.

"Splendid!" he cried; "the best slop-shop in Portsmouth couldn't match it! Cap and coat all in one! The fit perfect—and what a magnificent tail!"

At this point Ermigit caught sight of the gaping and glaring Ippegoo in the passage. With a bound he fell upon him, caught him by the hair, and dragged him in.

Of course there followed a deal of questioning, which the hapless youth tried to answer; but the fascination of the Kablunet was too much for him. He could do nothing but give random replies and stare; seeing which, Rooney suggested that the best way to revive him would be to give him something to eat.

R. M. Ballantyne

CHAPTER EIGHT

MRS. OKIOK'S LITTLE EVENING PARTY

In Eskimo land, as in England, power and industry result in the elevation and enrichment of individuals, though they have not yet resulted there, as here, in vast accumulations of wealth, or in class distinctions. The elevating tendency of superior power and practice is seen in the fact that while some hunters are nearly always pretty well off—"well-to-do," as we would express it—others are often in a state of poverty and semi-starvation. A few of them possess two establishments, and some even go the length of possessing two wives. It is but just to add, however, that these last are rare. Most Eskimo men deem one wife quite as much as they can manage to feed.

Our friend Okiok was what we may style one of the aristocracy of the land. He did not, indeed, derive his position from inheritance, but from the circumstance of his being a successful hunter, a splendid canoe-man, and a tremendous fighter.

When it is added that his fights were often single-handed against the Polar bear, it may be understood that both his activity and courage were great. He was not an angekok, for, like his friend Angut, he did not believe in wizards;

nevertheless he was very truly an angekok, in the sense of being an uncommonly wise man, and his countrymen, recognising the fact, paid him suitable respect.

Okiok possessed a town and a country mansion. That is to say, besides the solitary residence already mentioned, close to the great glacier, he owned the largest hut in the Eskimo village. It was indeed quite a palatial residence, capable of holding several families, and having several holes in it—or windows—which were glazed, if we may say so, with the scraped intestines of animals.

It was to this residence that Okiok drove on the afternoon of the day that he missed Ippegoo's visit.

On finding that most of the men had gone southward to hunt, he resolved to follow them, for his purpose was to consult about the Kablunet, who had so recently fallen like a meteor from the sky into their midst.

"But you will stop here, Nuna, with Nunaga, and tell the women all about the Kablunet, while I go south alone. Make a feast; you have plenty to give them. Here, help me to carry the things inside."

Okiok had brought quite a sledge-load of provisions with him, for it had been his intention to give a feast to as many of the community as could be got inside his hut. The carrying in of the supplies, therefore, involving as it did creeping on hands and knees through a low tunnel with each article, was not a trifling duty.

"Now," said he, when at last ready to start, "be sure that you ask the liars and the stupid ones to the feast, as well as the wise; and make them sit near you, for if these don't hear all about it from your own mouth they will be sure to carry away nonsense, and spread it. Don't give them the chance to invent."

While her husband was rattling away south over the hummocky sea in his empty sledge, Nuna lighted her lamps, opened her stores, and began to cook.

"Go now, Nunaga," she said, "and tell the women who are to feed with us to-night."

"Who shall I invite, mother?" asked pretty little Nunaga, preparing to set forth on her mission.

"Invite old Kannoa, of course. She is good."

"Yes, mother, and she is also griggy."

We may remark in passing that it is impossible to convey the exact meaning of the Eskimo word which we have rendered "griggy." Enough to say, once for all, that in difficult words and phrases we give as nearly as possible our English equivalents.

"And Kunelik," said Nuna, continuing to enumerate her guests; "I like the mother of Ippegoo. She is a pleasant little woman."

"But father said we were to ask liars," remarked Nunaga, with a sweet look.

"I'm coming to them, child," said Mrs Okiok, with a touch of petulance—the result of a gulp of lamp-smoke; "yes, you may ask Pussimek also. The wife of Simek is always full of wise talk, and her baby does not squall, which is lucky, for she cannot be forced to leave Pussi behind."

"But name the liars and stupid ones, mother," urged Nunaga, who, being a dutiful child, and anxious to carry out her father's wishes to the letter, stuck to her point.

"Tell Issek, then, the mother of Arbalik, to come," returned Nuna, making a wry face. "If she is not stupid, she is wicked enough, and dreadful at lies. And the sisters Kabelaw and Sigokow; they are the worst liars in all the village, besides being stupider than puffins. There, that will be enough for our first feed. When these have stuffed, we can have more. Too many at once makes much cooking and little talk. Go, my child."

An hour later, and the gossips of the Eskimo village were assembled round Mrs Okiok's hospitable lamp—she had no "board,"—the raised floor at the further end of the hut serving both for seat and table in the daytime and for bed at night. Of course they were all bursting with curiosity, and eager to talk.

But food at first claimed too much attention to permit of free conversation. Yet it must not be supposed that the company was gluttonous or greedy. Whatever Eskimos may feel at a feast, it is a point of etiquette that guests should not appear anxious about what is set before them. Indeed, they require a little pressing on the part of the host at first, but they always contrive to make amends for such self-restraint before the feast is over.

And it was by no means a simple feast to which that party sat down. There were dried herrings and dried seal's flesh, and the same boiled; also boiled auks, dried salmon, dried reindeer venison, and a much-esteemed dish consisting of half raw and slightly putrid seal's flesh, called *mikiak*— something similar in these respects to our own game. But the principal dish was part of a whale's tail in a high or gamey condition. Besides these delicacies, there was a pudding, or dessert, of preserved crowberries, mixed with "chyle" from the maw of the reindeer, with train oil for sauce.

[See note.]

Gradually, as appetite was satisfied, tongues were loosened, and information about the wonderful foreigner, which had been fragmentary at first, flowed in a copious stream. Then commentary and question began in right earnest.

"Have some more mikiak?" said Mrs Okiok to Pussimek.

"No," replied Mrs P, with a sigh.

These northern Eskimos did not, at least at the time of which we write, say "thank you"—not that there was any want of good feeling or civility among them, but simply because it was not customary to do so.

Mrs Okiok then offered some more of the delicacy mentioned to the mother of Ippegoo.

"No," said Kunelik, leaning back with a contented air against the wall; "I am pleasantly stuffed already."

"But tell me," cried Issek, the stern mother of Arbalik, "what does the Kablunet say the people eat in his own land?"

"They eat no whales," said Nuna; "they *have* no whales."

"No whales!" exclaimed Pussimek, with a 'huk' of surprise!

"No; no whales," said Nuna—"and no bears," she added impressively. "Ridroonee, (that's his name), says they eat a thing called bread, which grows out of the ground like grass."

"Eat grass!" exclaimed the mother of Arbalik.

"So he says, and also beasts that have horns—"

"Reindeer?" suggested Kunelik.

"No; the horns are short, with only one point to each; and the beasts are much heavier than reindeer. They have also great beasts, with no name in our language—hurses or hosses he calls them,—but they don't eat these; they make them haul sledges on little round things called weels—"

"*I* know," cried Sigokow; "they must be big dogs!"

"Huk!" exclaimed old Kannoa, who confined her observations chiefly to that monosyllable and a quiet chuckle.

"No," returned Nuna, becoming a little impatient under these frequent interruptions; "they are not dogs at all, but hurses— hosses—with hard feet like stones, and iron boots on them."

A general exclamation of incredulous surprise broke forth at this point, and the mother of Arbalik silently came to the conclusion that Nuna had at last joined the liars of the community, and was making the most of her opportunities, and coming out strong.

"Let there be no talk, and I will speak," said Nuna somewhat indignantly; "if you interrupt me again, I will send you all away to your huts!"

This threat produced silence, and a sniff from Arbalik's mother. Mrs Okiok went on:—

"The land, Ridroonee says, is very rich. They have all that they wish—and *more*!" ("Huk!" from the company)—

R. M. Ballantyne

"except a great many people, called poo-oor, who have not all that they wish—and who sometimes want a little more." (A groan of remonstrative pity from the audience.) "But they have not many seals, and they *never* eat them."

"Poo! I would not care to live there," said Pussimek.

"And no walruses at all," added Mrs Okiok.

"Boo! a miserable country!" exclaimed Ippegoo's mother.

"Then they have villages—so big!—oh!" Nuna paused from incapacity to describe, for Eskimos, being unable to comprehend large numbers, are often obliged to have recourse to illustration. "Listen," continued Nuna, holding up a finger; "if all the whales we catch in a year were to be cooked, they would not feed the people of their largest village for *one* day!"

The mother of Arbalik now felt that she had sufficient ground for the belief that Mrs Okiok was utterly demoralised and lost, in the matter of veracity. Mrs Okiok, looking at her, perceived this in her countenance, and dropped that subject with a soft smile of conscious innocence.

Thereupon curiosity broke forth again with redoubled violence.

"But what is the Kablunet like?" cried Kabelaw, as eagerly as if it were the first time of asking.

"I have told you six times," replied Nuna.

"Tell her again," cried the mother of Arbalik, with a sniff; "she's so used to lies that she finds it hard to take in *the truth*."

There was a sort of double hit intended here, which immensely tickled the Eskimos, who laughed heartily, for they are fond of a touch of sarcastic humour.

"Yes, tell her again," they cried unanimously—"for," added Pussimek, "we're not tired of it yet. Are we, Pussi?"

The query was addressed to her stark naked baby, which broke from a tremendous stare into a benignant laugh, that had the effect of shutting up its eyes at the same time that it opened its little mouth.

It must be remarked here that although we have called Pussi a baby, she was not exactly an infant. She could walk, and understand, and even talk. She did not, however, (desirable child!) use her tongue freely. In fact, Eskimo children seldom do so in the company of their elders. They are prone to listen, and gaze, and swallow, (mentally), and to reply only when questioned. But they seem to consider themselves free to laugh at will—hence Pussi's explosion.

"Well, then," continued Mrs Okiok good-naturedly, "I will tell you again. The Kablunet is a fine man. He must be very much finer when he is fat, for he is broad and tall, and looks strong; but he is thin just now—oh, so thin!—as thin almost as Ippegoo!"

Ippegoo's mother took this in good part, as, indeed, it was intended.

"But that will soon mend with stuffing," continued Nuna. "And his hair is brown—not black—and is in little rings; and there is nearly as much below his nose as above it, so that his mouth can only be seen when open. He carries needles and soft sinews, too, in his bag; but his needles are not fish-bones—they are iron; and the sinews are not like our sinews.

R. M. Ballantyne

They are—I know not what! He has a round thing also, made of white iron, in his pocket, and it is alive. He says, 'No, it is a dead thing,' but he lies, for one day when he was out I heard it speaking to itself in a low soft little voice, but I was afraid to touch it for fear it should bite."

("Lies again!" muttered Issek, the mother of Arbalik, to herself.)

"He says that it tells him about time," continued Nuna; "but how can it tell him about anything if it is dead? Alive and dead at the same time!"

"Impossible!" cried Pussimek.

"Ridiculous!" cried every one else.

"Huk!" ejaculated old Kannoa, wrinkling up her mild face and exposing her toothless gums in a stupendous chuckle.

"Yes, impossible! But I think he does not tell many lies," said Nuna apologetically. "I think he only does it a little. Then he goes on his knees every night before lying down, and every morning when he rises, and speaks to himself."

"Why?" cried every one in blazing astonishment.

"I know not," replied Nuna, "and he does not tell."

"He must be a fool," suggested Kunelik.

"I suppose so," returned Nuna, "yet he does not look like a fool."

At this point the description of Rooney's person and characteristics was interrupted by a tremendous splash. It was poor Pussi, who, having grown wearied of the conversation, had slipped from her mother's side, and while wandering in the background had tumbled into the oil-tub, from which she quickly emerged gasping, gazing, and glittering.

A mild remonstrance, with a good wipe down, soon put her to rights, and Nuna was about to resume her discourse, when the sound of rushing footsteps outside arrested her. Next moment a wild scrambling was heard in the tunnel—as of a giant rat in a hurry—and Ippegoo tumbled into the hut in a state of wild excitement, which irresistibly affected the women.

"What has happened?" demanded Nuna.

"Mother," gasped the youth, turning to the natural repository of all his cares and troubles, "he is coming!"

"Who is coming, my son?" asked Kunelik, in a quiet, soothing tone, for the pleasant little woman, unlike most of the others, was not easily thrown into a state of agitation.

"The Kablunet," cried Ippegoo.

"Where, when, who, how, which, what?" burst simultaneously from the gaping crowd.

But for some minutes the evidently exhausted youth could not answer. He could only glare and pant. By degrees, however, and with much patience, his mother extracted his news from him, piecemeal, to the following effect.

After having sat and gazed in mute surprise at the Kablunet for a considerable time, as already mentioned, and having devoured a good meal at the same time, Ippegoo had been closely questioned by Angut as to the reason of his unexpected visit. He had done his best to conceal matters, with which Angut, he said, had nothing to do; but somehow that wonderfully wise man had seen, as it were, into his brain, and at once became suspicious. Then he looked so fierce, and demanded the truth so sternly, that he, (Ippegoo), had fled in terror from the hut of Okiok, and did not stop till he had reached the top of a hummock, where he paused to recover breath. Looking back, he saw that Angut had already harnessed the dogs to his sledge, and was packing the Kablunet upon it—"All lies," interrupted Arbalik's mother, Issek, at this point. "If this is true, how comes it that Ippegoo is here first? No doubt the legs of the simple one are the best part of him, but every one knows that they could not beat the dogs of Angut."

"Issek is wise," said Kunelik pleasantly, "almost *too* wise!—but no doubt the simple one can explain."

"Speak, my son."

"Yes, mother, I can explain. You must know that Angut was in such a fierce hurry that he made his whip crack like the splitting of an iceberg, and the dogs gave such a yell and bound that they dashed the sledge against a hummock, and broke some part of it. What part of it I did not stop to see. Only I saw that they had to unload, and the Kablunet helped to mend it. Then I turned and ran. So I am here first."

There was a huk of approval at this explanation, which was given in a slightly exulting tone, and with a glance of mild defiance at Arbalik's mother.

But Issek was not a woman to be put down easily by a simpleton. She at once returned to the charge.

"No doubt Ippegoo is right," she said, with forced calmness, "but he has talked of a message to Okiok. I dare say the wife of Okiok would like to hear what that message is."

"Huk! That is true," said Nuna quickly.

"And," continued Issek, "Ippegoo speaks of the suspicions of Angut. What does he suspect? We would all like to know that."

"Huk! huk! That is also true," exclaimed every one.

"My son," whispered Kunelik, "silence is the only hope of a fool. Speak not at all."

Ippegoo was so accustomed to render blind and willing obedience to his mother that he instantly brought his teeth together with a snap, and thereafter not one word, good, bad, or indifferent, was to be extracted from the simple one.

From what he had revealed, however, it was evident that a speedy visit from the wonderful foreigner was to be looked for. The little party therefore broke up in much excitement, each member of it going off in bursting importance to spread the news in her particular circle, with exaggerations suitable to her special nature and disposition.

While they are thus engaged, we will return to the object of all their interest.

When Ippegoo fled from Angut, as already told, the latter worthy turned quickly to Rooney, and said—

"There is danger somewhere—I know not where or what; but I must leave you. Ermigit will take good care of Ridroonee till I come again."

R. M. Ballantyne

"Nay, if there is danger anywhere I will share it," returned Rooney, rising and stretching himself; "I am already twice the man I was with all this resting and feeding."

The Eskimo looked at the sailor doubtfully for a moment; but when action was necessary, he was a man of few words. Merely uttering the word "Come," he went out and harnessed his dog-team in a few minutes. Then, after wrapping the Kablunet carefully up in furs, he leaped on the fore-part of the sledge, cracked his whip, and went off at full speed.

"What is the danger that threatens, think you?" asked Rooney; "you must have some notion about it."

"I know not, but I guess," answered Angut, with a sternness that surprised his companion. "Ippegoo is a poor tool in the hands of a bad man. He comes from Ujarak, and he asks too earnestly for Nunaga. Ujarak is fond of Nunaga."

Rooney looked pointedly and gravely at Angut. That Eskimo returned the look even more pointedly and with deeper gravity. Then what we may term a grave smile flitted across the features of the Eskimo. A similar smile enlivened the features of the seaman. He spoke no word, but from that moment Rooney knew that Angut was also fond of Nunaga; and he made up his mind to aid him to the utmost of his capacity both in love and war—for sympathy is not confined to races, creeds, or classes, but gloriously permeates the whole human family.

It was at this point that the crash described by Ippegoo occurred. Fortunately no damage was done to the occupants of the sledge, though the vehicle itself had suffered fractures which it took them several hours to repair.

Having finished the repairs, they set off again at greater

speed than ever in the direction of the Eskimo village, accompanied by Ermigit and Tumbler, who, not caring to be left behind, had followed on a smaller sledge, and overtaken them.

* * * * *

Note: For further light on this interesting subject see *History of Greenland and the Moravian Brethren*, volume one, page 159. Longman, 1820.

R. M. Ballantyne

CHAPTER NINE

SHOWS THAT THE WISE ARE A MATCH FOR THE WICKED, AND EXHIBITS TUMBLER AND PUSSI IN DANGER

When Red Rooney and his friend reached the village, and found that most of the men had gone south to hunt, and that Nunaga was living in peace with her mother in her father's town mansion, their fears were greatly relieved, although Angut was still rendered somewhat anxious by the suspicion that mischief of some sort was brewing. Being resolved if possible to discover and counteract it, he told Rooney that he meant to continue his journey southward, and join the hunters.

"Good. I will rest here till you return," said the seaman, "for I feel that I'm not strong enough yet for much exertion."

"But Ridroonee promised to dwell with *me*," returned Angut, somewhat anxiously.

"So I did, and so I will, friend, when you come back. At present you tell me your hut is closed because you have no wife—no kinswoman."

"That is true," returned the Eskimo; "my mother is dead; my

father was killed; I have no brothers, no sisters. But when I am at home old Kannoa cooks for me. She is a good woman, and can make us comfortable."

"Just so, Angut. I'll be content to have the old woman for a nurse as long as I need one. Good luck to you; and, I say, keep a sharp look-out on Ujarak. He's not to be trusted, if I am any judge of men's faces."

Angut said no word in reply, but he smiled a grim smile as he turned and went his way.

Being much fatigued with his recent exertions, Red Rooney turned into Okiok's hut, to the great sorrow of the women and children, who had gathered from all parts of the village to gaze at and admire him.

"He is real—and alive!" remarked Kunelik in a low voice.

"And Nuna is *not* a liar," said the mother of Arbalik.

"Yes; he is tall," said one.

"And broad," observed another.

"But *very* thin," said Pussimek.

"No matter; he can stuff," said Kabelaw, with a nod to her sister Sigokow, who was remarkably stout, and doubtless understood the virtue of the process.

While this commentary was going on, the object of it was making himself comfortable on a couch of skins which Nuna had spread for him on the raised floor at the upper end of her hut. In a few minutes the wearied man was sound asleep, as was indicated by his nose.

No sooner did Mrs Okiok note the peculiar sound than she went out and said to her assembled friends—"*Now* you may come in; but—forget not—no word is to be spoken. Use your eyes and bite your tongues. The one who speaks shall be put out."

Under these conditions the multitude filed into the mansion, where they sat down in rows to gaze their fill in profound silence; and there they sat for more than an hour, rapt in contemplation of the wonderful sight.

"He snorts," was on the lips of Pussimek, but a warning glance from Nuna checked the sentence in the bud.

"He dreams!" had almost slipped from the lips of Kunelik, but she caught it in time.

Certainly these primitive people availed themselves of the permission to use their eyes; nay, more, they also used their eyebrows—and indeed their entire faces, for, the lips being sealed, they not only drank in Rooney, so to speak, with their eyes, but tried to comment upon him with the same organs.

Finding them very imperfect in this respect, they ventured to use their lips without sound—to speak, as it were, in dumb show—and the contortions of visage thus produced were indescribable.

This state of things was at its height when Rooney chanced to awake. As he lay with his face to the foe, the *tableau vivant* met his gaze the instant he opened his eyes. Rooney was quick-witted, and had great power of self-command. He reclosed the eyes at once, and then, through the merest chink between the lids, continued to watch the scene. But the wink had been observed. It caused an abrupt stoppage of the pantomime, and an intense glare of expectancy.

This was too much for Rooney. He threw up his arms, and gave way to a violent explosion of loud and hearty laughter.

If a bomb-shell had burst among the spectators, it could scarcely have caused greater consternation. A panic ensued. Incontinently the mother of Ippegoo plunged head first into the tunnel. The mother of Arbalik followed, overtook her friend, tried to pass, and stuck fast. The others, dashing in, sought to force them through, but only rammed them tighter. Seeing that egress was impossible, those in rear crouched against the furthest wall and turned looks of horror on the Kablunet, who they thought had suddenly gone mad. But observing that Nuna and her daughter did not share their alarm, they soon recovered, and when Rooney at last sat up and began to look grave, they evidently felt somewhat ashamed of themselves. Pussimek at last seized the mother of Ippegoo by the legs, and with a strong pull extracted her from the tunnel. Issek, being thus set free, quickly made her exit. The rest followed by degrees, until Rooney was left with Nuna and her daughter.

"Your friends have had a fright," remarked the sailor.

"They are easily frightened. Are you hungry?"

"Yes; I feel as if I could eat a white bear raw."

"So I expected," returned the little woman, with a laugh, as she placed a platter of broiled meat before her guest, who at once set to work.

Let us now return to Ippegoo. Having borrowed a sledge, he had driven off to the appointed place of rendezvous, before the arrival of Rooney and Angut, as fast as the team could take him. Arrived there, he found Ujarak awaiting him.

R. M. Ballantyne

"You have failed," said the wizard gravely.

"Yes, because Nunaga had left with her father and mother, and is now in the village. So is the Kablunet."

Whatever Ujarak might have felt, he took good care that his countenance should not betray him. Indeed this capacity to conceal his feelings under a calm exterior constituted a large element of the power which he had obtained over his fellows. Without deigning a reply of any kind to his humble and humbled follower, he stepped quietly into the sledge, and drove away to the southward, intending to rejoin the hunters.

Arrived at the ground, he set off on foot over the ice until he found a seal's breathing-hole. Here he arranged his spears, erected a screen of snow-blocks, and sat down to watch.

"Ippegoo," he said, at last breaking silence, "we must not be beaten."

"No, that must *not* be," replied his pupil firmly.

"This time we have failed," continued the wizard, "because I did not think that Okiok would leave his guest."

"I thought," said Ippegoo, somewhat timidly, "that your torngak told you everything."

"You are a fool, Ippegoo."

"I know it, master; but can you not make me more wise by teaching me?"

"Some people are hard to teach," said Ujarak.

"That is also true," returned the youth mournfully. "I know that you can never make me an angekok. Perhaps it would be better not to try."

"No. You are mistaken," said the wizard in a more cheerful tone, for he felt that he had gone too far. "You will make a good enough angekok in time, if you will only attend to what I say, and be obedient. Come, I will explain to you. Torngaks, you must understand, do not always tell all that they know. Sometimes they leave the angekok dark, for a purpose that is best known to themselves. But they always tell enough for the guidance of a wise man—"

"But—but—I am not a wise man, you know," Ippegoo ventured to remark.

"True; but when I have made you an angekok then you will become a wise man—don't you see?"

As the word angekok signifies "wise man," Ippegoo would have been a fool indeed had he failed to see the truism. The sight raised his spirits, and made him look hopeful.

"Well, then, stupid one, speak not, but listen. As I have before told you, I love Nunaga and Nunaga loves me—"

"I—I thought she loved Angut," said Ippegoo.

"O idiot," exclaimed the wizard; "did I not tell you that you cannot understand? The loves of angekoks are not as the loves of ordinary men. Sometimes one's torngak makes the girl seem uncertain which man she likes best—"

"Ye-yes; but in this case there *seems* no uncertainty, for she and Angut—"

"Silence! you worse than baby walrus!"

Ippegoo shut his mouth, and humbly drooped his eyelids.

After a few minutes, Ujarak, having swallowed his wrath, continued in a calm tone—

"This time we have failed. Next time we will be sure to succeed, and—"

"I suppose your torngak told—"

"Silence! weak-minded puffin!" thundered the wizard, to the great astonishment of a seal which came up at that moment to breathe, and prudently retired in time to save its life.

Once again the angekok with a mighty effort restrained his wrath, and after a time resumed—

"Now, Ippegoo, we dare not venture again to try till after the feast, for the suspicion which you have roused in Angut by the foolish wagging of your tongue must be allowed to die out. But in the meantime—though you cannot, *must* not, speak—you can listen, and you can get your mother to listen, and, when you hear anything that you think I ought to know, you will tell me."

"But if," said the pupil timidly, "I should only find out things that your torngak has already told you, what—"

He stopped short, for Ujarak, springing up, walked smartly away, leaving his follower behind to finish the question, and gather up the spears.

"Yes; he is right. I *am* a fool," murmured Ippegoo. "Yet his conduct does seem strange. But he is an angekok. That must be the reason."

Consoling himself with this reflection, the puzzled youth, putting the spears and hunting tackle on his shoulders, followed after his irate master towards the bay where the other hunters were encamped.

We turn now to two other actors in our tale, who, although not very important characters, deserve passing notice.

When Nuna's youngest son, little Tumbler, was brought to the Eskimo village, he made his appearance in the new black dress suit with which Rooney had clothed him—much to the surprise and delight of the whole community. Not long after arriving, he waddled away through the village in search of some piece of amusing mischief to do. On his ramble he fell in with a companion of about his own size, whose costume was that of a woman in miniature—namely, a short coat with a fully developed tail, which trailed on the ground with the approved fashionable swing. This was none other than Pussi, the little daughter of Simek, the great hunter. Now it chanced that there was a mutual liking—a strong bond of sympathy—between Tumbler and Pussi, which induced them always to play together when possible.

No sooner, therefore, did Tumbler catch sight of his friend than he ran after her, grasped her greasy little hand, and waddled away to do, in company with her, what mischief might chance to be possible at the time.

Immediately behind the village there stood a small iceberg, which had grounded there some years before, and was so little reduced in size or shape by the action of each brief summer's sun that it had become to the people almost as familiar a landmark as the solid rocks. In this berg there was a beautiful sea-green cavern whose depths had never yet

R. M. Ballantyne

been fathomed. It was supposed to be haunted, and was therefore visited only by the more daring and courageous among the children of the tribe. Tumbler and Pussi were unquestionably the most daring among these—partly owing to native bravery in both, and partly to profound ignorance and inexperience of danger.

"Let's go to ze g'een cave," suggested Tumbler.

Pussi returned that most familiar of replies—a nod.

We cannot, of course, convey the slightest idea of the infantine Eskimo lisp. As before said, we must be content with the nearest English equivalent.

The green cave was not more than half a mile distant from the village. To reach it the children had to get upon the sea-ice, and this involved crossing what has been termed the ice-foot—namely, that belt of broken up and shattered ice caused by the daily tides—at the point where the grounded ice meets that which is afloat. It is a chaotic belt, varying in character and width according to position and depth of water, and always more or less dangerous to the tender limbs of childhood.

Encountering thus an opportunity for mischievous daring at the very beginning of their ramble, our jovial hero and heroine proceeded to cross, with all the breathless, silent, and awesome delight that surrounds half-suspected wickedness—for they were quite old enough to know that they were on forbidden ground.

"Come, you's not frighted?" said Tumbler, holding out his hand, as he stood on the top of a block, encouraging his companion to advance.

"No—not fri—frighted—but—"

She caught the extended hand, slipped her little foot, and slid violently downward, dragging the boy along with her.

Scrambling to their feet, Pussi looked inclined to whimper, but as Tumbler laughed heartily, she thought better of it, and joined him.

Few of the riven masses by which they were surrounded were much above five or six feet thick; but as the children were short of stature, the place seemed to the poor creatures an illimitable world of icy confusion, and many were the slips, glissades, and semi-falls which they experienced before reaching the other side. Reach it they did, however, in a very panting and dishevelled condition, and it said much for Red Rooney's tailoring capacity that the black dress coat was not riven to pieces in the process.

"Look; help me. Shove me here," said Tumbler, as he laid hold of a block which formed the last difficulty.

Pussi helped and shoved to the best of her small ability, so that Tumbler soon found himself on a ledge which communicated with the sea-ice. Seizing Pussi by her top-knot of hair, he hauled while she scrambled, until he caught a hand, then an arm, then her tail, finally one of her legs, and at last deposited her, flushed and panting, at his side. After a few minutes' rest they began to run—perhaps it were more correct to say waddle—in the direction of "ze g'een cave."

Now it chanced that the said cave was haunted at that time, not by torngaks or other ghosts, but by two men, one of whom at least was filled with an evil spirit.

Ujarak, having ascertained that Okiok had joined the hunting

R. M. Ballantyne

party, and that the Kablunet had reached the village, resolved to make a daring attempt to carry off the fair Nunaga from the very midst of her female friends, and for this purpose sought and found his dupe Ippegoo, whom he sent off to the green cave to await his arrival.

"We must not go together," he said, "for we might be suspected; but you will go off to hunt seals to the south, and I will go out on the floes to consult my torngak."

"But, master, if I go to the south after seals, how can we ever meet at the green cave?"

"O stupid one! Do you not understand that you are only to pretend to go south? When you are well out of sight, then turn north, and make for the berg. You will find me there."

Without further remark the stupid one went off, and in process of time the master and pupil met at the appointed rendezvous.

The entrance to the cavern was light, owing to the transparency of the ice, and farther in it assumed that lovely bluish-green colour from which it derived its name; but the profound depths, which had never yet been fathomed, were as black as ebony—forming a splendid background, against which the icicles and crystal edges of the entrance were beautifully and sharply defined.

Retiring sufficiently far within this natural grotto to be safe from observation in the event of any one chancing to pass by, the wizard looked earnestly into the anxious countenance of the young man.

"Ippegoo," he said, with an air of unwonted solemnity, for, having made up his mind to a desperate venture, the wizard wished to subdue his tool entirely as well as promptly to his will; "Ippegoo, my torngak says the thing must be done to-night, if it is to be done at all. Putting off, he says, will perhaps produce failure."

"'Perhaps'!" echoed the youth, with that perplexed look which so frequently crossed his features when the wizard's words puzzled him. "I thought that torngaks knew every-thing, and never needed to say 'perhaps.'"

"You think too much," said Ujarak testily.

"Was it not yesterday," returned the pupil humbly, "that you told me to think well before speaking?"

"True, O simple one! but there are times to think and times not to think. Your misfortune is that you always do both at the wrong time, and never do either at the right time."

"I wish," returned Ippegoo, with a sigh, "that it were always the time not to think. How much pleasanter it would be!"

"Well, it is time to listen just now," said the wizard, "so give me your attention. I shall this night harness my dogs, and carry off Nunaga by force. And you must harness your dogs in another sledge, and follow me."

"But—but—my mother!" murmured the youth.

"Must be left behind," said the wizard, with tremendous decision and a dark frown; but he had under-estimated his tool, who replied with decision quite equal to his own—

"That *must* not be."

Although taken much by surprise, Ujarak managed

R. M. Ballantyne

to dissemble.

"Well, then," he said, "you must carry her away by force."

"That is impossible," returned Ippegoo, with a faint smile and shake of the head.

For the first time in his life the wizard lost all patience with his poor worshipper, and was on the point of giving way to wrath, when the sound of approaching footsteps outside the cave arrested him. Not caring to be interrupted at that moment, and without waiting to see who approached, Ujarak suddenly gave vent to a fearful intermittent yell, which was well understood by all Eskimos to be the laughter of a torngak or fiend, and, therefore, calculated to scare away any one who approached.

In the present instance it did so most effectually, for poor little Pussi and Tumbler were already rather awed by the grandeur and mysterious appearance of the sea-green cave. Turning instantly, they fled—or toddled—on the wings of terror, and with so little regard to personal safety, that Pussi found herself suddenly on the edge of an ice-cliff, without the power to stop. Tumbler, however, had himself more under command. He pulled up in time, and caught hold of his companion by the tail, but she, being already on a steep gradient, dragged her champion on, and it is certain that both would have gone over the ice precipice and been killed, if Tumbler had not got both heels against an opportune lump of ice. Holding on to the tail with heroic resolution, while Pussi was already swinging in mid-air, the poor boy opened wide his eyes and mouth, and gave vent to a series of yells so tremendous that the hearts of Ujarak and Ippegoo leaped into their throats, as they rushed out of the cavern and hastened to the rescue.

But another ear had been assailed by those cries. Just as Ippegoo—who was fleeter than his master—caught Tumbler with one hand, and Pussi's tail with the other, and lifted both children out of danger, Reginald Rooney, who chanced to be wandering in the vicinity, appeared, in a state of great anxiety, on the scene.

"Glad am I you were in time, Ippegoo," said the seaman, shouldering the little girl, while the young Eskimo put the boy on his back, "but I thought that you and Ujarak were away south with the hunters. What has brought you back so soon? Nothing wrong, I trust?"

"No; all goes well," returned Ippegoo, as they went towards the village. "We have only come back to—to—"

"To make preparation for the feast when they return," said the wizard, coming quickly to the rescue of his unready follower.

"Then they will be back immediately, I suppose?" said Rooney, looking pointedly at the wizard.

"Yes, immediately," answered Ujarak, without appearing to observe the pointed look, "unless something happens to detain them."

Suspecting that there was something behind this reply, the sailor said no more. Ujarak, feeling that he was suspected, and that his plan, therefore, must be given up for the time being, determined to set himself to work to allay suspicion by making himself generally useful, and giving himself up entirely to the festivities that were about to take place on the return of the men from their successful hunt.

CHAPTER TEN

RED ROONEY BECOMES A SPECTACLE
AND THEN A PRESIDENT

Late on the evening of the following day the fur-clad hunters arrived at their village with shouts of rejoicing—hairy and happy—for they brought with them many a carcass of walrus and seal wherewith to replenish their wardrobes and larders, and banish hunger and care from their dwellings for a considerable time to come.

Be not too ready, most refined reader, to condemn those people for their somewhat gross and low ideas of enjoyment. Remember that they were "to the manner born." Consider, also, that "things are not what they seem," and that the difference between you and savages is, in some very important respects at least, not so great as would at first sight appear. You rejoice in literature, music, fine art, etcetera; but how about one or two o'clock? Would these afford you much satisfaction at such a time?

"Bah!" you exclaim, "what a question! The animal wants must of course be supplied." True, most refined one, but a hunk of bread and a plate of soup would fully suffice for animal needs. Would your refined pleasures have as keen a relish for you if you had only to look forward to bread and water between six and nine? Answer, ye sportsmen, how would you get through your day's work if there were not a glorious dinner at the end of it? Speak, ye ballroom frequenters, how would you skip, even with the light of brilliant eyes to encourage you, if there were not what you call a jolly good supper somewhere in the background? Be honest, all of you, and confess—what you tacitly and obviously admit by your actions every day—that our mere animal wants are of vast importance, and that in our ministering to these the only difference between ourselves and the Eskimos is, a somewhat greater variety of viands, a little less of toil in obtaining them, a little more of refinement and cleanliness in the consumption of them, and, perchance, a little less of appetite.

We feel impelled thus to claim for our northern brothers some forbearance and a little genuine sympathy, because we have to record that their first act on arriving was to fly to the cooking-lamps, and commence a feast which extended far into the night, and finally terminated in lethargic repose.

But this was not the feast to which we have more than once referred. It was merely a mild preliminary whet. The hunters were hungry and tired after their recent exertions, as might have been expected, and went in for refreshment with a will. They did not, however, forget the Kablunet. Eager expectation was on tip-toe, and even hunger was forgotten for a short time in the desire to see the foreigner; but Okiok had made up his mind to give them only one glimpse—a sort of moral appetiser—and reserve the full display of his lion until the following day. Just before arriving at the village, therefore, he called a halt, and explained to the hunters that the Kablunet had been very much wearied by his recent journey, that he would not permit him to be disturbed that night; but as he was to dwell with Angut, and was at that time in his, (Okiok's), hut, they would have an opportunity of

R. M. Ballantyne

seeing him during his brief passage from the one hut to the other. They were, however, to be very careful not to crowd upon him or question him, and not to speak at all—in short, only to look!

This having been settled and agreed to, Okiok pushed on alone in advance, to prevent Rooney from showing himself too soon.

Arriving at his town residence, the Eskimo found his guest asleep, as usual, for the poor seaman found that alternate food and repose were the best means for the recovery of lost vigour.

Nuna was quietly cooking the seaman's next meal, and Nunaga was mending one of his garments, when Okiok entered. Both held up a warning finger when he appeared.

"Where is Tumbler?" he asked softly, looking round.

"Gone to the hut of Pussimek to play with Pussi," replied the wife; "we could not keep him quiet, so we—"

She stopped and looked solemn, for Rooney moved. The talking had roused him. Sitting up, he looked gravely first at Nunaga, then at her mother, then at her father, after which he smiled mildly and yawned.

"So you've got back, Okiok?"

"Yes, Ridroonee. And all the hunters are coming, with plenty to eat—great plenty!"

The women's eyes seemed to sparkle at these words, but they said nothing.

"That's a good job, old boy," said the seaman, rising. "I think I'll go out and meet them. It will be dark in a short time."

Here Okiok interposed with an earnest petition that he would not go out to the people that night, explaining that if he were to sit with them during supper none except the gluttons would be able to eat. The rest would only wonder and stare.

Of course our seaman was amenable to reason.

"But," he said, with a humorous glance, "would it not be good for them—especially for the gluttons—to be prevented from eating too much?"

It was evident from the blank look of his visage that Okiok did not understand his guest. The idea of an Eskimo eating too much had never before entered his imagination.

"How can a man eat too much?" he asked. "Until a man is quite full he is not satisfied. When he is quite full, he wants no more; he can *hold* no more!"

"That says a good deal for Eskimo digestion," thought our hero, but as he knew no native word for digestion, he only laughed and expressed his readiness to act as his host wished.

Just then the noise of cracking whips and yelping dogs was heard outside.

"Remain here," said Okiok; "I will come again."

Not long after the hospitable man's exit all the noise ceased, but the seaman could hear murmuring voices and stealthy footsteps gathering round the hut. In a few minutes Okiok returned.

R. M. Ballantyne

"Angut is now ready," he said, "to receive you. The people will look at you as you pass, but they will not disturb you."

"I'm ready to go—though sorry to leave Nuna and Nunaga," said the gallant Rooney, rising.

The sounds outside and Okiok's words had prepared him for some display of curiosity, but he was quite taken aback by the sight that met his eyes on emerging from the tunnel, for there, in absolute silence, with wide expectant eyes and mouths a-gape, stood every man, woman, and child capable of motion in the Eskimo village!

They did not stand in a confused group, but in two long lines, with a space of four or five feet between, thus forming a living lane, extending from the door of Okiok's hut to that of Angut, which stood not far distant.

At first our seaman felt an almost irresistible inclination to burst into a hearty fit of laughter, there seemed something so absurdly solemn in this cumulative stare, but good feeling fortunately checked him; yet he walked with his host along the lane with such a genuine expression of glee and good-will on his manly face that a softly uttered but universal and emphatic "Huk!" assured him he had made a good first impression.

When he had entered the abode of Angut a deep sigh of relief escaped from the multitude, and they made up for their enforced silence by breaking into a gush of noisy conversation.

In his new abode Red Rooney found Angut and old Kannoa, with a blazing lamp and steaming stove-kettle, ready to receive him.

Few were the words of welcome uttered by Angut, for Eskimos are not addicted to ceremonial; nevertheless, with the promptitude of one ever ready to learn, he seized his visitor's hand, and shook it heartily in the manner which Rooney had taught him—with the slight mistake that he shook it from side to side instead of up and down. At the same time he pointed to a deerskin seat on the raised floor of the hut, where Kannoa had already placed a stone dish of smoking viands.

The smile which had overspread Rooney's face at the handshaking faded away as he laid his hand on the old woman's shoulder, and, stooping down, gazed at her with an expression of great tenderness.

Ah! Rooney, what is there in that old wrinkled visage, so scarred by the rude assaults of Time, yet with such a strong touch of pathos in the expression, that causes thy broad bosom to swell and thine eagle eyes to moisten? Does it remind thee of something very different, yet wonderfully like, in the old country?

Rooney never distinctly told what it was, but as he had left a much—loved grandmother at home, we may be permitted to guess. From that hour he took a tender interest in that little old woman, and somehow—from the expression of his eye, perhaps, or the touch of his strong hand—the old creature seemed to know it, and chuckled, in her own peculiar style, immensely. For old Kannoa had not been overburdened with demonstrative affection by the members of her tribe, some of whom had even called her an old witch—a name which had sent a thrill of great terror through her trembling old heart, for the doom of witches in Eskimo land in those days was very terrible.

Next day, being that of the great feast, the entire village

R. M. Ballantyne

bestirred itself with the first light of morning. Men and women put on their best garments, the lamps were kindled, the cooking-kettles put on, and preparations generally commenced on a grand scale.

Awaking and stretching himself, with his arms above his head and his mouth open, young Ermigit yawned vociferously.

"Hah! how strong I feel," he said, "a white bear would be but a baby in my hands!"

Going through a similar stretch-yawny process, his brother Norrak said that he felt as if he had strength to turn a walrus inside out.

"Come, boys, turn yourselves out o' the house, and help to cut up the meat. It is not wise to boast in the morning," said Okiok.

"True, father," returned Norrak quietly, "but if we don't boast in the morning, the men do it so much all the rest of the day that we'll have no chance."

"These two will be a match for you in talk before long," remarked Nuna, after her sons had left.

"Ay, and also in body," returned the father, who was rather proud of his well-grown boys. "Huk! what is Tumbler putting on?" he asked in astonishment.

"The dress that the Kablunet made for him," said Nunaga, with a merry laugh. "Doesn't it fit well? My only fear is that if Arbalik sees him, he will pierce him with a dart before discovering his mistake."

"What are you going to begin the day with?" asked Nuna, as

she stirred her kettle.

"With a feed," replied Okiok, glancing slyly at his better half.

"As if I didn't know that!" returned the wife. "When did Okiok ever do anything before having his morning feed?"

"When he was starving," retorted the husband promptly.

This pleasantry was received with a giggle by the women.

"Well, father, and what comes after the morning feed?" asked Nunaga.

"Kick-ball," answered Okiok.

"That is a hard game," said the wife; "it makes even the young men blow like walruses."

"Ay, and eat like whales," added the husband.

"And sleep like seals," remarked Nunaga.

"And snore like—like Okioks," said Nuna.

This was a hard hit, being founded on some degree of truth, and set Okiok off in a roar of laughter.

Becoming suddenly serious, he asked if anything had been seen the day before of Ujarak the angekok.

"Yes, he was in the village in the evening," replied Nuna as she arranged the food on platters. "He and Ippegoo were found in the green cave yesterday by the Kablunet. He was out about the ice-heaps, and came on them just as Tumbler

R. M. Ballantyne

saved Pussi, and Ippegoo saved them both."

"Tumbler saved Pussi!" exclaimed the Eskimo, looking first at his daughter and then at his wife.

"Yes; Pussi was tumbling over an ice-cliff," said Nunaga, "and Tumbler held on to her."

"By the tail," said Nuna. "So Ippegoo rushed out of the cave, and saved them both. Ujarak would have been too late. It seems strange to me that his torngak did not warn him in time."

"Torngaks must be very hard-hearted," said Okiok, with a look and tone of contempt that he did not care to conceal. "But what were they doing in the cave?"

"Who knows?" replied Nuna. "These two are always plotting. Ridroonee says they looked as if worried at having been discovered. Come, fall-to. You must be strong to-day if you would play kick-ball well."

Okiok glanced with a look of care upon his brow at Nunaga, shook his head gravely once or twice in silence, and began breakfast.

After the meal was over he sallied forth to join in the sports, which were soon to begin. Going first to the hut of Angut, he found the most of his countrymen and women surrounding Red Rooney, who, having finished breakfast, was seated on a sledge conversing with Angut and Simek, and others of the chief men of the tribe. All the rest were gazing and listening with greedy eyes and ears.

"Hi! Okiok," exclaimed the sailor heartily, as he rose and held out his hand, which his former host shook heartily, to the great surprise and delight of the crowd; "have you joined the gluttons, that you take so long to your morning feed? or have you slept longer than usual, to make you a better match for the young men?"

"No; I was in dreamland," answered the Eskimo, with profound gravity, which his countrymen knew quite well was pretended; "and I met a torngak there, who told me that the Kablunet needed much sleep as well as food, and must not be roused by me, although other fools might disturb him."

"How kind of the torngak!" returned Rooney. "But he was not polite, for if he spoke to you of 'other' fools, he must have thought of you as *one* fool. Was he your own torngak?"

"No; I have no torngak. He was my grandmother's. And he told me that the Kablunet was a great angekok, and would have a torngak of his own soon. Moreover, he said the games must begin at once—so come along, Ippegoo."

As he spoke, Okiok caught the slender youth in his powerful arms, laid him gently on his back, flung some snow in his face, and then ran away.

Ippegoo, entering at once into the spirit of the fun, arose and gave chase. Excelling in speed as much as his opponent did in strength, the youth soon overtook him, managed to trip him up, and fell on the top of him. He was wildly cheered by the delighted crowd, and tried to punish Okiok; but his efforts were not very successful, for that worthy put both his mittened hands over his head, and, curling himself up like a hedgehog, lay invulnerable on the ice. Poor Ippegoo had not strength either to uncoil, or lift, or even move his foe, and failed to find a crevice in his hairy dress into which he might stuff snow.

R. M. Ballantyne

After a few minutes Okiok straightened himself out, jumped up, and scurried off again over the ice, in the direction of the berg of the green cave, followed by the entire village.

It was on a level field of ice close to the berg referred to that the game of kick-ball was to be played. As Rooney was not yet strong enough to engage in rough play, a pile of deerskins was placed on a point of the berg, slightly higher than the heads of the people, and he was requested to mount thereon. There, as on a throne, he presided over the games, and became the gazing-stock of the tribe during the intervals of play. But these intervals were not numerous or prolonged, for most of the players were powerful men and boys, so thoroughly inured, by the nature of their lives, to hardship and vigorous action in every possible position of body that their muscles were always in the condition of those of a well-trained athlete. Even Ippegoo, with all his natural defects of mind and body, was by no means contemptible as a player, in those games, especially, which required agility and powers of endurance.

First they had a game of hand-ball. It was very simple. The players, who were not selected, but entered the lists at their own pleasure, divided themselves into two parties, which stood a little apart from each other. Then an ordinary hand-ball was tossed into the air by Okiok, who led one of the parties. Simek, the mighty hunter, led the other. These men, although approaching middle age, were still at the height of their strength and activity, and therefore fitting leaders of the younger men in this as well as the more serious affairs of life.

It seemed to Rooney at first as if Okiok and his band were bent on having all the fun to themselves, for they began to toss the ball to each other, without any regard to their opponents. But suddenly Simek and some of his best men made a rush into the midst of the other party with shouts and amazing bounds. Their object was to catch or wrest the ball from Okiok's party, and throw it into the midst of their own friends, who would then begin to amuse themselves with it until their opponents succeeded in wresting it from them.

Of course this led to scenes of violent action and wild but good-humoured excitement. Wrestling and grasping each other were forbidden in this game, but hustling, tripping up, pushing, and charging were allowed, so that the victory did not always incline either to the strong or the agile. And the difficulty of taking the ball from either party was much greater than one might suppose.

For full half an hour they played with the utmost energy, insomuch that they had to pause for a few seconds to recover breath. Then, with one accord, eyes were turned to the president, to see how he took it.

Delight filled every bosom, for they saw that he was powerfully sympathetic. Indeed Rooney had become so excited as well as interested in the game, that it was all he could do to restrain himself from leaping into the midst of the struggling mass and taking a part. He greeted the pause and the inquiring gaze with a true British cheer, which additionally charmed as well as surprised the natives. But their period of rest was brief.

Simek had the ball at the time. He suddenly sent it with a wild "Huk! hoo-o-o!" whirling into the air. The Kablunet was instantly forgotten. The ball came straight down towards a clumsy young man, who extended his hands, claw-like, to receive it. At that moment Ippegoo launched himself like a thunderbolt into the small of the clumsy youth's back, and sent him sprawling on the snow amid shouts of laughter, while Norrak leaped neatly in, and, catching the ball as it rebounded, sent it up again on the same side. As it went up straight and came down perpendicularly, there was a concentric rush from all sides. Ujarak chanced to be the buffer who received the shock, and his big body was well able to sustain it. At the same moment he deftly caught the ball.

"Ho! his torngak helps him!" shouted Okiok ironically.

"So he does," cried the wizard, with a scoffing laugh, as he hurled the ball aloft; "why does not your torngak help *you*?"

There was a loud titter at this, but the laugh was turned in favour of the other side when Ermigit caught the ball, and sent it over to the Okiok band, while their leader echoed the words, "So he does," and spun the ball from him with such force that it flew over all heads, and chanced to alight in the lap of Red Rooney. It could not have landed better, for that worthy returned it as a point-blank shot which took full effect on the unexpectant nose of Ermigit.

The spirited lad was equal to the occasion. Although water rose unbidden to his eyes, he caught the ball, and with a shout of laughter flung it into the midst of his own side. Thus the play went on fast and furious, until both sides were gasping. Then with one consent they stopped for a more prolonged rest—for there was no winning or losing at this game. Their only aim was to see which side could get hold of the ball oftenest and keep it longest until all were exhausted.

But the fun did not cease although the game did, for another and quieter game of strength was instituted. The whole party drew closer round their president, and many of them mounted to points of vantage on the berg, on the sides of which groups of the women and children had already taken up positions.

It may be remarked here that the snow-covered ice on which the game of ball had been played was like a sheet of white marble, but not so hard, for a heavy stamp with a heel could produce an indentation, though no mark was left by the ordinary pressure of a foot.

The competitors in the game of strength, or rather, of endurance, were only two in number. One was Okiok's eldest son, Norrak, the other the clumsy young man to whom reference has been already made. The former, although the smaller and much the younger of the two, was remarkably strong for his age.

These two engaged in a singular style of boxing, in which, strange to say, the combatants did not face each other, nor did they guard or jump about. Stripped to the waist, like real heroes of the ring, they walked up to each other, and the clumsy youth turned his naked back to Norrak, who doubled his fist, and gave him a sounding thump thereon. Then Norrak wheeled about and submitted to a blow, which was delivered with such good-will that he almost tumbled forward. Again he turned about, and the clumsy one presented his back a second time; and thus they continued to pommel each other's backs until they began to pant vehemently. At last Norrak hit his adversary such a whack on the right shoulder that he absolutely spun him round, and caused him to roll over on his back, amid the plaudits of the assembly.

The clumsy one rose with a somewhat confused look, but was not allowed to continue the battle. There was no such thing as fighting it out "to the bitter end" among these hilarious Eskimos. In fact, they were playing, not fighting.

At this point Simek approached Rooney with a smiling countenance, and said—

R. M. Ballantyne

"There is another game of strength which we sometimes play, and it is the custom to appoint a man to choose the players. Will the Kablunet act this part to-day?"

Of course our seaman was quite ready to comply. After a few moments' consideration, he looked round, with a spice of mischief in his heart, but a smile on his countenance, and said—

"What could be more agreeable than to see the striving of two such good friends as Angut my host and Ujarak the angekok?"

There was a sudden silence and opening of eyes at this, for every one was well aware that a latent feeling of enmity existed between these two, and their personal strength and courage being equally well-known, no one up to that time had ventured to pit these two against each other. There was no help for it now, however. They were bound in honour, as well as by the laws of the community, to enter into conflict. Indeed they showed no inclination to avoid the trial, for Angut at once stepped quietly into the space in front of the president, and began to strip off his upper garments, while Ujarak leaped forward with something of a bounce, and did the same.

They were splendid specimens of physical manhood, both of them, for their well-trained muscles lay bulging on their limbs in a way that would have gladdened the sculptors of Hercules to behold. But there was a vast difference in the aspect of the two men. Both were about equal in height and breadth of shoulder, but Angut was much the slimmer and more elegant about the waist, as well as considerably lighter than his adversary. It was in the bearing of Angut, however, that the chief difference lay. There was a refinement of physiognomy and a grace of motion about him of which the other was utterly destitute; and it was plain that while the wizard was burning to come off victorious, the other was only willing, in a good-humoured way, to comply with the demands of custom. There was neither daring, defiance, contempt, nor fear in his countenance, which wore its wonted aspect of thoughtful serenity.

After this description of the champions, we feel almost unwilling to disappoint the reader by saying that the game or trial was the reverse of martial or noble. Sitting down on the hard snow, they linked their legs and arms together in a most indescribable manner, and strove to out-pull each other. There was, indeed, much more of the comic than the grand in this display, yet, as the struggle went on, a feeling of breathless interest arose, for it was not often that two such stalwart frames were seen in what appeared to be a mortal effort. The great muscles seemed to leap up from arm and thigh, as each made sudden and desperate efforts—right and left—sometimes pulling and sometimes pushing back, in order to throw each other off guard, while perspiration burst forth and stood in beads upon their foreheads.

At last Ujarak thrust his opponent back to the utmost extent of his long arms, and, with a sudden pull, raised him almost to his feet.

There was a gasp of excitement, almost of regret, among the onlookers, for Angut was a decided favourite.

But the pull was not quite powerful enough. Angut began to sink back to his old position. He seemed to feel that now or never was his chance. Taking advantage of his descending weight, he added to it a wrench which seemed to sink his ten fingers into the flesh of Ujarak's shoulders; a momentary check threw the latter off his guard, and next instant Angut not only pulled him over, but hurled him over his own head, and rolled him like a porpoise on the snow!

A mighty shout hailed the victory as the wizard arose and retired crestfallen from the scene, while the victor gravely resumed his coat and mingled with the crowd.

Ujarak chanced, in retiring, to pass close to Okiok. Although naturally amiable, that worthy, feeling certain that the wizard was playing a double part, and was actuated by sinister motives in some of his recent proceedings, could not resist the temptation to whisper—

"Was your torngak asleep, that he failed to help you just now?"

The whisper was overheard by some of the women near, who could not suppress a subdued laugh.

The wizard, who was not at that moment in a condition to take a jest with equanimity, turned a fierce look upon Okiok.

"I challenge you," he said, "to a singing combat."

"With all my heart," replied Okiok; "when shall it be?"

"To-morrow," said the wizard sternly.

"To-morrow let it be," returned Okiok, with the cool indifference of an Arctic hunter, to the immense delight of the women and others who heard the challenge, and anticipated rare sport from the impending duel.

CHAPTER ELEVEN

THE HAIRY ONES FEAST AND ARE HAPPY

Lest the reader should anticipate, from the conclusion of the last chapter, that we are about to describe a scene of bloodshed and savagery, we may as well explain in passing that the custom of duelling, as practised among some tribes of the Eskimos, is entirely intellectual, and well worthy of recommendation to those civilised nations which still cling fondly and foolishly to the rapier and pistol.

If an Eskimo of the region about which we write thinks himself aggrieved by another, he challenges him to a singing and dancing combat. The idea of taking their revenge, or "satisfying their honour," by risking their lives and proving their courage in mortal combat, does not seem to have occurred to them—probably because the act would be without significance among men whose whole existence is passed in the daily risk of life and limb and proof of courage.

Certainly the singing combat has this advantage, that intellect triumphs over mere brute force, and the physically weak may prove to be more than a match for the strong.

But as this duel was postponed to the following day, for the very good reason that a hearty supper and night of social enjoyment had first to be disposed of, we will turn again to the players on the ice-floe.

"Come, Angut," said Rooney, descending from his throne or presidential chair, and taking the arm of his host; "I'm getting cold sitting up there. Let us have a walk together, and explain to me the meaning of this challenge."

They went off in the direction of the sea-green cave, while Simek organised a game of kick-ball.

"Okiok tells me," continued Rooney, "that there is to be no fighting or bloodshed in the matter. How is that?"

Angut expounded, as we have already explained, and then asked—

"Have they no singing combats in your land?"

"Well, not exactly; at least not for the purpose of settling quarrels."

"How, then, are quarrels settled?"

"By law, sometimes, and often by sword—you would call it spear—and pistol. A pistol is a thing that spouts fire and kills. Nations occasionally settle their quarrels in the same way, and call it war."

Angut looked puzzled—as well he might!

"When two men quarrel, can killing do any good?" he asked.

"I fear not," answered the seaman, "for the mere gratification of revenge is not good. But they do not always kill. They sometimes only wound slightly, and then they say that honour is satisfied, and they become friends."

"But—but," said the still puzzled Eskimo, "a wound cannot prove which quarreller is right. Is it the one who wounds that is thought right?"

"No."

"Is it then the wounded one?"

"O no. It is neither. The fact is, the proving of who is right and who is wrong has nothing to do with the matter. All they want is to prove that they are both very brave. Often, when one is slightly wounded—no matter which—they say they are satisfied."

"With what are they satisfied?"

"That's more than I can tell, Angut. But it is only a class of men called *gentlemen* who settle their quarrels thus. Common fellows like me are supposed to have no honour worth fighting about!"

The Eskimo looked at his companion, supposing that he might be jesting, but seeing that he was quite grave and earnest, he rejoined in an undertone—

"Then my thoughts have been wrong."

"In what respect, Angut?"

"It has often come into my mind that the greatest fools in the world were to be found among the Innuit; but there must be greater fools in the lands you tell of."

As he spoke the sound of child-voices arrested them, and one

R. M. Ballantyne

was heard to utter the name of Nunaga. The two men paused to listen. They were close to the entrance to the ice-cave, which was on the side of the berg opposite to the spot where the games were being held, and the voices were recognised as those of Pussi and Tumbler. With the indomitable perseverance that was natural to him, the latter had made a second attempt to lead Pussi to the cave, and had been successful.

"What is he goin' to do?" asked Pussi, in a voice of alarm.

"Goin' to run away vid sister Nunaga," replied Tumbler. "I heard Ippegoo say dat to his mudder. Ujarak is goin' to take her away, an' nebber, nebber come back no more."

There was silence after this, silence so dead and prolonged that the listeners began to wonder. It was suddenly broken. Evidently the horrified Pussi had been gathering up her utmost energies, for there burst from the sea-green depths of the cave a roar of dismay so stupendous that Angut and our seaman ran hastily forward, under the impression that some accident had occurred; but the children were sitting there all safe—Tumbler gazing in surprise at his companion, whose eyes were tight shut and her mouth wide-open.

The truth is that Pussi loved and was beloved by Nunaga, and the boy's information had told upon her much more powerfully than he had expected. Of course Tumbler was closely questioned by Angut, but beyond the scrap of information he had already given nothing more was to be gathered from him. The two friends were therefore obliged to rest content with the little they had learned, which was enough to put them on their guard.

Ere long the sinking of the sun put an end to the games, but not before the whole community had kick-balled themselves into a state of utter incapacity for anything but feeding.

To this process they now devoted themselves heart and soul, by the light of the cooking-lamps, within the shelter of their huts. The feast was indeed a grand one. Not only had they superabundance of the dishes which we have described in a previous chapter, but several others of a nature so savoury as to be almost overpowering to the poor man who was the honoured guest of the evening. But Red Rooney laid strong constraint on himself, and stood it bravely.

There was something grandly picturesque and Rembrandtish in the whole scene, for the smoke of the lamps, combined with the deep shadows of the rotund and hairy figures, formed a background out of which the animated oily faces shone with ruddy and glittering effect.

At first, of course, little sound was heard save the working of their jaws; but as nature began to feel more than adequately supplied, soft sighs began to be interpolated and murmuring conversation intervened. Then some of the more moderate began to dally with tit-bits, and the buzz of conversation swelled.

At this point Rooney took Tumbler on his knee, and began to tempt him with savoury morsels. It is only just to the child, (who still wore his raven coat), to say that he yielded readily to persuasion. Rooney also amused and somewhat scandalised his friends by insisting on old Kannoa sitting beside him.

"Ho! Ujarak," at last shouted the jovial Simek, who was one of those genial, uproarious, loud-laughing spirits, that can keep the fun of a social assembly going by the mere force and enthusiasm of his animal spirits; "come, tell us about that wonderful bear you had such a fight with last moon, you remember?"

"Remember!" exclaimed the wizard, with a pleased look, for there was nothing he liked better than to be called on to relate his adventures—and it must be added that there was nothing he found easier, for, when his genuine adventures were not sufficiently telling, he could without difficulty expand, exaggerate, modify, or even invent, so as to fit them for the ears of a fastidious company.

"Remember!" he repeated in a loud voice, which attracted all eyes, and produced a sudden silence; "of course I remember. The difficulty with me is to forget—and I would that I could forget—for the adventure was ho-r-r-ible!"

A low murmur of curiosity, hope, and joyful expectation, amounting to what we might style applause, broke from the company as the wizard dwelt on the last word.

You see, Eskimos love excitement fully as much as other people, and as they have no spirituous drinks wherewith to render their festivities unnaturally hilarious, they are obliged to have recourse to exciting tales, comic songs, games, and other reasonable modes of creating that rapid flow of blood, which is sometimes styled the "feast of reason and the flow of soul." Simek's soul flowed chiefly from his eyes and from his smiling lips in the form of hearty laughter and encouragement to others—for in truth he was an unselfish man, preferring rather to draw out his friends than to be drawn out by them.

"Tell us all about it, then, Ujarak," he cried. "Come, we are ready. Our ears are open—yes; they are very *wide* open!"

There was a slight titter at this sly reference to the magnitude of the lies that would have to be taken in, but Ujarak's vanity rendered him invulnerable to such light shafts. After glaring round with impressive solemnity, so as to deepen the silence and intensify the expectation, he began:—

"It was about the time when the ravens lay their eggs and the small birds appear. My torngak had told me to go out on the ice, far over the sea in a certain direction where I should find a great berg with many white peaks mounting up to the very sky. There, he said, I should find what I was to do. It was blowing hard at the time; also snowing and freezing. I did not wish to go, but an angekok *must* go forward and fear nothing when his torngak points the way. Therefore I went."

"Took no food? no sleigh? no dogs?" asked Okiok in surprise.

"No. When it is a man's duty to obey, he must not think of small things. It is the business of a wise man to do or to die."

There was such an air of stern grandeur about Ujarak as he gave utterance to this high-flown sentiment, that a murmur of approval burst from his believers, who formed decidedly the greater part of the revellers, and Okiok hid his diminished head in the breast of his coat to conceal his laughter.

"I had no food with me—only my walrus spear and line," continued the wizard. "Many times I was swept off my feet by the violence of the gale, and once I was carried with such force towards a mass of upheaved ice that I expected to be dashed against it and killed, but just as this was about to happen the—"

"Torngak helped—eh?" interrupted Okiok, with a simple look.

"No; torngaks never help while we are above ground. They only advise, and leave it to the angekok's wisdom and courage to do the rest," retorted the wizard, who, although roused to wrath by these interruptions of Okiok, felt that his character would be damaged if he allowed the slightest appearance of it to escape him.

"When, as I said, I was about to be hurled against the berg of ice, the wind seemed to bear me up. No doubt it was a long hollow at the foot of the ice that sent the wind upwards, but my mind was quick. Instead of resisting the impulse, I made a bound, and went up into the air and over the berg. It was a very low one," added the wizard, as a reply to some exclamations of extreme surprise—not unmingled with doubt—from some of his audience.

"After that," continued Ujarak, "the air cleared a little, and I could see a short way around me, as I scudded on. Small bergs were on every side of me. There were many white foxes crouching in the lee of these for shelter. Among them I noticed some white bears. Becoming tired of thus scudding before the wind, I made a dash to one side, to get under the shelter of a small berg and take rest. Through the driving snow I could see the figure of a man crouching there before me. I ran to him, and grasped his coat to check my speed. He stood up—oh, *so* high! It was not a man," (the wizard deepened his voice, and slowed here)—"it—was—a—white—bear!"

Huks and groans burst at this point from the audience, who were covered with the perspiration of anxiety, which would have been cold if the place had not been so warm.

"I turned and ran," continued the angekok; "the bear followed. We came to a small hummock of ice. I doubled round it. The bear went past—like one of Arbalik's arrows—

sitting on its haunches, and trying to stop itself in vain, for the wind carried it on like an oomiak with the sail spread. When the bear stopped, it turned back, and soon came up with me, for I had doubled, and was by that time running nearly against the wind. Then my courage rose! I resolved to face the monster with my walrus spear. It was a desperate venture, but it was my duty. Just then the snow partly ceased, and I could see a berg with sloping sides. 'Perhaps I may find a point of vantage there that I have not on the flat ice,' I thought, and away I ran for the sloping berg. It was rugged and broken. Among its masses I managed to dodge the bear till I got to the top. Here I resolved to stand and meet my foe, but as I stood I saw that the other side of the berg had been partly melted by the sun. It was a clear steep slope from the top to the bottom. The bear was scrambling up, foaming in its fury, with its eyes glaring like living lamps, and its red mouth a-gape. Another thought came to me—I have been quick of thought from my birth! Just as the bear was rising to the attack, I sat down on the slope, and flew rather than slid to the bottom. It was an awful plunge! I almost shut my eyes in horror—but—but—kept them open. At the bottom there was a curve like a frozen wave. I left the top of this curve and finished the descent in the air. The crash at the end was awful, but I survived it. There was no time for thought. I looked back. The bear, as I expected, had watched me in amazement, and was preparing to follow—for bears, you know, fear nothing. It sat down at the top of the slope, and stuck its claws well into the ice in front of it. I ran back to the foot of the slope to meet it. Its claws lost hold, and it came down thundering, like a huge round stone from a mountain side. I stood, and, measuring exactly its line of descent, stuck the butt of my spear into the ice with the point sloping upwards. Then I retired to see the end, for I did not dare to stand near to it. It happened as I had wished: the bear came straight on my spear. The point went in at the breast-bone, and came out at the small of the back; but the bear was not checked. It went on, taking the spear along with it, and sending out streams of blood like the spouts of a dying whale. When at last it ceased to roll, it lay stretched out upon the ice—dead!"

The wizard paused, and looked round. There was a deep-drawn sigh, as if the audience had been relieved from a severe strain of attention. And so they had; and the wizard accepted that involuntary sigh as an evidence of the success of his effort to amuse.

"How big was that bear?" asked Ippegoo, gazing on his master with a look of envious admiration.

"How big?" repeated Ujarak; "oh, as big—far bigger than—than—the—biggest bear I have ever seen."

"Oh, then it was an *invisible* bear, was it?" asked Okiok in surprise.

"How? What do you mean?" demanded the wizard, with an air of what was meant for grave contempt.

"If it was bigger than the *biggest* bear you have ever seen," replied Okiok, with a stupid look; "then you could not have seen *it*, because, you know, it could not well be bigger than itself."

"Huk! that's true," exclaimed one, while others laughed heartily, for Eskimos dearly love a little banter.

"Boh! ba! boo!" exclaimed Simek, after a sudden guffaw; "that's not equal to what *I* did to the walrus. Did I ever tell it you, friends?—but never mind whether I did or not. I'll tell it to our guest the Kablunet now."

The jovial hunter was moved to this voluntary and abrupt offer of a story by his desire to prevent anything like angry feeling arising between Okiok and the wizard. Of course the company, as well as Rooney, greeted the proposal with pleasure, for although Simek did not often tell of his own exploits, and made no pretension to be a graphic story-teller, they all knew that whatever he undertook he did passably well, while his irrepressible good-humour and hilarity threw a sort of halo round all that he said.

"Well, my friends, it was a terrible business!"

Simek paused, and looked round on the company with a solemn stare, which produced a smothered laugh—in some cases a little shriek of delight—for every one, except the wizard himself, recognised in the look and manner an imitation of Ujarak.

"A dreadful business," continued Simek; "but I got over it, as you shall hear. I too have a torngak. You need not laugh, my friends. It is true. He is only a little one, however—about so high, (holding up his thumb), and he never visits me except at night. One night he came to me, as I was lying on my back, gazing through a hole in the roof at our departed friends dancing in the sky. [See note.] He sat down on the bridge of my nose, and looked at me. I looked at *him*. Then he changed his position, sat down on my chin, and looked at me over my nose. Then he spoke.

"'Do you know White-bear Bay?' he asked."

"'Know it?' said I—'do I know my own mother?'"

"'What answer is that?' he said in surprise."

"Then I remembered that torngaks—especially little ones—

R. M. Ballantyne

don't understand jokes, nothing but simple speech; so I laughed."

"'Don't laugh,' he said, 'your breath is strong.' And that was true; besides, I had a bad cold at the time, so I advised him to get off my chin, for if I happened to cough he might fall in and be swallowed before I could prevent it.

"'Tell me,' said he, with a frown, 'do you know White-bear Bay?'"

"'Yes!' said I, in a shout that made him stagger."

"'Go there,' said he, 'and you shall see a great walrus, as big as one of the boats of the women. Kill it.'"

"The cold getting bad at that moment, I gave a tremendous sneeze, which blew my torngak away—"

A shriek of delight, especially from the children, interrupted Simek at this point. Little Tumbler, who still sat on Rooney's knee, was the last to recover gravity, and little Pussi, who still nestled beside Nunaga, nearly rolled on the floor from sympathy.

Before the story could be resumed, one of the women announced that a favourite dish which had been for some time preparing was ready. The desire for that dish proving stronger than the desire for the story, the company, including Simek, set to work on it with as much gusto as if they had eaten nothing for hours past!

* * * * *

Note. Such is the Eskimo notion of the Aurora Borealis.

CHAPTER TWELVE

COMBINES STORY-TELLING (IN BOTH SENSES) WITH FASTING, FUN, AND MORE SERIOUS MATTERS

The favourite dish having been disposed of, Simek continued his story.

"Well," said he, "after my little torngak had been blown away, I waited a short time, hoping that he would come back, but he did not; so I got up, took a spear in my hand, and went off to White-bear Bay, determined to see if the little spirit had spoken the truth. Sure enough, when I got to the bay, there was the walrus sitting beside its hole, and looking about in all directions as if it were expecting me. It was a giant walrus," said Simek, lowering his remarkably deep voice to a sort of thunderous grumble that filled the hearts of his auditors with awe in spite of themselves, "a—most—awful walrus! It was bigger,"—here he looked pointedly at Okiok—"than—than the very *biggest* walrus I have ever seen! I have not much courage, friends, but I went forward, and threw my spear at it." (The listeners gasped.) "It missed!" (They groaned.) "Then I turned, and, being filled with fear, I ran. Did you ever see me run?"

"Yes, yes," from the eager company.

R. M. Ballantyne

"No, my friends, you never saw me run! Anything you ever saw me do was mere walking—creeping—standing still, compared with what I did then on that occasion. You know I run fast?" ("Yes, yes.") "But that big walrus ran faster. It overtook me; it overturned me; it *swallowed* me!"

Here Simek paused, as if to observe how many of them swallowed that. And, after all, the appeal to their credulity was not as much overstrained as the civilised reader may fancy, for in their superstitious beliefs Eskimos held that there was one point in the training of a superior class of angekoks which necessitated the swallowing of the neophyte by a bear and his returning to his friends alive and well after the operation! Besides, Simek had such an honest, truthful expression of countenance and tone of voice, that he could almost make people believe anything he chose to assert. Some there were among his hearers who understood the man well, and guessed what was coming; others there were who, having begun by thinking him in jest, now grew serious, under the impression that he was in earnest; but by far the greater number believed every word he said. All, however, remained in expectant silence while he gravely went on:—

"My friends, you will not doubt me when I say that it was very hot inside of that walrus. I stripped myself, but was still too hot. Then I sat down on one of his ribs to think. Suddenly it occurred to me to draw my knife and cut myself out. To my dismay, I found that my knife had been lost in the struggle when I was swallowed. I was in despair, for you all know, my friends, how impossible it is to cut up a walrus, either from out or inside, without a knife. In my agony I seized the monster's heart, and tried to tear it; but it was too hard-hearted for that. The effort only made the creature tremble and jump, which I found inconvenient. I also knew from the curious muffled sound outside that it was roaring. I sat down again on a rib to consider. If I had been a real angekok, my torngak no doubt would have helped me at that time—but he did not."

"How could you have a torngak at all if you are not a *real* angekok?" demanded the wizard, in a tone that savoured of contempt.

"You shall hear. Patience!" returned Simek quietly, and then went on:—

"I had not sat long when I knew by the motions of the beast that he was travelling over the ice—no doubt making for his water-hole. 'If he gets into the sea,' I thought, 'it will be the end of me.' I knew, of course, that he could not breathe under water, and that he could hold his breath so long that before he came up again for fresh air I should be suffocated. My feelings became dreadful. I hope, my friends, that you will never be in a situation like it. In my despair I rushed about from the head to the tail. I must have hurt him dreadfully in doing so—at least I thought so, from the way he jumped about. Once or twice I was tossed from side to side as if he was rolling over. You know I am a man of tender heart. My wife says that, so it must be true; but my heart was hardened by that time; I cared not. I cared for nothing!

"Suddenly I saw a small sinew, in the form of a loop, close to the creature's tail. As a last hope, without knowing why, I seized it and tugged. The tail, to my surprise, came slightly inwards. I tugged again. It came further in. A new thought came to me suddenly. This was curious, for, you know, that never since I was a little child have my thoughts been quick, and very seldom new. But somehow the thought came— without the aid of my torngak too! I tugged away at that tail with all my might. It came further and further in each tug. At last I got it in as far as the stomach. I was perspiring all over. Suddenly I felt a terrific heave. I guessed what that was. The walrus was sick, and was trying to vomit his own tail! It was awful! Each heave brought me nearer to the mouth. But now the difficulty of moving the mass that I had managed to get inside had become so great that I felt the thing to be quite beyond my power, and that I must leave the rest to nature. Still, however, I continued the tugging, in order to keep up the sickness—also to keep me employed, for whenever I paused to recover breath I was forced to resume work to prevent my fainting away altogether, being so terrified at the mere thought of my situation. To be inside a walrus is bad enough, but to be inside of a sick walrus!—my friends, I cannot describe it.

"Suddenly there was a heave that almost rent the ribs of the creature apart. Like an arrow from a bow, I was shot out upon the ice, and with a clap like thunder that walrus turned inside out! And then," said Simek, with glaring solemnity, "I awoke—for it was all a dream!"

There was a gasp and cheer of delight at this, mingled with prolonged laughter, for now the most obtuse even among the children understood that Simek had been indulging in a tale of the imagination, while those whose wits were sharper saw and enjoyed the sly hits which had been launched at Ujarak throughout. Indeed the wizard himself condescended to smile at the conclusion, for the tale being a dream, removed from it the only objectionable part in his estimation, namely, that any torngak, great or small, would condescend to have intercourse with one who was not an angekok.

"Now," cried Okiok, starting up, "bring more meat; we are hungry again."

"Huk! huk!" exclaimed the assenting company.

"And when we are stuffed," continued Okiok, "we will be

glad to hear what the Kablunet has to tell about his own land."

The approval of this suggestion was so decided and hearty, that Red Rooney felt it to be his duty to gratify his hospitable friends to the utmost of his power. Accordingly he prepared himself while they were engaged with the second edition of supper. The task, however, proved to be surrounded with difficulties much greater than he had expected. Deeming it not only wise, but polite, to begin with something complimentary, he said:—

"My friends, the Innuits are a great people. They work hard; they are strong and brave, and have powerful wills."

As these were facts which every one admitted, and Rooney uttered them with considerable emphasis and animation; the statement of them was received with nods, and huks, and other marks of approval.

"The Innuits are also hospitable," he continued. "A Kablunet came to them starving, dying. The Great Spirit who made us all, and without whose permission nothing at all can happen, sent Okiok to help him. Okiok is kind; so is his wife; also his daughter. They took the poor Kablunet to their house. They fed—they stuffed—him. Now he is getting strong, and will soon be able to join in kick-ball, and pull-over, and he may perhaps, before long, teach your great angekok Ujarak some things that he does not yet know!"

As this was said with a motion in one eye which strongly resembled a wink, the audience burst into mingled applause and laughter. To some, the idea of their wise man being taught anything by a poor benighted Kablunet was ridiculous. To others, the hope of seeing the wizard's pride humbled was what is slangily termed "nuts." Ujarak himself

R. M. Ballantyne

took the remark in good part, in consequence of the word "great" having been prefixed to his title.

"But," continued the seaman, with much earnestness, "having said that I am grateful, I will not say more about the Innuit just now. I will only tell you, in few words, some things about my own country which will interest you. I have been asked if we have big villages. Yes, my friends, we have very big villages—so big that I fear you will find it difficult to understand what I say."

"The Innuit have big understandings," said Simek, with a bland smile, describing a great circle with his outspread arms; "do not fear to try them."

"Well, one village we have," resumed Rooney, "is as broad as from here to the house of Okiok under the great cliff, and it is equally long."

The "huks" and "hois!" with which this was received proved that, big as their understandings were, the Eskimos were not prepared to take in so vast an idea.

"Moreover," said the seaman, "because there is not enough of space, the houses are built on the top of each other—one—two—three—four—even five and six—one standing on the other."

As each number was named, the eyes of the assembly opened wider with surprise, until they could open no further.

"Men, women, and children live in these houses; and if you were to spread them all over the ice here, away as far as you can see in every direction, you would not be able to see the ice at all for the houses."

"*What* a liar!" murmured the mother of Arbalik to the mother of Ippegoo.

"Dreadful!" responded the latter.

"Moreover," continued Rooney, "these people can put their words and thoughts down on a substance called paper and send them to each other, so that men and women who may be hundreds of miles away can talk with each other and understand what they say and think, though they cannot hear or see each other, and though their words and thoughts take days and moons to travel."

The breathless Eskimos glanced at each other, and tried to open their eyes wider, but, having already reached the utmost limit, they failed. Unfortunately at that moment our hero was so tickled by the appearance of the faces around him, that he smiled. In a moment the eyes collapsed and the mouths opened.

"Ha! ha-a-a!" roared Simek, rubbing his hands; "the Kablunet is trying to beat my walrus."

"And he has succeeded," cried Angut, who felt it his duty to stand up for the credit of his guest, though he greatly wished that he had on this occasion confined himself to sober truth.

A beaming expression forthwith took the place of surprise on every face, as it suddenly dawned upon the company that Ridroonee was to be classed with the funny dogs whose chief delight it is to recount fairy tales and other exaggerated stories, with a view to make the men shout, the women laugh, and the children squeak with amusement.

"Go on," they cried; "tell us more."

Rooney at once perceived his mistake, and the misfortune that had befallen him. His character for veracity was shaken. He felt that it would be better to say no more, to leave what he had said to be regarded as a fairy tale, and to confine himself entirely to simple matters, such as an Eskimo might credit. He looked at his friend Angut. Angut returned the look with profound gravity, almost sorrow. Evidently his faith in the Kablunet was severely shaken. "I'll try them once more," thought Rooney. "It won't do to have a vast range of subjects tabooed just because they won't believe. Come, I'll try again."

Putting on a look of intense earnestness, which was meant to carry irresistible conviction, he continued—

"We have kayaks—oomiaks—in my country, which are big enough to carry three or four times as many people as you have in this village."

Another roar of laughter greeted this statement.

"Isn't he a good liar?" whispered Arbalik's mother.

"And so grave about it too," replied Kunelik.

Red Rooney stopped.

The mother of Ippegoo, fearing he had divined her thoughts, was overwhelmed, and tried to hide her blushing face behind Issek.

"They don't believe me," said the seaman in a low voice to Okiok.

"Of course they don't. You might as well tell us that the world is round, when we *see* that it is flat!"

Rooney sighed. He felt depressed. The impossibility of his ever getting these people to understand or believe many things was forced upon him. The undisguised assurance that they looked upon him as the best liar they had ever met with was unsatisfactory.

"Besides all this, my friends," he cried, with a feeling and air of reckless gaiety, "we have grand feasts, just as you have, and games too, and dances, and songs—"

"Songs!" shouted Simek, with an excited look; "have you songs? can you sing?"

"Well, after a fashion I can," returned Rooney, with a modest look, "though I don't pretend to be much of a dab at it. Are you fond o' singin'?"

"Fond!" echoed Simek, with a gaze of enthusiasm, "I love it! I love it *nearly* as much as I love Pussimek; better, far, than I love blubber! Ho! sing to us, Ridroonee."

"With all my heart," said Rooney, starting off with all his lung-power, which was by no means slight.

"Rule Britannia," rendered in good time, with tremendous energy, and all the additional flourishes possible, nearly drove the audience wild with delight. They had never heard anything like it before.

"That beats *you*, Okiok," said Simek.

"That is true," replied Okiok humbly.

"What! does *he* sing?" asked Rooney.

"Yes; he is our maker of songs, and sings a little."

R. M. Ballantyne

"Then he must sing to me," cried the sailor. "In my land the man who sings last has the right to say who shall sing next. I demand a song from Okiok."

As the company approved highly of the demand, and Okiok was quite willing, there was neither difficulty nor delay. The good-natured man began at once, with an air of humorous modesty, if we may say so.

Eskimos, as a rule, are not highly poetical in their sentiments, and their versification has not usually the grace of rhyme to render it agreeable, but Okiok was an exception to the rule, in that he could compose verses in rhyme, and was much esteemed because of this power. In a tuneful and moderate voice he sang. Of course, being rendered into English, his song necessarily loses much of its humour, but that, as every linguist knows, is unavoidable. It was Red Rooney who translated it, which will account for the slightly Hibernian tone throughout. I fear also that Rooney must have translated rather freely, but of course at this late period of the world's history it is impossible to ascertain anything certain on the point. We therefore give the song for what it is worth.

OKIOK'S SONG

I.

A seal once rowled upon the sea
Beneath the shining sun,
Said I, "My friend, this very day
Your rowlin' days are done."
"No, no," said he, "that must not be,"
(And splashed the snowy foam),
"Beneath the wave there wait for me
A wife and six at home."

II.

"A lie!" said I, "so you shall die!"
I launched my whistling spear;
Right up his nose the weapon goes,
And out behind his ear.
He looked reproachful; then he sank;
My heart was very sore,
For down, and down, and down he went.
I never saw him more.

III.

Then straight from out the sea arose
A female seal and six;
"O kill us now, and let our blood
With that of father's mix.
We cannot hunt; we dare not beg;
To steal we will not try;
There's nothing now that we can do
But blubber, burst, and die."

IV.

They seized my kayak by the point,
They pulled me o'er the sea,
They led me to an island lone,
And thus they spoke to me:
"Bad man, are there not bachelors
Both old and young to spare,
Whom you might kill, and eat your fill,
For all the world would care?"

V.

"Why stain your weapon with the blood

R. M. Ballantyne

Of one whose very life
Was spent in trying to provide
For little ones and wife?"
They paused and wept, and raised a howl.
(The youngest only squealed).
It stirred the marrow in my bones,
My very conscience reeled.

VI.

I fell at once upon my knees,
I begged them to forgive;
I said I'd stay and fish for them
As long as I should live.
"And marry me," the widow cried;
"I'd rather not," said I
"But that's a point we'd better leave
To talk of by and by."

VII.

I dwelt upon that island lone
For many a wretched year,
Serving that mother seal and six
With kayak, line, and spear.
And strange to say, the little ones
No bigger ever grew;
But, strangest sight of all, they changed
From grey to brilliant blue.

VII.

"O set me free! O set me free!"
I cried in my despair,
For by enchantments unexplained
They held and kept me there.

Red Rooney 157

"I will. But promise first," she said,
"You'll never more transfix
The father of a family,
With little children six."

IX.

"I promise!" Scarce the words had fled,
When, far upon the sea,
Careering gaily homeward went
My good kayak and me.
A mist rolled off my wond'ring eyes,
I heard my Nuna scream—
Like Simek with his walrus big,
I'd only had a dream!

The reception that this peculiar song met with was compound, though enthusiastic. As we have said, Okiok was an original genius among his people, who had never before heard the jingle of rhymes until he invented and introduced them. Besides being struck by the novelty of his verses, which greatly charmed them, they seemed to be much impressed with the wickedness of killing the father of a family; and some of the Eskimo widows then present experienced, probably for the first time in their lives, a touch of sympathy with widowed seals who happened to have large families to provide for.

But there was one member of the company whose thoughts and feelings were very differently affected by the song of this national poet—this Eskimo Burns or Byron—namely the wizard Ujarak. In a moment of reckless anger he had challenged Okiok to combat, and, knowing that they would be called on to enter the arena and measure, not swords, but intellects, on the morrow, he felt ill at ease, for he could not hope to come off victorious. If it had been the ordinary battle

R. M. Ballantyne

of wits in blank verse, he might have had some chance he thought, but with this new and telling jingle at the end of alternate lines, he knew that he must of a surety fail. This was extremely galling, because, by the union of smartness, shrewd common sense, and at times judicious silence, he had managed up to that time to maintain his supremacy among his fellows. But on this unlucky day he had been physically overcome by his rival Angut, and now there was the prospect of being intellectually beaten by Okiok.

"Strange!" thought the wizard; "I wonder if it was my intention to run away with Nunaga that brought this disgrace upon me."

"It was," said a voice very close to him.

The wizard looked round quickly, but no one seemed to be thinking of him.

It was the voice of Conscience. Ujarak felt uneasy, and stifled it at once. Everybody can do that without much difficulty, as the reader knows, though nobody has ever yet succeeded in killing Conscience outright. He then set himself to devise some plan for escaping from this duel. His imagination was fertile. While the revellers continued to amuse themselves with food, and song, and story, the wizard took to thinking.

No one thought his conduct strange, or sought to disturb him, for angekoks belong to a privileged class. But think as hard and as profoundly as he could, no way of escape presented itself until the evening was far advanced, and then, without an appreciable effort of thought, a door seemed to fly open, and that door was—Ippegoo.

"Yes," thought the wizard; "that will do. Nothing could be

better. I'll make him an angekok."

It may be needful to explain here that the creation of an angekok is a serious matter. It involves much ceremonial action on the part of him who operates, and preparation on the part of him who is operated on. Moreover, it is an important matter. When once it has been decided on, nothing can be allowed to interfere with it. All other things—save the unavoidable and urgent—must give way before it.

He would announce it that very night. He would boldly omit some of the preliminary ceremonial. The morrow would be a day of preparation. Next day would be the day of the ceremony of induction. After that it would be necessary for him to accompany the new-made wizard on his first journey to the realm of spirits. Thus the singing duel would have to be delayed. Ultimately he would manage to carry off Nunaga to the land of the southern Eskimo; thus he would be able to escape the ordeal altogether, and to laugh at Okiok and his jingling rhymes.

When he stood up and made the announcement, declaring that his torngak had told him that another angekok must be created, though who that other one was had not yet been revealed to him, there was a slight feeling of disappointment, for Eskimos dearly love a musical combat; but when he pointed out that after the ceremonies were over, the singing duel might then come off, the people became reconciled to the delay. Being by that time exhausted in body and mind, they soon after retired to rest.

Ere long oblivion brooded over the late hilarious crew, who lay down like bundles of hair in their festal garments, and the northern lights threw a flickering radiance over a scene of profound quietude and peace.

R. M. Ballantyne

CHAPTER THIRTEEN

MISCHIEF HATCHING

At early dawn next morning Ippegoo was awakened from a most refreshing slumber by a gentle shake of the shoulder.

"Oh! not yet, mother," groaned the youth in the drowsiest of accents; "I've only just begun to sleep."

He turned slowly on the other side, and tried to continue his repose, but another shake disturbed him, and a deep voice said, "Awake; arise, sleepy one."

"Mother," he murmured, still half asleep, "you have got the throat s-sickness v-v-very bad," (referring to what we would style a cold).

A grim smile played for a moment on the visage of the wizard, as he gave the youth a most unmotherly shake, and said, "Yes, my son, I am very sick, and want you to cure me."

Ippegoo was wide awake in a moment. Rising with a somewhat abashed look, he followed his evil genius out of the hut, where, in another compartment, his mother lay, open-mouthed, singing a song of welcome to the dawning day through her nose.

Ujarak led the youth to the berg with the sea-green cave. Stopping at the entrance, he turned a stern look on his pupil, and pointing to the cavern, uttered the single word— "Follow."

As Ippegoo gazed into the sea-green depths of the place— which darkened into absolute blackness, with ghostly projections from the sides, and dim icicles pendent from the invisible roof, he felt a suspicion that the cave might be the vestibule to that dread world of the departed which he had often heard his master describe.

"You're not going far, I hope," he said anxiously; "remember I am not yet an angekok."

"True; but you are yet a fool," returned the wizard contemptuously. "Do you suppose I would lead you to certain death for no good end? No; but I will make you an angekok to-night, and after that we may explore the wonders of the spirit-world together. I have brought you here to speak about that, for the ears of some people are very quick. We shall be safe here. You have been long enough a fool. The time has arrived when you must join the ranks of the wise men. Come."

Again he pointed to the cave, and led the way into its dim sea-green interior.

Some men seek eagerly after honours which they cannot win; others have honours which they do not desire thrust upon them. Ippegoo was of the latter class. He followed humbly, and rather closely, for the bare idea of being alone in such a place terrified him. Although pronounced a fool, the poor fellow was wise enough to perceive that he was utterly unfitted, physically as well as mentally, for the high honour to which Ujarak destined him; but he was so thoroughly under the power of his influence that he felt resistance or refusal to be impossible. He advanced, therefore, with a heavy heart. Everything around was fitted to chill his ambition, even if he had possessed any, and to arouse the terrors of his weak and superstitious mind.

When they had walked over the icy floor of the cave until the entrance behind them seemed no larger than a bright star, the wizard stopped abruptly. Ippegoo stumbled up against him with a gasp of alarm. The light was so feeble that surrounding objects were barely visible. Great blocks and spires and angular fragments of ice projected into obser- vation out of profound obscurity. Overhead mighty and grotesque forms, attached to the invisible roof, seemed like creatures floating in the air, to which an imagination much less active than that of Ippegoo might easily have given grinning mouths and glaring eyes; and the atmosphere of the place was so intensely cold that even Eskimo garments could not prevent a shudder.

The wizard turned on his victim a solemn gaze. As he stood facing the entrance of the cavern, there was just light enough to render his teeth and the whites of his eyes visible, though the rest of his features were shadowy.

"Ippegoo," he said in a low voice, "the time has come—"

At that moment a tremendous crash drowned his voice, and seemed to rend the cavern in twain. The reverberating echoes had not ceased when a clap as of the loudest thunder seemed to burst their ears. It was followed for a few seconds by a pattering shower, as of giant hail, and Ippegoo's very marrow quailed.

It was only a crack in the berg, followed by the dislodgement of a great mass, which fell from the roof to the floor below—fortunately at some distance from the spot on which the Eskimos stood.

"Bergs sometimes rend and fall asunder," gasped the trembling youth.

Ujarak's voice was unwontedly solemn as he replied—

"Not in the spring-time, foolish one. Fear not, but listen. To-night you must be prepared to go through the customs that will admit you to the ranks of the wise men."

"Don't you think," interposed the youth, with a shiver, "that it would be better to try it on some one else—on Angut, or Okiok, or even Norrak? Norrak is a fine boy, well-grown and strong, as well as clever, and I am such a fool, you know."

"You have said truth, Ippegoo. But all that will be changed to-morrow. Once an angekok, your foolishness will depart, and wisdom will come."

The poor youth was much cheered by this, because, although he felt utterly unfit for the grave and responsible character, he had enough of faith in his teacher to believe that the needed change would take place,—and change, he was well aware, could achieve wonders. Did he not see it when the change from summer to winter drove nearly all the birds away, converted the liquid sea into a solid plain, and turned the bright day into dismal night? and did he not feel it when the returning summer changed all that again, sent the sparkling waves for his light kayak to dance upon, and the glorious sunshine to call back the feathered tribes, to open the lovely flowers, to melt the hard ice, and gladden all the land? Yes, he knew well what "change" meant, though it

R. M. Ballantyne

never occurred to him to connect all this with a Creator who changes not. In this respect he resembled his master.

"Besides," continued the wizard in a more confidential tone, which invariably had the effect of drawing the poor youth's heart towards him, "I cannot make whom I will an angekok. It is my torngak who settles that; I have only to obey. Now, what I want you to do is to become very solemn in your manner and speech from this moment till the deed is finished. Will you remember?"

Ippegoo hesitated a moment. He felt just then so unusually solemn that he had difficulty in conceiving it possible to become more so, but remembering the change that was about to take place, he said brightly, "Yes, I'll remember."

"You see," continued his instructor, "we must get people to suppose that you are troubled by a spirit of some sort—"

"Oh! only to suppose it," cried Ippegoo hopefully. "Then I'm not *really* to be troubled with a spirit?"

"Of course you are, foolish man. But don't you understand people must see that you are, else how are they to know it?"

Ippegoo thought that if he was really to be troubled in that way, the only difficulty would be to prevent people from knowing it, but observing that his master was getting angry, he wisely held his tongue, and listened with earnest attention while Ujarak related the details of the ordeal through which he was about to pass.

At the time this conversation was being held in the sea-green cave, Okiok, rising from his lair with a prodigious yawn, said to his wife—

"Nuna, I go to see Kunelik."

"And what may ye-a-o-u—my husband want with the mother of Ippegoo?" asked Nuna sleepily, but without moving.

"I want to ye-a-o-u—ask about her son."

"Ye-a-a-o-o-u!" exclaimed Nuna, turning on her other side; "go, then," and she collapsed.

Seeing that his wife was unfit just then to enter into conversation, Okiok got up, accomplished what little toilet he deemed necessary in half a minute, and took his way to the hut of Ippegoo's mother.

It is not usual in Eskimo land to indulge in ceremonious salutation. Okiok was naturally a straightforward and brusque man. It will not therefore surprise any one to be told that he began his interview with—

"Kunelik, your son Ippegoo is a lanky fool!"

"He is," assented Kunelik, with quiet good-humour.

"He has given himself," continued Okiok, "spirit and body, to that villain Ujarak."

"He has," assented Kunelik again.

"Where is he now?"

"I do not know."

"But me knows," said a small sweet little child-voice from the midst of a bundle of furs.

R. M. Ballantyne

It was the voice of Pussi. That Eskimo atom had been so overcome with sleep at the breaking up of the festivities of the previous night that she was unable to distinguish between those whom she loved and those for whom she cared not. In these circumstances, she had seized the first motherly tail that came within her reach, and followed it home. It chanced to belong to Kunelik, so she dropped down and slept beside her.

"*You* know, my dear little seal?" said Okiok in surprise.

"Yes, me knows. When I was 'sleep, a big man comes an' stump on my toes—not much, only a leetle. Dat wokes me, an' I see Ujiyak. He shooks Ip'goo an' bose hoed out degidder."

Okiok looked at Kunelik, Kunelik looked at Okiok, and both gravely shook their heads.

Before they could resume the conversation, Ippegoo's voice was heard outside asking if his mother was in.

"Go," said Kunelik; "though he is a fool, he is wise enough to hold his tongue when any one but me is near."

Okiok took the hint, rose at once, and went out, passing the youth as he entered, and being much struck with the lugubrious solemnity of his visage.

"Mother," said Ippegoo, sitting down on a skin beside the pleasant little woman, "it comes."

"What comes, my son?"

"I know not."

"If you know not, how do you know that it comes?" asked Kunelik, who was slightly alarmed by the wild manner and unusual, almost dreadful, gravity of her boy.

"It is useless to ask me, mother. I do not understand. My mind cannot take it in, but—but—it comes."

"Yes; when is it coming?" asked Kunelik, who knew well how to humour him.

"How can I tell? I—I think it has come *now*," said the youth, growing paler, or rather greener; "I think I feel it in my breast. Ujarak said the torngak would come to-day, and to-night I am to *be—changed*!"

"Oho!" exclaimed Kunelik, with a slight touch of asperity, "it's a torngak that is to come, is it? and Ujarak says so? Don't you know, Ippe, that Ujarak is an idiot!"

"Mother!" exclaimed the youth remonstratively, "Ujarak an idiot? Impossible! He is to make me an angekok to-night."

"You, Ippe! You are not more fit for an angekok than I am for a seal-hunter."

"Yes, true; but I am to *be—changed*!" returned the youth, with a bright look; then remembering that his *role* was solemnity, he dropped the corners of his mouth, elongated his visage, turned up his eyes, and groaned.

"Have you the stomach twist, my boy?" asked his mother tenderly.

"No; but I suppose I—I—am changing."

"No, you are not, Ippe. I have seen many angekoks made.

R. M. Ballantyne

There will be no change till you have gone through the customs, so make your mind easy, and have something to eat."

The youth, having had no breakfast, was ravenously hungry, and as the process of feeding would not necessarily interfere with solemnity, he agreed to the proposal with his accustomed look of satisfaction—which, however, he suddenly nipped in the bud. Then, setting-to with an expression that might have indicated the woes of a lifetime, he made a hearty breakfast.

Thereafter he kept moving about the village all day in absolute silence, and with a profound gloom on his face, by which the risibility of some was tickled, while not a few were more or less awe-stricken.

It soon began to be rumoured that Ippegoo was the angekok-elect. In the afternoon Ujarak returned from a visit, as he said, to the nether world, and with his brother wizards—for there were several in the tribe—confirmed the rumour.

As evening approached, Rooney entered Okiok's hut. No one was at home except Nuna and Tumbler. The latter was playing, as usual, with his little friend Pussi. The goodwife was busy over the cooking-lamp.

"Where is your husband, Nuna?" asked the sailor, sitting down on a walrus skull.

"Out after seals."

"And Nunaga?"

"Visiting the mother of Arbalik."

The seaman looked thoughtfully at the lamp-smoke for a few moments.

"She is a hard woman, that mother of Arbalik," he said.

"Issek is not so hard as she looks," returned Mrs Okiok; "her voice is rough, but her heart is soft."

"I'm glad to hear you speak well of her," said Rooney, "for I don't like to think ill of any one if I can help it; but sometimes I can't help it. Now, there's your angekok Ujarak: I cannot think well of him. Have you a good word to say in his favour?"

"No, not one. He is bad through and through—from the skin to the bone. I know him well," said Nuna, with a flourish of her cooking-stick that almost overturned the lamp.

"But you may be mistaken," remarked Rooney, smiling. "You are mistaken even in the matter of his body, to say nothing of his spirit."

"How so?" asked Nuna quickly.

"You said he is bad through and through. From skin to bone is not through and through. To be quite correct, you must go from skin to marrow."

Nuna acknowledged this by violently plunging her cooking-stick into the pot.

"Well now, Nuna," continued Rooney, in a confidential tone, "tell me—"

At that moment he was interrupted by the entrance of the master of the mansion, who quietly sat down on another skull close to his friend.

"I was just going to ask your wife, Okiok, what she and you think of this business of making an angekok of poor Ippegoo," said Rooney.

"We think it is like a seal with its tail where its head should be, its skin in its stomach, and all its bones outside; all nonsense—foolishness," answered Okiok, with more of indignation in his look and tone than he was wont to display.

"Then you don't believe in angekoks?" asked Rooney.

"No," replied the Eskimo earnestly; "I don't. I think they are clever scoundrels—clever fools. And more, I don't believe in torngaks or any other spirits."

"In that you are wrong," said Rooney. "There is one great and good Spirit, who made and rules the universe."

"I'm not sure of that," returned the Eskimo, with a somewhat dogged and perplexed look, that showed the subject was not quite new to him. "I never saw, or heard, or tasted, or smelt, or felt a spirit. How can I know anything about it?"

"Do you believe in your own spirit, Okiok?"

"Yes, I must. I cannot help it. I am like other men. When a man dies there is something gone out of him. It must be his spirit."

"Then you believe in other men's spirits as well as your own spirit," said Rooney, "though you have never seen, heard, tasted, smelt, or felt them?"

For a moment the Eskimo was puzzled. Then suddenly his

countenance brightened.

"But I *have* felt my own," he cried. "I have felt it moving within me, so that it made me *act*. My legs and arms and brain would not go into action if they were dead, if the spirit had gone out of them."

"In the very same way," replied the seaman, "you may *feel* the Great Spirit, for your own spirit could not go into action so as to cause your body to act unless a greater Spirit had given it life. So also we may feel or understand the Great Spirit when we look at the growing flowers, and hear the moving winds, and behold the shining stars, and feel the beating of our own hearts. I'm not much of a wise man, an angekok—which they would call *scholar* in my country— but I know enough to believe that it is only 'the fool who has said in his heart, There is no Great Spirit.'"

"There is something in what you say," returned the Eskimo, as the lines of unusually intense thought wrinkled his brow; "but for all that you say, I think there are no torngaks, and that Ujarak is a liar as well as a fool."

"I agree with you, Okiok, because I think you have good reason for your disbelief. In the first place, it is well-known that Ujarak is a liar, but that is not enough, for liar though he be, he *sometimes* tells the truth. Then, in the second place, he is an ass—hum! I forgot—you don't know what an ass is; well, it don't matter, for, in the third place, he never gave any proof to anybody of what he and his torngak are said to have seen and done, and, strongest reason of all, this familiar spirit of his acts unwisely—for what could be more foolish than to choose out of all the tribe a poor half-witted creature like Ippegoo for the next angekok?"

A gleaming glance of intelligent humour lighted up Okiok's

R. M. Ballantyne

face as he said—

"Ujarak is wiser than his torngak in that. He wants to make use of the poor lad for his own wicked ends. I know not what these are—but I have my suspicions."

"So have I," broke in Nuna at this point, giving her pot a rap with the cooking-stick by way of emphasis.

Rooney laughed.

"You think he must be watched, and his mischief prevented?" he said.

"That's what I think," said Okiok firmly.

"Tell me, what are the ceremonies to be gone through by that poor unwilling Ippegoo, before he can be changed into a wise man?"

"Oh, he has much to do," returned Okiok, with his eyes on the lamp-flame and his head a little on one side, as if he were thinking. "But I am puzzled. Ujarak is cunning, though he is not wise; and I am quite sure he has some secret reason for hurrying on this business. He is changing the customs, and that is never done for nothing."

"What customs has he changed?" asked Rooney.

"The customs for the young angekok before he gets a torngak," replied the Eskimo.

Okiok's further elucidation of this point was so complex that we prefer to give the reader our own explanation.

Before assuming the office of an angekok or diviner, an

Eskimo must procure one of the spirits of the elements for his own particular familiar spirit or torngak. These spirits would appear to be somewhat coquettish and difficult to win, and marvellous tales are related of the manner in which they are wooed. The aspirant must retire for a time to a desert place, where, entirely cut off from the society of his fellows, he may give himself up to fasting and profound meditation. He also prays to Torngarsuk to give him a torngak. This Torngarsuk is the chief of the good spirits, and dwells in a pleasant abode under the earth or sea. He is not, however, supposed to be God, who is named Pirksoma, i.e. "He that is above," and about whom most Eskimos profess to know nothing. As might be expected, the weakness of body and agitation of mind resulting from such exercises carried on in solitude throw into disorder the imaginative faculty of the would-be diviner, so that wonderful figures of men and monsters swim before his mental vision, which tend to throw his body into convulsions—all the more that he labours to cherish and increase such symptoms.

How far the aspirants themselves believe in these delusions it is impossible to tell; but the fact that, after their utmost efforts, some of them fail to achieve the coveted office, leads one to think that some of them are too honest, or too strong-minded, to be led by them. Others, however, being either weak or double-minded, are successful. They assert that, on Torngarsuk appearing in answer to their earnest petition, they shriek aloud, and die from fear. At the end of three days they come to life again, and receive a torngak, who takes them forthwith on a journey to heaven and hell, after which they return home full-fledged angekoks, prepared to bless their fellows, and guide them with their counsels.

"Now, you must know," said Okiok, after explaining all this, "what puzzles me is, that Ujarak intends to alter the customs at the beginning of the affair. Ippegoo is to be made an angekok to-night, and to be let off all the fasting and hard thinking and fits. If I believed in these things at all, I should think him only a half-made angekok. As it is, I don't care a puff of wind what they make of poor Ippegoo—so long as they don't kill him; but I'm uneasy because I'm afraid the rascal Ujarak has some bad end in view in all this."

"I'm *quite* sure of it," muttered Nuna, making a stab with her stick at the contents of her pot, as if Ujarak's heart were inside.

At that moment Nunaga entered, looking radiant, in all the glory of a new under-garment of eider-duck pelts and a new sealskin upper coat with an extra long tail.

"Have you seen Angut lately?" asked Rooney of the young girl.

"Yes," she replied, with a modest smile that displayed her brilliant teeth; "he is in his own hut."

"I will go and talk with him on this matter, Okiok," said the seaman. "Meanwhile, do you say nothing about it to any one."

CHAPTER FOURTEEN

SOLEMN AND MYSTERIOUS DOINGS ARE BROUGHT TO A VIOLENT CLOSE

Angut was seated at the further end of his abode when his friend entered, apparently absorbed in contemplation of that remarkable specimen of Eskimo longevity, the grandmother of Okiok.

"I have often wondered," said Angut, as the seaman sat down beside him, "at the contentment and good-humour and cheerfulness, sometimes running into fun, of that poor old woman Kannoa."

"Speak lower," said Rooney in a soft voice; "she will hear you."

"If she does, she will hear no evil. But she is nearly deaf, and takes no notice."

"It may be so; poor thing!" returned the sailor in a tender tone, as he looked at the shrivelled-up old creature, who was moving actively round the never-idle lamp, and bending with inquiring interest over the earthen pot, which seemed to engross her entire being. "But why do you wonder?"

"I wonder because she has so little to make her contented, and so much to ruin her good-humour and cheerfulness, and to stop her fun. Her life is a hard one. She has few relations to care for her. She is very old, and must soon grow feeble, and then—"

"And then?" said Rooney, as the other paused.

"Then she knows not what follows death—who does know?—and she does not believe in the nonsense that our people invent. It is a great mystery."

The Eskimo said the last words in a low voice and with a wistful gaze, as if he were rather communing with himself than conversing with his friend. Rooney felt perplexed. The thoughts of Angut were often too profound for him. Not knowing what to say, he changed the subject by mentioning the object of his visit.

At once Angut turned, and gave undivided attention to the subject, while the seaman described his recent conversation with Okiok. As he concluded, a peculiar look flitted across Angut's countenance.

"I guess his reason," he said.

"Yes; what may it be, think you?"

"He fears to meet Okiok in a singing duel."

Rooney laughed. "Well, you know best," he said; "I daresay you are right. Okiok is a sharp fellow, and Ujarak is but a blundering booby after—"

A low chuckle in the region of the lamp attracted their attention at this point. They looked quickly at Kannoa, but that ancient's face was absolutely owlish in its gravity, and her little black eyes peered into her pot with a look of intense inquiry that was almost philosophic. Resuming their belief that she was as deaf as a post, or an iceberg, Rooney and Angut proceeded to discuss Ujarak and his probable plans without any regard to her. After having talked the matter over for some time, Angut shook his head, and said that Ujarak must be closely watched.

"More than that," said Rooney, with decision; "he must be stultified."

The seaman's rendering of the word "stultified" into Eskimo was curious, and cannot easily be explained, but it was well understood by Angut, and apparently by Kannoa, for another chuckle came just then from the culinary department. Again the two men glanced at the old woman inquiringly, and again were they baffled by that look of owlish intensity at the stewing meat.

"She hears," whispered Rooney.

"Impossible," replied Angut; "a dead seal is not much deafer."

Continuing the conversation, the seaman explained how he thought it possible to stultify the wizard, by discrediting him in the eyes of his own people—by foiling him with his own weapons,—and himself undertook to accomplish the task of stultification.

He was in the act of concluding his explanation when another chuckle burst upon them from the region of the lamp. This time there was no attempt at concealment, for there stood old Kannoa, partly enveloped in savoury steam, her head thrown back, and her mouth wide-open.

With a laugh Rooney leaped up, and caught her by the arm.

"You've heard what I've been saying, mother?"

"Ye-yes. I've heard," she replied, trying to smother the laughter.

"Now, look here. You must promise me not to tell *anybody*," said the seaman earnestly, almost sternly.

"Oh, I not tell," returned the old woman; "I love not Ujarak."

"Ah! just so; then you're pretty safe not to tell," said Rooney.

"No fear of Kannoa," remarked Angut, with a pleasant nod; "she never tells anything to anybody."

Satisfied, apparently, with this assurance, the seaman took the old woman into his counsels, congratulating himself not a little on having found an ally in the very hut in which it had been arranged that the mysterious performance was to take place. Shortly after that Angut left.

"Now, Kannoa," said Rooney, after some preliminary talk, "you remember the big white bear that Angut killed two moons ago?"

"Remember it? Ay," said Kannoa, licking her lips; "it was the fattest and best bear I ever chewed. Huk! it *was* good!"

"Well, where is that bear's skin?"

The old dame pointed to a corner of the hut where the skin lay. Rooney went and picked it up, and laid it at the upper end of the hut farthest from the door.

"Now, mother," said he; "you'll not touch that skin. Let it lie there, and let no one touch it till I come again. You understand?"

"Yes," answered Kannoa, with a look so intensely knowing that it made the seaman laugh.

"But tell me," said the old woman, becoming suddenly grave, and laying her thin scraggy hand on the man's arm; "why do you call me mother?"

"Oh, it's just a way we have in my country when—when we feel kindly to an old woman. And I do feel kindly to you, Kannoa," he added, with sudden warmth and energy of look and tone, "because you are so like my own grandmother— only she was younger than you, and much better-looking."

Rooney meant no rudeness by the last remark, but, having observed the straightforward simplicity of his new friends in saying exactly what they meant, he willingly adopted their style.

Kannoa seemed much pleased with the explanation.

"It is strange," she said pathetically, "that I should find you so very like my husband."

"Indeed!" returned the seaman, who did not feel flattered by the compliment; "is it long since he died?"

"O yes; long, long—very long," she answered, with a sigh. "Moons, moons, moons without number have passed since that day. He was as young as you when he was killed, but a far finer man. His face did not look dirty like yours—all over with hair. It was smooth and fat, and round and oily. His cheeks were plump, and they would shine when the sun was up. He was also bigger than you—higher and wider. Huk! he was grand!"

Although Rooney felt inclined to laugh as he listened to this description, he restrained himself when he observed the tears gathering in the old eyes. Observing and appreciating the look of sympathy, she tightened her clutch on the seaman's arm and said, looking wistfully up in his face—

"Has Ridroonee ever felt something in here,"—she laid a hand on her withered bosom—"as if it broke in two, and then went dead for evermore? That is what I felt the day they brought my man home; he was so kind. Like my son Okiok, and Angut."

As the seaman looked down at the pitiful old soul that had thus broken the floodgates of a long silence, and was pouring out her confidences to him, he felt an unusual lump in his throat. Under a sudden impulse, he stooped and kissed the wrinkled brow, and then, turning abruptly, left the hut.

It was well he did so, for by that time it was nearly dark, and Kannoa had yet to arrange the place for the expected meeting.

As the time drew near, the night seemed to sympathise with the occasion, for the sky became overcast with clouds, which obliterated the stars, and rendered it intensely dark.

The chief performer in the approaching ceremony was in a fearful state of mind. He would have done or given anything to escape being made a wise man. But Ujarak was inexorable. Poor Ippegoo sought comfort from his mother, and, to say truth, Kunelik did her best for him, but she could not resist the decrees of Fate—i.e. of the wizard.

"Be a man, my son, and all will go well," she said, as he sat beside her in her hut, with his chin on his breast and his thin hands clasped.

"O mother, I *am* such a fool! He might let me off. I'll be disgraced forever."

"Not you, Ippe; you're not half such a fool as he is. Just go boldly, and do your best. Look as fierce and wild as you can, and make awful faces. There's nothing like frightening people! Howl as much as possible, and gasp sometimes. I have seen a good deal done in that way. I only wish they would try to make an angekok of *me*. I would astonish them."

The plucky little woman had to stop here for a moment to chuckle at her own conceit, but her poor son did not respond. He had got far beyond the point where a perception of the ludicrous is possible.

"But it is time to go now, my son. Don't forget your drum and the face-making. You know what you've got to do?"

"Yes, yes, I know," said Ippegoo, looking anxiously over his shoulder, as if he half expected to see a torngak already approaching him; "I know only too well what I've got to do. Ujarak has been stuffing it into me the whole day till my brain feels ready to burst."

The bitter tone in which the poor youth pronounced his master's name suggested to his mother that it would not require much more to make the worm turn upon its tormentor. But the time had arrived to send him off, so she was obliged to bring her questions and advices to an abrupt close.

As Ippegoo walked towards the dreaded hut, he was

R. M. Ballantyne

conscious of many glaring eyes and whispered words around him. This happily had the effect of stirring up his pride, and made him resolve to strive to do his part creditably.

At the door of the hut two dark figures glided swiftly in before him. One he could perceive was Angut; the other he thought looked very like the Kablunet "Ridroonee." The thought gave him some comfort—not much, indeed, but anything that distracted his mind for an instant from the business in hand afforded him comfort.

He now braced himself desperately to the work. Seizing the drum which he had been told not to forget, he struck it several times, and began to twist his body about violently. There was just light enough to show to onlookers that the poor youth was whirling himself round in contortions of the most surprising kind. This he did for the purpose of working himself up to the proper pitch of enthusiasm.

There seems little doubt that the mere exertion of great muscular effort, coupled with a resolute wish and intention to succeed in some object, has a powerful tendency to brace the energies of the human mind. Ippegoo had not contorted himself and beaten his drum for many minutes when his feeling of warmth and physical power began to increase. The feeling seemed to break on his mind as a revelation.

"Ho!" he thought, "here it comes; it comes at last! Ujarak told the truth—I am becoming one of the wise men."

So delighted was the poor fellow with the idea, and with the strong hope created thereby, that his blood began to course more rapidly and his heart to beat high. Under the impulse, he gave vent to a yell that drew a nod of gratified approval from his mother, and quite astonished those who knew him best. Redoubling his twistings and drummings, he soon wore himself out, and ere long fell down in a state of temporary exhaustion.

Having thus, according to instruction, worked himself up to the proper pitch of enthusiasm, Ippegoo lay still and panted. Ujarak then, coming forward, led him into Angut's hut, which was lighted as usual with several cooking-lamps. The people flocked in after them till it was nearly full; but spaces in the centre and upper end were kept comparatively free. Near the lamp the Kablunet was seen seated, observing the proceedings with much gravity; Okiok sat near him.

When all were seated, the wizard led his pupil into the centre space, and, making him sit down, bent him forward until his head was between his legs. He fastened it in that position, and then tied his hands behind his back. All the lights were now extinguished, for no one is allowed to witness the interview of the unfinished angekok with the torngak, nor to move a finger for fear of disturbing him.

The room being now in the state which is described as darkness just visible, Ippegoo began to sing a song, in which all joined. Presently he took to groaning by way of variety; then he puffed and gasped, and in a quavering voice entreated his torngak to come. Spirits, however, like human creatures, are not always open to entreaty. At all events, Ippegoo's torngak refused to appear.

In such circumstances it is usual for an aspirant to writhe about until he brings on a sort of *fit*, during the continuance of which his soul goes off to fetch the obstinate torngak. After a short time he returns with him, laughing loudly for joy, while a rustling noise, resembling the wings of birds as they swoop about the roof, is heard.

But Ippegoo was not a sufficiently wise man to get through

R. M. Ballantyne

this part of the programme. True, he wrought himself into a wonderful state of excitement, and then humbly lay down on his side to have a fit. But the fit would not come. He tried his best to have it. He wished with all his heart for it, but all his efforts were vain.

"O why won't you come to me, torngak?" demanded the poor youth, with a pitiful whine.

"Because you are wise enough already," said a low voice, which startled the audience very much, and sent a thrill of alarm, not unmingled with surprise, to the hearts of Ippegoo and his master.

The voice seemed to come from the outside of the hut.

"Ask him to come inside and speak to us," whispered Ujarak, who was a good deal more surprised even than his pupil at this unexpected turn of affairs.

"Won't you come in, torngak?" said Ippegoo timidly. "It is very cold outside. You will be more comfortable inside, and we shall hear you better. I suppose you can come as easily through the wall as by—"

"Stop your stupid tongue!" growled Ujarak.

At that moment a deep unearthly voice was heard inside the hut. Every one trembled, and there ensued a silence so oppressive as to suggest the idea that all present were holding their breath, and afraid to move even by a hair's-breadth.

Suddenly there was a faint murmur, for at the upper end of the hut a dark form was seen slowly to arise. It must be remembered that there was barely light enough to render darkness visible. No features could be distinguished on this apparition, but it gradually assumed the form of a gigantic bear, rising nearly to the roof, and with its great forelegs extended, as if it were brooding over the assembly. Every one remained perfectly still, as if spell-bound.

Only one of the audience was sceptical. Being himself a master of deception, Ujarak suspected some trick, and slowly approached the giant bear with the intention of testing its reality—in some trepidation, however, for he was naturally superstitious. When he had drawn near enough to touch it, he received a tremendous blow on the forehead, which laid him flat on his back in a partially stunned condition, with his head in Pussimek's lap. That amiable woman considerately allowed it to remain there, and as the wizard felt mentally confused he did not care to change his position.

Presently a low musical voice broke upon the assembly. We need scarcely say that it was that of our hero, Red Rooney, but so changed in character and tone as to be quite unrecognisable by the company, most of whom, indeed, were not yet very familiar with it. Even his more intimate friends, Angut and the Okiok family, were startled by it. In fact, the seaman, besides being something of a mimic, possessed a metallic bass voice of profound depth, which, like most bass voices, was capable of mounting into the higher latitudes of tone by means of a falsetto. He utilised his gifts on the present occasion.

"Ippegoo," he said solemnly and very slowly, "I am not your torngak. I am an angekok, and as I chanced to be passing by your hut in my wanderings, I stopped to hear. I have heard enough to be able to tell you that you shall never be an angekok. Nor shall you ever have a torngak. You do not need one. You are wise enough already, much wiser than your master, who is no better than a miserable puffin. Is it not the

R. M. Ballantyne

duty of one who would be an angekok to go away and live alone for many days fasting, and praying, and meditating? Has not Ujarak advised you to change the ancient customs? Pooh! he is a fool. You cannot succeed now. All the spirits of water, earth, and air have been insulted. This assembly must break up. You must leave off trying. You may all be thankful that the ice does not burst up and crush you; that the sky does not fall upon you; that the great sea does not roll its maddest waves over you. Up, all of you—Begone!"

Rooney finished off with a roar so deep and fearsome that the very rafters trembled. A pile of wood, stones, and earthenware, previously prepared for the purpose, was tipped over, and fell with a most awful crash. At the same moment the seaman culminated in a falsetto shriek that might have shamed a steam whistle.

It was enough. Had the tunnel entrance of the hut been long and strong, suffocation to many must have been the result, for they went into it pell-mell, rolling rather than running. Fortunately, it was short and weak. Ujarak and Simek, sticking in it, burst it up, and swept it away, thus clearing the passage for the rest. The last to disappear was Kunelik, whose tail flapped on the door-post like a small pistol-shot as she doubled round it and scrambled out, leaving Rooney, Angut, Kannoa, and Ippegoo to enjoy the situation.

CHAPTER FIFTEEN

A GREAT SINGING DUEL
INTERRUPTED BY A CATASTROPHE

When the lamps were rekindled by Kannoa, it was discovered that the old lady's nostrils were twitching and her throat contracting in a remarkable manner, with smothered laughter. Very different was the condition of Ippegoo, who still lay bound in the middle of the room. Fear and surprise in equal proportions seemed to have taken possession of him. Rooney, having dropped the bear-skin, approached him, while Angut stood beside the lamp looking on with a sort of serious smile.

"Now, Ippegoo," said the sailor, stooping and cutting his bonds, "I set you free. It is to be hoped also that I have freed you from superstition."

"But where is the bear-angekok?" asked the bewildered youth.

"I am the bear-angekok."

"Impossible!" cried Ippegoo.

To this Rooney replied by going back to his bear-skin,

R. M. Ballantyne

spreading it over himself, getting on a stool so as to tower upwards, spreading out his long arms, and saying in his deepest bass tones—

"Now, Ippegoo, do you believe me?"

A gleam of intelligence flashed on the youth's countenance, and at that moment he became more of a wise man than he had ever before been in his life, for he not only had his eyes opened as to the ease with which some people can be deceived, but had his confidence in the infallibility of his old tyrant completely shaken. He reasoned somewhat thus—

"If Ujarak's torngak was good and true, it would have told him of the deceit about to be practised on him, and would not have allowed him to submit to disgrace. If it did not care, it was a bad spirit. If it did not know, it was no better than a man, and not worth having—so I don't want to have one, and am very glad I have escaped so well."

The poor fellow shrank from adding, "Ujarak must be a deceiver;" but he began to think that Red Rooney might not have been far wrong after all when he called him a fool.

Ippegoo was now warned that he must keep carefully out of the wizard's way, and tell no one of the deceit that had been practised. He promised most faithfully to tell no one, and then went straight home and told his mother all about it—for it never for a moment occurred to the poor fellow to imagine that he was meant to conceal it from his mother!

Fortunately Kunelik was a wise little woman. She knew how to keep her own counsel, and did not even by nod or look insinuate to any one that she was in possession of a secret.

"Now, then, Angut, what is the next thing to be done?" asked

Rooney, after Ippegoo had left.

"Make Ujarak fight his duel," said Angut.

"What! the singing duel with Okiok?"

"Yes. The people have set their hearts on the thing, and Ujarak will try to escape. He will perhaps say that his torngak has told him to go hunting to-morrow. But our customs require him to keep his word. My fear is that he will sneak off in the night. He is a sly fox."

"I will stop that," said Rooney.

"How?"

"You shall see. Come with me to the hut of Ujarak."

On reaching the hut, they found its owner, as had been expected, sharpening his spears, and making other arrangements for a hunting expedition.

"When do you start?" asked Rooney.

"Immediately," replied the wizard.

"Of course *after* the duel," remarked Angut quietly.

The wizard seemed annoyed.

"It is unfortunate," he said, with a vexed look. "My torngak has told me of a place where a great number of seals have come. They may leave soon, and it would be such a pity to lose them."

"That is true," said Angut; "but of course you cannot break

R. M. Ballantyne

our customs. It would ruin your character."

"Of course, of course I will not break the custom," returned Ujarak quickly; "unless, indeed, my torngak *orders* me to go. But that is not likely."

"I want to ask you," said Rooney, sitting down, "about that trip you had last year to the land of the departed. They tell me you had a hard time of it, Ujarak, and barely escaped with your life."

The sly seaman had spread a net with which the wizard could at all times be easily caught. He had turned him on to a tune at which he was always willing to work with the persistency of an organ-grinder. The wizard went on hour after hour with unwearied zeal in his narrations, being incited thereto by a judicious question now and then from the seaman, when he betrayed any symptom of flagging. At last Angut, who had often heard it before, could stand it no longer, and rose to depart. Having already picked up the Kablunet's mode of salutation, he held out his hand, and said "Goo'-nite."

"Good-night, friend," returned Rooney, grasping the proffered hand. "I can't leave till I've heard the end of this most interesting story, so I'll just sleep in Ujarak's hut, if he will allow me, and thus avoid disturbing you by coming in late. Good-night."

"Goo'-nite," responded Angut, and vanished from the scene.

The wizard heaved a sigh. He perceived that his little plan of gliding away in the hours of darkness was knocked on the head, so, like a true philosopher, he resigned himself to the inevitable, and consoled himself by plunging into intricacies of fabulous adventure with a fertility of imagination which surprised even himself—so powerful is the influence of a sympathetic listener.

When Ujarak at last discovered that his guest had fallen into a profound slumber, he brought his amazing narrative to an abrupt close, and, wrapping himself in a reindeer-skin, resigned himself to that repose which was so much needed to fit him for the combat of the approaching day.

It was a brilliant sunny morning when Red Rooney awoke from a startling dream, in which he had been wrestling with monstrous creatures in the depths of ocean as well as in the bowels of the earth.

The wizard was still locked in apparently dreamless slumber. Unwilling to disturb him, the seaman glided quietly out, and clambered to the top of a cliff, whence a magnificent sea-view was revealed to his wondering gaze.

There are times when the atmosphere of this earth seems to be rarefied and freshened with celestial zephyrs, which not only half intoxicate the spirit, but intensify the powers of hearing and vision, so that gentle sounds which are very far off come floating to us, and mingle softly with those that are near at hand, while objects are seen at such immense distances that one feels as if the world itself had suddenly grown larger. To these influences were added on this occasion a sea which absolutely glittered with the icy gems that decked her calm and waveless bosom. It was not only that millions of white and glittering peaks, with facets and edges gleaming like diamonds, rose into the blue sky, but here and there open lanes of water, and elsewhere lakes and little ponds upon the melting ice caught the full orb of the rising sun, and sent its reflection into the man's eyes with dazzling refulgence, while the ripple or rush of ice-born water-falls and the plaintive cries of wild-fowl gave variety and animation to the scene. In a mind less religiously

R. M. Ballantyne

disposed than that of our seaman, the sights and sounds would have irresistibly aroused grateful thoughts to our Creator. On Rooney the effect was almost overpowering, yet, strange to say, it drew no word of thanksgiving from his lips. Clasping his hands and shutting his eyes, he muttered with bowed head the words, "God, be merciful to me a sinner!"

Perhaps the recognition of the Father's great goodness and condescension, coupled with his own absolute unworthiness, and the impulse which called those words forth, was nearly the highest act of worship which the sailor could have offered.

Far below, under the sheltering cliff, the huts of the Eskimo village could be seen like little black specks dotting the still snow-covered land; and the voices of children could be heard in faint but merry shouts and peals of laughter, as their owners, like still smaller specks, romped about. One of those specks Rooney recognised, from its intense blackness, to be his friend Tumbler, and a smaller and lighter speck he guessed to be Pussi, from the circumstance of its persistently following and keeping close to the raven-clad hero.

The pleased look with which Rooney at first regarded the children slowly passed away, and was replaced by one of profound sadness; for how could he escape dejection when he thought of a sweet Irish wife and little ones, with a dear old grandmother, whom he had left in the old country, and who must long before that time have given him up as dead?

His melancholy thoughts were dissipated by a sudden increase in the shouting of the little ones. On regarding them attentively, he observed that they scattered themselves in the direction of the several huts, and disappeared therein.

Well did Rooney know that the movement meant breakfast,

and having a personal interest in that game, he left his perch and the glorious view, and hastened down.

After breakfast the entire community went with one consent to witness the singing combat. It was to take place on the ice near the scene of the recent kick-ball game, close to the berg of the sea-green cave. The people were much elated, for these savages were probably as much influenced by brilliant spring weather as civilised folk are, though not given to descant so much on their feelings. They were also in that cheerful frame of mind which results from what they correctly referred to as being stuffed; besides, much fun was expected from the contest. Lest our readers should anticipate similar delight, we must repeat that Eskimos are a simple folk, and easily pleased.

"Won't it be a tussle?" remarked Issek, who marched in the centre of a group of women.

"It will, for Ujarak is tough. He is like a walrus," responded an admirer of the wizard.

"Poo!" exclaimed the mother of Ippegoo contemptuously; "he can indeed roar like the walrus, but he can do nothing else."

"Yes; and his strength goes for nothing," cried a sympathiser, "for it is his brain, not his body, that has got to work."

"We shall see," said Kabelaw, whose sister remarked—"if we are not blind."

This mild observation was meant for a touch of pleasantry. Little touches of pleasantry often passed between these "lying sisters," as they were called, and they not infrequently culminated in touches of temper, which must have been the reverse of pleasant to either.

Arrived at the arena, a ring was formed, and the wisdom as well as amiability of these poor people was shown by their putting the children in front, the little women in the second row, the tall women in the third, and the men behind.

In a few minutes Ujarak bounded into the centre of the circle, with a small drum or tambourine in one hand, which he beat vigorously with the other. Okiok followed more sedately, armed with a similar musical instrument, and retired to one side of the arena, for the wizard, perhaps because he was the challenger, had the right to begin.

A good authority on the Eskimo tongue says: "The language is not easily translatable, the brevity and force of a single sentence requiring to be rendered in many words of another tongue." The same authority also informs us that angekoks "speak in a metaphorical style sometimes, in order to exhibit their assumed superiority in learning and penetration." It will not be expected, therefore, that our translation should convey more than a general idea of the combat.

Ujarak's first act, after bounding into the ring and drumming, was to glare at his adversary. Okiok returned the glare with interest, and, being liberal, threw a sneer of contempt into the bargain. Ujarak then glared round at the audience, and began his song, which consisted merely of short periods, without rhyme or measure, but with a sort of rhythmic musical cadence. He commenced with the chorus—"Amna ajah ajah hey!" which was vociferously repeated by his supporters among the audience.

What these words, mean—whether they represent our "fal lal la" or "runity iddity"—we have not been able to ascertain, but they came in at irregular intervals, greatly to the satisfaction of the audience, thus:—

"Amna ajah ajah hey!
There was once a man—a man
(So it is said, but we are not sure),
A puffin perhaps he was—or a stupid spirit
Made in the likeness of a man;
Amna ajah ajah hey!"

Here the wizard not only accompanied the chorus with the drum, but with a species of dance, which, being a clumsy man, he performed in an extremely elephantine manner. After a few moments he went on:—

"This man—this puffin—was a liar:
A liar, because he was a teller of lies.
Did he not one time say that seals had come,
And that birds were in the air?
And when we went to look, no seals or birds were there.
Amna ajah ajah Hey!"

The extreme vigour with which the last word was uttered resulted from the wizard having tripped in his dance, and come down heavily on the ice, to the immense delight of his opponents and the children. But Ujarak rose, and quelling the laugh with a look of dignity, continued:—

"Worse than a liar was this foolish puffin.
He hunted badly. When he flung the spear
The seals would laugh before they went away.
Sometimes he missed, sometimes he tipped the nose,
Sometimes hit the wrong animal,
And sometimes touched the tail.
Amna ajah ajah hey!"

This verse was a hit, for Okiok was known to be but an

indifferent marksman with the throwing-spear; yet such was his industry and his ability to approach very near to his prey, that he was the reverse of a bad hunter. But men in all lands are prone to shut their eyes to the good, and to open them very wide to the evil, that may be said of an adversary. Consequently at this point the chorus was given with great vigour by the wizard faction, and the wizard himself, having worked himself into a breathless condition by the mental effort and the furious dance, deemed it a fitting occasion to take his first rest.

The custom in those duels is for each combatant to devote a quarter of an hour or so to the attack, and then make way for his opponent, who at once steps forward and begins his counter-attack. After a short time he in like manner gives way, and his foe returns. Thus they proceed until one is exhausted or overwhelmed; and he who has the last word gains the victory, after which the dispute is held as settled, and they frequently become better friends than before.

There was something in the expression of Okiok as he stepped sedately into the ring which gladdened his friends and distressed his opponents. Unlike the wizard, he was well formed, and all his movements were comparatively elegant, so that in his case the conventional bit of dance at the end of periods was pleasant to the eye, while his peculiar advantage of rhyming power rendered his performance grateful to the ear. After a little drumming he began:—

"Why must I step within this ring,
To jump and dance, and drum and sing?
You all know well that Okiok
Was never made an angekok.
Amna ajah ajah hey!"

"Amna ajah ajah hey!" yelled the hunter's admirers, with enthusiasm.

> "But Ujarak's the man of skill,
> To kick or wrestle, sing or kill;
> He bids me meet him here to-day.
> Poor Okiok! he must obey.
> My Torngak, come here, I say!
> Thus loud I cried the other day—
> 'You always come to Ujarak;
> Thou come to me, my Torngak!'
> But he was deaf, and would not hear,
> Although I roared it in his ear.
> At last he said, 'No, Okiok,
> For you are not an angekok!'
> Amna ajah ajah hey!"

Here the hunter, after a neat pirouette and tickling of the drum, changed his tone to a soft insinuating whine:

> "'Tis true I'm not an angekok;
> I'm only hunter Okiok.
> But Torngak, dear Torngak,
> Don't go away. O do come back!
> If you'll be mine, and stick to me
> For evermore, I'll stick to thee.
> And every single thing I do
> I'll come and ask advice from you;
> Consult you morning, noon, and night;
> Consult you when I hunt or fight;
> Consult you when I sing and roar;
> Consult you when I sleep and snore;
> Consult you more than Ujarak—
> My Tor—Tor—Tor—Tor—Torngak!"

A roar of laughter and a stupendous "Amna ajah ajah hey!"

R. M. Ballantyne

greeted this flight, while Okiok gravely touched his drum, and performed a few more of his graceful evolutions.

> "'No, no,' he said; 'I'll never make
> So gross and stupid a mistake.
> One man there is who tried to do it—
> He thinks the spirits never knew it—
> He tried to make an angekok-stew
> Out of a lad named Ippegoo!'"

Here another yell of delight was followed by the chorus, and Okiok was about to resume, when a terrific rending sound seemed to paralyse every one. Well did they know that sound. It was the rending of the solid ice on which they stood. The advancing spring had so far weakened it that a huge cake had broken off from the land-ice, and was now detached. A shriek from some of the women drew attention to the fact that the disruption of the mass had so disturbed the equilibrium of the neighbouring berg that it was slowly toppling to its fall. A universal stampede instantly took place, for the danger of being crushed by its falling cliffs and pinnacles was very great. Everything but personal safety was forgotten in the panic that ensued. Red Rooney was almost swept off his legs in the rush. Women and children were overturned, but fortunately not hurt. A very few minutes sufficed to take them all clear of danger; but the succeeding crashes produced such an inconceivable roar that the terrified villagers ran on until close to the place where the ice had cracked off, and where a lane of water about three feet wide presented itself.

Over this went men, women, and children at a flying leap—all except poor little Pussi. That fat little thing would have been left behind had not the mere force of the rush carried her on in a half running, half rolling way. Being unable to manage the jump, she went in with a plunge, and disappeared.

A wild scream from the nearest female caused every one to stop and run back.

"Pussi!" exclaimed Nunaga, pointing wildly to the water.

"Where—where did she go in?" cried Rooney.

"She must have gone under the ice!" gasped the poor girl.

As she spoke a bubble of air rose to the surface. Next moment the seaman cleft the cold black water and disappeared.

Then with a thrill of alarm the Eskimos observed that the great ice-cake which had broken off was being driven shoreward by the rising tide, and that the lane of water was rapidly closing.

But they were not kept long in suspense. Another moment, and Rooney appeared with little Pussi in his arms. They were instantly seized by Okiok and Angut, and dragged violently out—not much too soon, for only a few seconds after they were rescued the ice closed with a grinding crash, that served to increase the fervency of the "Thank God!" with which the seaman hailed their deliverance.

The child was not quite insensible, though nearly so. Rooney seized her in his arms, and ran as fast as he could towards the village, whither the fleet-footed Ippegoo had already been sent to prepare skins and warm food for the reception of rescued and rescuer.

R. M. Ballantyne

CHAPTER SIXTEEN

THE REBELLION OF THE WORM
AND THE FALL OF THE WIZARD

The event which had so suddenly interrupted the singing duel was a matter of secret satisfaction to Ujarak, for he felt that he was no match for Okiok, and although he had intended to fight the battle out to the best of his ability, he knew that his ultimate defeat was so probable that its abrupt termination before that event was a piece of great good-fortune.

Still, his position was unsatisfactory, for, in addition to the fact that his credit as a genuine angekok had been sadly shaken because of Ippegoo's failure, he was well aware that the combat which had been interrupted was only postponed. What was to be done in the circumstances became, therefore, the urgent question of the hour. In great perplexity he sought out his poor victim Ippegoo—with something of the feeling, no doubt, that induces a drowning man to clutch at a straw—and silently walked with him to a secluded spot near the neighbouring cliffs.

"Ippegoo," he said, turning round abruptly; "it is certain that you will never be an angekok."

"I don't want to be one," returned the simpleton quietly.

The wizard looked at him in surprise.

"What do you mean?" he asked sharply.

"I mean that if the torngak you were going to get for me is no better than your own, he is a fool, and I would rather not have him."

This unexpected rebellion of the worm which he had so often twisted round his finger was too much for Ujarak in his then irascible condition. He flew into a violent rage, grasped the handle of his knife, and glared fiercely at his pupil.

Ippegoo returned the look with a quiet smile.

This was perplexing. There are few things more trying to passionate men than uncertainty as to how their bursts of anger will be received. As a rule such men are merely actors. No doubt their rage may be genuine, but the manner in which they will display their anger depends very much on who are their witnesses, and what their opponents. Rage which fumes at some trifling insult, and tears off the coat, resolved on fighting, when a timid wife seeks to soothe, is likely to assume a very different appearance and follow some other course of action when a prize-fighter pulls the nose, and invites it to "do its worst."

If Ippegoo had winced, or stood on the defensive, or stepped back, or shown the slightest sign of fear, it is probable that the strong and lawless man would have stabbed him to the heart in the first impulse of his anger, for the poor youth was well acquainted with all his secrets and most of his bad intentions. But the motionless figure and the smiling face not only surprised—it alarmed—Ujarak. It seemed so unnatural.

R. M. Ballantyne

What powers of sudden onslaught might not lie hidden within that calm exterior? what dynamitic capacities of swift explosion might not underlie that fearless expression?

"Ippegoo," he said, stifling his anger with a painful effort, "are you going to turn against your best friend?"

"My mother is my best friend," answered the youth stoutly.

"You are right; I made a mistake."

"Why does your torngak let you make so many mistakes?"

Again a rush of anger prompted the wizard to sacrifice his quondam pupil, and once more the youth's imperturbable coolness overawed him. Bad as he was, Ujarak could not kill a smiling victim.

"Ippegoo," said the wizard, suddenly changing his tone, and becoming intensely earnest, "I see what is the matter. Angut and the Kablunet have bewitched you. But now, I tell my torngak to enter into your heart, and unbewitch you. Now, do you not feel that he has done it?"

The youth, still smiling, shook his head.

"I knew it," continued the wizard, purposely misunderstanding the sign. "You are all right again. Once more I lay my commands on you. Listen. I want you to go at once and tell Nunaga that *Angut* wants to see her alone."

"Who?" asked Ippegoo in surprise.

"Angut."

"What! your rival?"

"Yes; my rival. My torngak tells me that Angut wants to meet her—alone, mind—out on the floes at Puffin Island this afternoon."

"Are—are you sure your torngak has made no mistake?" asked the youth, with something of his old hesitancy.

"Quite sure," replied Ujarak sternly. "Now, will you give her my message?"

"Angut's message, you mean."

"Yes, yes; I mean Angut's message," said the wizard impatiently. "You'll be *sure* to do what I tell you, won't you?"

"Quite sure," replied Ippegoo, the smile again overspreading his visage as he turned and quitted the spot.

Half an hour later he entered Okiok's hut in quest of Nunaga, but only her mother was there. She told him that the girl had gone off with a sledge along the coast to Moss Bay to fetch a load of moss to stuff between the logs of the hut where they required repairing, and that she had taken Kabelaw as well as Tumbler and Pussi with her.

"That's good," said Ippegoo, "then she can't and won't go to Puffin Island. I said I would tell her that Angut wants to meet her there alone."

"Who told you to tell her that?" asked Nuna.

"A fool," answered Ippegoo, promptly.

"He must indeed have been a fool," returned Nuna, "for Angut has just been helping Nunaga to harness the dogs, and he is now with my husband in his own hut."

R. M. Ballantyne

This information caused the messenger to shut his eyes, open his mouth, and laugh silently, with evident enjoyment.

"I intended to deliver my message," he said, on recovering composure, "for I promised to do so; and I also meant to tell Nunaga that the message was a *big lie*."

At this amazing depth of slyness on his part, Ippegoo fell into another hearty though inaudible laugh, after which he went off to communicate his news to Okiok and Angut, but these worthies having gone out to visit some snares and traps, no one knew whither, he was obliged to seek counsel of Simek.

On hearing of the plot that seemed to be hatching, that jovial hunter at once ordered his sledge to be got ready, and started off, with two stalwart sons and his nephew Arbalik, for Moss Bay, to warn Nunaga of her enemy's intentions, and to fetch her home. But alas! for even the best laid of human plans.

It so happened that one of the Eskimo youths, who was rather inclined to tease Nunaga, had set a snow-trap for Arctic foxes about two miles from the village. As the spot was not much out of the way, the girl resolved to turn aside and visit the trap, take out the fox, if one chanced to be caught, and in any case set the trap off, or put a bit of stick into it by way of fun. The spot chanced to be only a short distance beyond the place where the wizard had met Ippegoo, but the sea-shore there was so covered with hummocks of ice that Nunaga had approached without being observed by either the wizard or the pupil. It was not more than a few minutes after Ippegoo had left on his errand to herself that she came suddenly in sight of Ujarak. He was seated, as if in contemplation, on a rock at the base of the cliff.

Suspecting no evil, Nunaga stopped her team of dogs. It was

her father's best team, consisting of the swiftest and most enduring animals in the village. The wizard observed this as he rose up and approached, rejoicing to think that Fortune had favoured him. And truly Fortune—or rather, God—was indeed favouring the wicked man at that time, though not in the way that he imagined.

In a few moments Ujarak's plans were laid. The opportunity was too good to be lost.

"Where goes Nunaga to-day?" he asked quietly, on reaching the sledge.

"To Moss Bay," answered Nunaga.

"Has Nunaga forgotten the road?" asked Ujarak, with a slight look of surprise. "This is not the way to Moss Bay."

"It is not far out of the way," said Kabelaw, who was the more self-assertive of the two lying sisters; "we go to visit a trap, and have no time to waste with *you*."

As she spoke she seized the heavy Eskimo whip out of Nunaga's hand, and brought it smartly down on the backs of the whole team, which started off with a yelp, and also with a bound that well-nigh left Tumbler and Pussi behind. But she was not quick enough for Ujarak, who exclaimed with a laugh, as he leaped on to the sledge and assumed the place of driver—

"I too am fond of trapping, and will go with you."

He took the whip from Kabelaw, and guided the team.

A few minutes, at the speed they were going, brought them close to a point or cape which, in the form of a frowning cliff two or three hundred feet high, jutted out into the sea. To round this, and place the great cape between them and the village, was Ujarak's aim. The ice was comparatively smooth and unbroken close to the land.

"See!" exclaimed Nunaga, pointing towards the bushes on shore; "the trap is there. That is the place."

Ujarak paid no heed to her. The die was cast. He had taken the first step, and must now go through with it at all hazards. Plying the cruel whip, so as to make the dogs run at their utmost speed, he drove on until the other side of the cape was gained. Then he relaxed the speed a little, for he knew that no shriek, however loud, could penetrate the cliffs that lay between him and the Eskimo village.

Taking up a walrus-line with a running noose on it that lay on the sledge beside him, the wizard turned, dropped the noose suddenly over Kabelaw, and drew it tight, so as to pin her arms to her sides. Almost before she could realise what had occurred, he took a quick turn of the same line round Nunaga, drew the girls together, and fastened them to the sledge. They knew now full well, but too late, that Ujarak meant mischief. Screaming at the utmost pitch of their voices, they struggled to free themselves, but were too well secured for that.

The wizard now glanced at the children. For a few moments he was perplexed. They could be of no use on a long journey, and might be troublesome—besides, they would have to be fed. There was one sure and easy method of getting rid of them. He grasped his knife-handle.

The women observed the movement, and became instantly silent with horror.

But the bold free air of Tumbler and the soft innocent look of Pussi were too much for the wizard. He abandoned the half-formed thought, and, turning to the women, said in a low, stern voice—

"If you cry or struggle again, these shall die."

This was enough. The poor creatures remained perfectly silent and still after that, while the wizard guided the dogs out upon the floes on a totally different route from that which led to Moss Bay.

Coming to a place where the ice had been cut up into many tracks by the Eskimos' sledges during the winter work of traffic to and from the hunting-grounds, Ujarak availed himself of the opportunity to lose, as it were, his own track among the others, so that, in the sure event of pursuit, the pursuers might be effectually baffled. The only point he had to consider after that was the necessity of diverging from the track with such care that the point of divergence should be impossible to find.

In this he was again favoured by circumstances. Having driven at full speed straight out from the land in a westerly direction, he came to a place where the ice had been considerably broken up, so that the old tracks ended abruptly in many places where lanes of water had opened up. A sharp frost had set these lanes and open spaces fast again, and the new ice was just strong enough to bear a sledge. There was some risk in venturing on it, but what of that? Nothing bold can be successfully carried out in this world without more or less of risk! At a spot where the confusion of tracks was very great, he turned at a sharp angle, got upon a sheet of new ice, and went off at greater speed than ever towards the far-south.

His aim was to travel some hundreds of miles, till he reached

R. M. Ballantyne

the Kablunet settlements on the south-western shores of Greenland, in regard to which, various and strange reports had reached the northern Eskimos from time to time. He said nothing, however, to his captives, but after driving some twenty miles or so—which he did in a couple of hours—he cast off their bonds, and bade them make themselves comfortable. The poor creatures were only too glad to avail themselves of the permission, for, although spring had set in, and the cold was not very severe, their constrained position had benumbed their limbs.

Tumbler and Pussi, after gazing for a considerable time at each other in a state of blank amazement at the whole proceedings, had finally dropped off to sleep on a pile of deerskins. Nunaga and Kabelaw, wrapping themselves in two of these, leaned against each other and conversed in low whispers.

And now the wizard began in good earnest a journey, which was destined to lead him, in more ways than one, far beyond the point at which he originally aimed.

He plied the whip with vigour, for well did he know that it was a race for life. If any of the men of his tribe should overtake him, he felt assured that death would be his portion.

The dogs, as we have said, were splendid animals. There were ten of them, resembling wolves both in size and appearance, each being fastened to the sledge by a single independent line. The vehicle itself was Okiok's hunting-sledge, having spears, bow and arrows, lines, bladders, etcetera, attached to it, so that, although there were no provisions on it except one small seal, which its owner had probably thought was not worth removing, the wizard knew that he possessed all the requisites for procuring a supply. The women, being also well aware of this, were filled with anxiety, for their one hope of rescue lay in their friends discovering their flight and engaging in instant and hot pursuit.

Never since the commencement of his career had Ujarak displayed such anxiety to increase the distance between himself and his tribe. Never since that long-lashed, short-handled, heavy whip was made, had it given forth such a rapid series of pistol-like reports, and never since they were pups had those ten lanky wolfish dogs stretched out their long legs and scampered over the Arctic sea as they did on that occasion. The old ice was still sufficiently firm and smooth to afford a good road, and the new ice was fortunately strong enough to bear, for the pace was tremendous. With "the world before him where to choose," and death, as he imagined, on the track behind, the wizard's spirit had risen to the point of "neck or nothing." Mile after mile was passed at highest speed and in perfect silence, except when broken by the crack of whip and yelp of dogs. Occasional roughnesses in the way were crashed over. Small obstructions were taken in flying leaps, which rendered it necessary for the poor women to cling to each other, to the sledge, and to the children, to prevent their being hurled off. Once or twice a hummock which it seemed possible to leap turned out to be too high, and obliged the driver to turn aside with such violence that the sledge went for a few seconds on one runner, and all but turned over. This at last induced some degree of caution, for to break the vehicle at the beginning of the journey would have been almost certainly fatal to the enterprise.

And oh! how earnestly Nunaga longed for a spill! In her despair, poor thing, it did not occur to her that at such a pace an upset might break the necks of the whole party.

Towards sunset they rounded a high cape, beyond which was a deep and wide bay. On this the sun shone apparently on what appeared to be open water. For one moment a look of alarm flitted over the wizard's face, as he glanced quickly shoreward to see whether the ground-ice was passable; but it was only for a moment, for immediately he perceived that the light had dazzled and deceived him. It was not water, but new ice—smooth and refulgent as a mirror. The fringe of old ice on shore was disrupted and impassable. There was therefore only one course open to him.

Knitting his brows and clenching his teeth, Ujarak resolved to take it at all hazards. Bringing the cruel lash to bear with extreme violence, he sent the dogs howling out upon the glassy surface. At first they slipped and sprawled a good deal, but soon gathered themselves well together. They were accustomed to such work, and the friction of the sledge being reduced, they skimmed along with ease.

Although strong enough to bear, the ice undulated terribly as they swept over it, and sent forth rending sounds, which cannot be conceived by those whose experience of young ice has been derived chiefly from lakelets and ponds. Dogs in such circumstances are apt to become terrified and to stop, in which case immersion is almost certain. But Ujarak gave his team no time to think. With lash and voice he urged them on until they were nearly frantic. The undulations became greater as they advanced, and the rending sounds continuous. Still the wizard plied his whip and shouted. Indeed it was his only chance. At the other side of the bay the old ice still adhered to the shore. If that could be reached, they would be safe. Eagerly the women strained their eyes, and even stretched out their hands as if to grasp the shore, for the fear of instant death had banished all other thoughts. A few minutes more, and Ujarak, standing up in his eagerness, flourishing the great whip, and shouting at the pitch of his voice, drove the yelling dogs off the crackling sheet of ice to a place of safety on the solid floe.

It did not require the wizard's altered tone to inform the sagacious animals that the danger was past. Down they flopped at once to rest, panting vehemently, and with tongues out; but they were not permitted to rest long, Ujarak's fear of pursuit was so great. Even while securing on the sledge the articles that had been disarranged, he could not help casting frequent suspicious glances in the direction from which they had come, for guilt is ever ready to anticipate retribution even when it is far distant. As soon as the fastenings were arranged he prepared to continue the flight.

"Where do you take us to?" asked Kabelaw, in a tone of humility which was very foreign to her nature.

"You shall know that in time," was the stern reply.

Nunaga was too much frightened to speak, but little Tumbler was not.

"Bad—bad man!" he exclaimed, with a fierce look that caused the wizard for a moment to smile grimly.

Little Pussi was so horrified at the reckless presumption of the remark, that she hid her face in Nunaga's lap and did not venture to look up for some time.

Getting on the sledge without another word, the wizard gave a hint to the dogs which was so unmistakable that they sprang up and resumed their journey at full gallop. Slowly the sun went down, and sea and berg and snow-clad cliff grew grey in the light of departing day. Still the panting team sped on over the frozen sea. Soon it became too dark to travel with safety. The pace was slackened. The run became a canter, then a trot, and then a walk. At last the driver stopped, jumped off the sledge, and ordered the women to get out the seal and feed the dogs. He also gave them permission to help themselves, but as there was no lamp or fire, it was evident that he meant them to eat their supper raw.

Leaving them while thus engaged, he walked away out of sight.

"I won't have raw seal," said Tumbler, in that tone of petulant resolve which tells of spoilt-childism.

"An' me won't too," said Pussi, profiting by example.

"But there's nothing else," said Nunaga, gently.

"Yes, there is. I have got some cold seal in my boots—from this morning's breakfast," said Kabelaw, extracting a goodly-sized morsel; "I never go on a journey, however short, without a bit of cooked meat."

Lest the reader should be perplexed here, we may explain that some Eskimo ladies often make the wide tops of their long sealskin boots do duty for pockets.

The party was still engaged in discussing the delicacy referred to, and commenting in pitiable tones on their situation, when Ujarak returned, bade them resume their places, jumped on the sledge, and continued to advance. In half an hour the moon rose in a clear sky. The stars shone brightly, and to add to the beauty of the scene, the aurora borealis played and shot about vividly overhead, enabling them to resume a rapid gallop.

It was not till the night was far advanced, and his dogs were nearly worn-out, and full sixty miles lay between him and his native village, that Ujarak felt himself to be comparatively safe, and halted for a prolonged rest.

Without a word, he made for himself a shelter with a bear-skin under a low bush, devoured a lump of raw seal's flesh, and then went to sleep, leaving the women to look after themselves, the dogs, and the children, as best they might. Fortunately, they were well able to do so, and, being very weary, were not long in doing it. While they went about the work, however, they could not help remarking the unusually morose and surly manner of their master, and expressed the opinion that he was already troubled with that mental complaint to which we give the name of remorse.

And they were right. Bad as the wizard was, he had hitherto kept within the bounds of Eskimo propriety; but now at last he had overstepped those bounds and become a criminal—an outlaw. By one hasty act he had cut, for ever, the cords which had united him to his kindred.

CHAPTER SEVENTEEN

TELLS OF DESPAIR AND A WILD PURSUIT

On discovering that Nunaga and the children were not at Moss Bay, and that there were no fresh sledge tracks in that region to tell of their whereabouts, Simek drove back to the village at a wild scamper, in a state of mind very much the reverse of jovial. His hope was that the girl might have been to some other locality, and had perhaps returned during his absence; but the first glance at Nuna put that hope to flight, for the poor woman was in a state of terrible anxiety.

Cheery little Kunelik and her mild son did their best to comfort her, but without success, for she knew well the determined character of the man who had probably carried off her children.

"Has she not come back?" demanded Simek, appearing, like an infuriated Polar bear, at the inside opening of the passage to Okiok's mansion.

"No," gasped Nuna.

Simek said no more, but backed out faster than he had come in. Ippegoo followed him.

"Run, Ippe; tell all the men to get all their sledges and dogs ready, and come here to me."

Ippegoo ran off at once, while the energetic hunter rearranged the fastenings of his own sledge and team as if for a long journey.

He was thus engaged when Okiok and Angut were seen approaching the village at an easy trot. Evidently they knew nothing of what had occurred. Simek ran out to meet them. A few words sufficed to explain. The news seemed to stun both men at first, but the after-effect on each was wonderfully different. The blood rushed to Okiok's face like a torrent. He clenched his hands and teeth, glared and stamped, and went on like one deranged—as indeed for the moment he was. Angut, on the other hand, was perfectly self-possessed and subdued, but his heaving chest, quivering nostrils, compressed lips, and frowning brows told that a volcano of emotion raged within.

Turning suddenly to Okiok, he seized him by both arms as if his hands were vices.

"Listen," he said, with a sort of subdued intensity, that had the effect of quieting his friend; "get out your sledge and dogs."

"All are ready," interposed Simek, eagerly.

Angut waited for no more, but, leaving his friends, ran off at full speed towards the village. Okiok and Simek leaped on their respective sledges and followed.

On arriving, it was found that most of the active men of the tribe were already assembled, with dogs harnessed, provisions and hunting-gear strapped down, and all ready for a journey of any length.

To these Angut gave directions in a tone and manner that deeply impressed his friends. Not that he was loud or eager or violent; on the contrary, he was unusually calm, but deadly pale, and with an air of tremendous resolution about him that made the men listen intently and obey with promptitude. In a very few minutes he had sent off one and another in almost every direction, with instructions where to go, what to do, and how and when to return, in the event of failure. Then he leaped on his own sledge, and turned to Red Rooney, who was standing by.

"Ridroonee," he said, in a somewhat sad tone, "I go to find Nunaga. If I succeed not, you will see me no more."

He held out his hand to take farewell in the Kablunet's fashion.

"What say you?" exclaimed Rooney, taken by surprise, "Nonsense! see you no—Pooh!—hold on a bit."

He ran into his friend's hut, and quickly returned with his bear-skin sleeping-bag and a small wallet which contained his little all.

"Now then," he cried, jumping on the sledge, "away you go as soon as you like. I'm with 'ee, lad."

Angut shook his head.

"But the Kablunet is not yet strong enough to travel," said the Eskimo, doubtfully.

"The Kablunet is strong enough to pitch you over his head; and he'll do it too, if you don't drive on."

With another doubtful look and shake of the head, Angut seized his whip. The dogs, knowing the signal well, sprang up. At that moment Angut observed the little eyes of Kannoa peering at him wistfully.

"Come," he said, holding out a hand.

The old woman's visage beamed with joy, as she seized the hand, and scrambled on the sledge. Then the lash came round with the wonted crack. The dogs winced, but did not suffer, for Angut was merciful to his beasts, and away they went at full speed—Okiok having dashed off in similar fashion with his two sons and Simek in another direction a few minutes before them.

North, south, east, and west, on land and sea, did those Eskimos search for tracks of the fugitives; but the whole immediate neighbourhood was so cut up in all directions by the daily out-going and in-coming of their own hunters, that the discovering of a special track was not easy—indeed, almost impossible. All day they sped over the ice and snow in widening circles. When night came, they waited till the moon arose, and then continued the search. It was not till the forenoon of the following day that the unsuccessful searchers began to drop in one by one, worn-out and disheartened.

Nuna and the other women had breakfast ready for them. Little was said, for the women were depressed, and the men, after eating, immediately sought much-needed repose. It was nearly evening before Okiok and his sons returned.

"No sign anywhere," he said in reply to his poor wife's mute inquiry. "Ippegoo," he added, turning to the youth, whose woe-begone expression at another time would have been ludicrous, "I will sleep for some time. Let the dogs be well fed all round, and be ready to start with me when the moon rises."

Without another word, he stretched himself on the floor, pillowed his head on a deerskin, and went to sleep almost on the instant.

Meanwhile Angut had driven straight to Moss Bay. His search was not one of a wild haphazard nature. Despite the agitation of his breast, his mind was clear and his head cool. Judging that Nunaga must at least have started for her intended destination, whatever might afterwards have induced her to change her mind, he drove slowly along, observing with a lynx eye everything that looked in the slightest degree like a divergence from the route. The consequence was, that on reaching the place where the divergence had actually taken place, he pulled up, and got off the sledge to examine.

"You're right," remarked Rooney, who accompanied his friend, while old Kannoa remained with the dogs. "It's easy to see that a sledge has turned off here."

"Quite easy," responded the Eskimo, with suppressed eagerness; "we will follow."

Running back, they turned the dogs into the fresh track, and soon came to the place where Ujarak had joined the women. Angut pointed to the footprints with a gleam of unusual ferocity in his eyes. For some time they could easily follow the track, and went along at a rapid pace; but when it led them to the point where it joined other tracks, the difficulty of following became great. Of course Angut at once understood the object of this ruse, and became more attentive to every mark that seemed in the remotest degree to indicate another divergence, but failed to hit upon the spot, and finally came to a halt when far out on the floes where drift had obliterated the old sledge-marks, and a recent track could not have escaped notice. Then he made a wide circular sweep, which was meant to cut across all the tracks that radiated from the village.

In this manoeuvre he was more successful.

Towards evening he came upon a recent track which led straight to the southward.

"Got him at last!" exclaimed Rooney, with a shout of excitement and satisfaction.

"I think so," said Angut, as he went down on his knees and carefully examined the marks on the floe. His opinion was clearly shown by his starting up suddenly, jumping on the sledge again, flourishing his whip savagely, and setting off at a pace that obliged Rooney to seize the lashings with both hands and hold on tight. Old Kannoa did the same, and stuck to the sledge like a limpet, with her chin resting on her knees and her sharp little eyes gazing anxiously ahead.

Soon they came to the rough ground that had tried the quality of the wizard's sledge, and the vehicle bumped over the ice at such a rate that the poor old woman was almost pitched out.

"Hallo! hold on!" cried Rooney, as they went over a hummock with a crash that made Kannoa gasp, "you'll kill the poor thing if you—"

He stopped short, for another crash almost tumbled himself over the stern of the vehicle.

Angut was roused to desperation. He scarcely knew what he was doing, as he lashed the yelping team furiously, hoping that when he should pass the cape ahead of him he would come in sight of the fugitives.

R. M. Ballantyne

"Here, catch hold of me, old woman," cried Rooney, putting an arm round the poor creature's waist; "sit on my legs. They'll act something like a buffer to your old bones."

Kannoa gave a sort of lively chuckle at the novelty of the situation, let go her hold of the sledge, and made a sudden plunge at Rooney, grasping him tight round the neck with both arms. She was little more than a baby in the seaman's huge grasp, nevertheless, having only one arm to spare, and with a sledge that not only bumped, but swung about like a wild thing, he found her quite as much as he could manage.

The night had fairly set in when the cape was rounded, so that nothing could be distinguished, not even the track they had been following—and travelling became dangerous.

"No use to push on, Angut," remarked Rooney, as his friend pulled up; "we must have patience."

"Yes; the moon will be up soon," returned his friend; "we will now rest and feed."

The resting meant sitting there in the dark on the side of the sleigh, and the feeding consisted in devouring a lump of seal's flesh raw. Although not very palatable, this was eminently profitable food, as Angut well knew. As for Rooney, he had learned by that time to eat whatever came in his way with thankfulness—when hungry, and not to eat at all when otherwise.

The moon rose at last, and revealed the sheet of glassy ice which had previously disconcerted Ujarak. Angut also beheld it with much concern, and went on foot to examine it. He returned with an anxious look.

"They have crossed," he said moodily, "but the ice has

cracked much, and my sledge is, I fear, heavier than theirs."

"We can walk, you know, and so lighten it," said Rooney.

"No; it is only by a dash at full speed that we can do it. Will my friend run the risk?"

"He would not be your friend if he were not willing," returned the seaman gravely; "but what about Kannoa? It's not fair to risk her life."

"We cannot leave her behind," said Angut, with a perplexed glance at the cowering figure on the sledge. "She could not return to the village on foot. That would be greater risk to her than going on with us."

At this point the old woman looked up with a sort of pleasant grin, and croaked—

"Kannoa is not heavy. Take her with you. She is quite willing to live or die with Angut and Ridroonee."

With a slight smile the Eskimo resumed his place and whip. Rooney patted Kannoa on the head as he sat down beside her, and called her a "brave old girl."

Another moment, and the dogs were out on the glassy plain, galloping as well as they could, and yelping as much from fear of the rending and bending ice as the cracking whip.

They had not advanced twenty yards when one of the sledge-runners broke through. This brought them to a sudden halt. Next moment the sledge went down, and Angut found himself struggling with the dogs in the sea. Fortunately Rooney, being near the back part of the sledge, was able to roll off in a sort of back-somersault before the vehicle was

R. M. Ballantyne

quite submerged. Even in the act he did not forget Kannoa. He made a blind grasp at her in passing, but found her not, for that remarkable woman, at the first alarm, and being well aware of what was coming, had sprawled off at the rear, and was already on the ice in safety.

The two now set to work to rescue Angut and the dogs. The former had cut the latter free from the sledge, so that it was not difficult to haul them out along with their master. For it must be remembered that, although the thin ice had failed to bear the sledge, it was sufficiently strong to support the individuals singly.

To get the sledge out of the water was, however, a matter of much greater difficulty, but they accomplished it in the course of an hour or so. The process of doing this helped to dry Angut's garments, which was fortunate. It was also fortunate that the sharp spring frost, which had set fast the space of open water, had by that time given way, so that there was no fear of evil consequences from the ducking either to dogs or man.

But now came the serious question, What was to be done?

"It is of no use trying it again," said Angut, in a frame of mind amounting almost to despair.

"Could we not send Kannoa back with the sledge, and you and I make sail after them on foot?" asked Rooney.

Angut shook his head despondingly.

"Of no use," he said; "they have the best dogs in our village. As well might a rabbit pursue a deer. No; there is but one course. The land-ice is impassable, but the floes out on the sea seem still to be fast. If they break up while we are on them we shall be lost. Will Ridroonee agree to take old Kannoa back to her friends, and I will go forward with the sledge alone?"

"What say you, Kannoa?" asked Rooney, turning to the old woman with a half-humorous look.

"Kannoa says she will live or die with Angut and Ridroonee," she replied firmly.

"You're a trump!" exclaimed the seaman in English. Then, turning to the Eskimo—

"You see, Angut, it's impossible to get rid of us, so up anchor, my boy, and off we go seaward. The truth is, I ought to feel more in my element when we get out to sea."

Seeing that they were resolved, Angut made no further objection, but, directing the dogs' heads away from the land, flourished his long whip over them, and set off at as break-neck a pace as before over the seaward ice-floes.

R. M. Ballantyne

CHAPTER EIGHTEEN

A TERRIBLE ENCOUNTER, DISASTROUS RESULTS, AND SINGULAR TERMINATION

Let us return now to the wizard and his captives.

After travelling for several days at the utmost possible speed, the guilty man began to feel at ease as regarded pursuit, and commenced to advance at a more reasonable rate, giving the poor dogs time for sufficient rest, and going out once or twice on the floes to procure fresh supplies of seal-flesh for himself and his party.

The thaw which had by that time set steadily in had not broken up the old ice to the southward, so that no more thin ice or open water was met with. But although he had thus begun to take things more easily, Ujarak did not by any means waste time. The wretched man was very morose, even savage, insomuch that he would scarcely reply to the questions which were timidly put to him at times by the women. It was evident that he repented of his hasty flight, and no doubt was rendered desperate by the reflection that the matter was by that time past remedy.

One morning, on rounding one of those bluff precipitous capes which jut out from the western coast of Greenland into

Baffin's Bay, they came unexpectedly in sight of a band of Eskimos who were travelling northwards.

Ujarak pulled up at once, and for some moments seemed uncertain what to do. He had not yet been observed, so that there was a possibility of turning aside, if he were so disposed, and hiding among the rugged masses of ice which lined the bottom of the cliffs. Before he could make up his mind, however, on the subject, a loud shout from the Eskimos showed that he had been observed.

Turning sharply, and with a savage scowl, to the women, he said in a low voice—

"If you say that I have run away with you, I will kill you and the children."

A smile of contempt flickered on the face of Kabelaw at the moment. Observing it, the wizard added—

"There will be no escape for *you*. Your death will be certain, for even if these people were to kill me, and carry you back to the village, my torngak would follow you and kill you."

He said no more, for he knew well that he had said enough.

At first sight of the Eskimo band, Kabelaw's heart had leaped for joy, because she at once made up her mind to explain how matters stood, and claim protection, which she had no doubt they would grant. But some Eskimos, not less than many civilised people, are deeply imbued with superstition, and the bare idea of an invisible torngak pursuing her to the death—in the possibility of which she and Nunaga more or less believed—was too much for her. In fear and trembling she made up her mind to be silent, and submit to her fate. It need scarcely be added, so did her more timid companion.

R. M. Ballantyne

"Where do you come from?" asked the leader of the party when they met.

"From the far-away *there*," replied the wily wizard, pointing northward. "I do not ask where *you* come from."

"Why not?" demanded the leader, in some surprise.

"Because I know already," answered Ujarak, "that you come from the far-away *there*," pointing southward; "and I know that, because I am an angekok. You have come from a spot near to the land where the Kablunets have settled, and you are bringing iron and other things to exchange with my kinsmen for horns of the narwhal and tusks of the walrus."

Knowing as he did from rumour that Eskimos from the Moravian settlements were in the habit of travelling northward for the purposes of barter, (though they had not up to that time travelled so far north as his own tribe), and observing bundles of hoop-iron on the sledges, it did not require much penetration on the part of a quick mind like that of Ujarak to guess whence the strangers had come, and what their object was. Nevertheless, the leader and most of the party who had circled round the wizard and his sledge, opened their eyes in amazement at this smart statement of their affairs.

"My brother must indeed be a great angekok, for he seems to know all things. But we did not come from *near* the land where the Kablunets have built their huts. We have come *from* it," said the matter-of-fact leader.

"Did I not say that?" returned Ujarak promptly.

"No; you said near it—whereas we came from it, from inside of itself."

"Inside of itself must be very near it, surely!" retorted the wizard, with a grave look of appeal to those around him.

A laugh and nod of approval was the reply, for Eskimos appreciate even the small end of a joke, however poor, and often allow it to sway their judgment more powerfully than the best of reasoning—in which characteristic do they not strongly resemble some people who ought to know better? The matter-of-fact leader smiled grimly, and made no further objection to the wizard's claim to correct intelligence.

"Now," continued Ujarak, for he felt the importance of at once taking and keeping the upper hand, "my tribe is not far from here; but they are going away on a hunting expedition, so you must lose no time, else they will be gone before you arrive. They want iron very much. They have horns and tusks in plenty. They will be glad to see you. My torngak told me you were coming, so I came out a long way to meet you. I brought my wives and children with me, because I want to visit the Kablunets, and inquire about their new religion."

He paused for a moment or two, to let his tissue of lies have full effect, but the very matter-of-fact leader took advantage of the pause to ask how it was that if he, Ujarak, had been told by his torngak of the coming of the trading party, he had failed to tell his tribe *not* to go on a hunting expedition, but to await their arrival.

"Ha! ho!" exclaimed several of the Eskimos, turning a sharp gaze upon the wizard, as much as to say, "There's a puzzler for you, angekok!"

But Ujarak, although pulled up for a moment, was not to be overturned easily. "Torngaks," he said, "do not always reveal all they know at once. If they did, angekoks would only have to listen to all they had to tell on every subject, and there would be an end of it; they would have no occasion to use their judgments at all. No; the torngaks tell what they choose by degrees. Mine told me to leave my tribe, and visit the Kablunets. On the way he told me more, but not *all*."

This explanation seemed quite satisfactory to some, but not to all of them. Seeing this, the wizard hastened to turn their minds from the subject by asking how far it was to the land of the Kablunets.

"Four suns' journey," replied the leader.

"It is the same to the village of my kindred," exclaimed Ujarak, getting quickly on his sledge. "I must hasten on, and so must you. Time must not be wasted."

With a flourish of his whip, he started his team at full speed, scattering the Eskimos right and left, and scouring over the ice like the wind.

For a moment or two the leader of the band thought of pursuit, but seeing at a glance that none of his teams were equal to that of Ujarak, and feeling, perhaps, that it might be dangerous to pursue an angekok, he gave up the idea, and resumed his northward route.

For two days more the wizard continued his journey, encamping each night at sunset, eating his supper apart, making his bed of bearskins in the lee of a shrub or under the shelter of an overhanging cliff, and leaving his captives to make themselves comfortable as best they could on the sledge. This they did without difficulty, all of them being well accustomed to rough it, and having plenty of bear and deerskins to keep them warm. The dogs also contributed to this end by crowding round the party, with deep humility of expression, as close as they were allowed to come.

At the end of these two days an incident occurred which totally changed the aspect of affairs.

On the morning of the third day they started with the dawn, and drove steadily southward for a couple of hours. They had just traversed a small bay, and were close to the high cape which formed its southern extremity, when one of the bars of the sledge broke, rendering a halt necessary. Breaking the gloomy silence which he had so long maintained, the wizard spoke:

"Go," he said, "cook some food under the cliffs there. I will mend the sledge."

The women replied, not by words, but by the more emphatic method of at once obeying the order. Kabelaw seized and shouldered a large piece of raw seal's flesh. Nunaga took up little Pussi with one hand, and the materials for producing fire with the other, and followed her companion. Tumbler brought up the rear, staggering under the weight of the cooking-lamp.

They had only a couple of hundred yards to go. In a few minutes Kabelaw was busy under the cliffs producing fire, in the usual Eskimo fashion with two pieces of dry wood, while her friend set up the lamp and sliced the meat. The children, inheriting as they did the sterling helpful propensities of their parents, went actively about, interfering with everything, in their earnest endeavours to assist.

"Isn't he strange?" remarked Kabelaw, glancing in the direction of Ujarak, as she diligently twirled the fire-stick between her palms; "so different from what he was."

"I think," said Nunaga, pouring oil into the lamp, "that he is sorry for what he has done."

"No; him not sorry," said Tumbler, as he assisted Pussi to rise, for she had tripped and fallen; "him not sorry—him sulky."

Kabelaw took no notice of this juvenile observation, but, blowing the spark which she had at last evoked into a flame, expressed some doubt as to Ujarak's repentance, and said she had never seen him in a state of sorry-tude before. Whereupon Tumbler pertly rejoined that *he* had often seen him in a state of sulky-tude!

The damage to the sledge was slight. It was soon repaired, and the wizard brought it round with him to the spot where breakfast was being got ready.

This was the first time he had eaten with them since the flight began. His manner, however, was not much changed. He was still silent and gloomy, though once or twice he condescended to make a remark or two about the weather.

When a man talks upon the weather, the ice is fairly broken—even in Arctic regions—and from that well-nigh universal starting-point Ujarak went on to make a few more remarks. He did so very sternly, however, as though to protest against the idea that he was softening to the smallest extent.

"Nunaga," he said, holding up a finger, "in two suns, or less, we shall arrive at the land where the Kablunets have built houses and settled down."

We may explain that the wizard here referred to the Moravians, who had about that time sent out their first mission to Greenland. Of course he knew nothing of the object those self-sacrificing men had in view in thus establishing themselves in Greenland, only vague rumours having at that time reached his distant tribe. All he knew was that they were Kablunets, or foreigners, and that they had something mysterious to tell about the God of the Kablunets.

Nunaga received Ujarak's information in silence, and waited for more.

"And now," he continued, "I want you to say when you arrive there that you are my wife."

"But I am *not* your wife," returned Nunaga gently, yet firmly.

The wizard frowned, then he glared fiercely, then he looked sad, then there settled on his visage a sulky look which gradually faded away, leaving nothing but a simple blank behind. After that he opened his lips, and was about to speak, when Nunaga opened her pretty eyes to their widest, also her pretty mouth, and gave vent to a tremendous shriek, which, reverberating among the cliffs, caused all the creatures around her, canine and human, to leap electrically to their feet.

To account for this we must take the reader round to the other side of the cliff, at the foot of which the party sat enjoying their breakfast.

There, all ignorant of the human beings so near at hand, sauntered an enormous Polar bear. It seated itself presently on its haunches, and swayed itself gently to and fro, with its head on one side, as if admiring the Arctic scenery. There was not much more than a space of five hundred yards between the parties, but owing to the great promontory which formed an effectual screen between them, and the fact that the light air blew from the land to the sea, neither bear nor dogs had scented each other.

It seemed as if Bruin had only just got out of bed, for his little eyes blinked sleepily, his motions were exceedingly slow, and his yawns were frequent as well as remonstrative in tone. Doubtless bears, like men, dislike early rising!

Having gazed at the scenery long enough, and shaken off its lethargy to some extent, the bear began probably to think of food. Then it arose, sauntered round the promontory, and presented itself to the more than astonished gaze of Nunaga, who was the only one that chanced to sit facing in its direction.

The resulting shriek and its consequences seemed to have a petrifying effect on the animal, for it stood stock still for some moments, and simply gazed. This condition of things was instantly changed by three of the dogs breaking their traces, and rushing wildly at the animal. With two nimble pats of its great paws it sent two of the dogs into the air, almost killing them, while the third it dismissed, yelling hideously, with a bad tear in its flank.

Quick as thought, Ujarak set the other dogs free, and the whole pack ran open-mouthed at their natural foe, but another dog being promptly sent away howling, the rest were cowed, and confined themselves to barking furiously round their powerful foe.

Apparently this was an old bear, confident perhaps in its strength, and used, it might be, to dog-assaults, for it paid no further attention to its canine opponents, but advanced with a very threatening aspect towards the sledge.

It is pretty well-known that two Eskimo men of average strength and courage are more than a snatch for the Polar bear, if armed with spears. The mode of attack is simple. The two men separate. The one who arranges to be the slayer of the animal advances on its left side; the other on its right. Thus the victim's attention is distracted; it becomes undecided which foe to attack first. The hunter on the right settles the question by running in, and giving him a prick with the spear. Turning in fury on this man, the bear exposes its left side to the full force of a deadly thrust of the spear, which usually reaches the heart, and finishes it. The chances, however, are very much in favour of the bear when the man is alone. Hence, single hunters are not fond of attacking a Polar bear, except when unusually strong and courageous, as well as confident of their dexterity.

Now it happened that Ujarak, although strong and courageous enough, was not over-confident of his dexterity. With a tried comrade, he would readily have faced any bear in the Arctic regions, but on this occasion he felt he had to depend entirely on himself.

Seizing a spear quickly, he looked at the approaching animal, and glanced uneasily at Nunaga.

"If I am killed," he said, "you will have to defend the children."

There was a tone of pathos in the voice, which showed that no touch of selfish fear influenced the man.

Hitherto the women and children had stood absolutely horror-struck and helpless, but the vigorous nature of Kabelaw came to her aid.

"We will help you," she suddenly cried, catching up two spears, and thrusting one into the hands of Nunaga; "two women may perhaps be equal to one man."

R. M. Ballantyne

The wizard smiled grimly in spite of circumstances at this heroic action, but there was no time for reply, as the bear was already close to them.

Poor, timid Nunaga, trembling from skin to marrow, had just courage enough to grasp her spear and follow Kabelaw. The latter understood well how to act. She had often seen her own kinsmen do the work that was required of her. As for the two little ones, they continued throughout to stand limp and motionless, with eyes and mouths wide-open.

Of course Kabelaw ran to the right, and Ujarak to the left of the foe. Advancing, as in duty bound, a step or two ahead of her male friend, the former proceeded to prick the bear; but when the monster rose on his hind legs, and towered to a height of eight feet, if not more, her heart failed her. Nevertheless, she made a gallant thrust, which might have at least incommoded the animal had not the spear received a blow which not only sent it spinning out of the woman's hand, but hurled poor Kabelaw herself on the ice, a small lump of which cut open her temple, and rendered her for the moment insensible. At the same instant the wizard took prompt advantage of his opportunity, and delivered what should have been the death-wound. But the very energy of the man foiled him, for the spear entered too near the shoulder, and stuck upon the bone.

The fall of Kabelaw had the peculiar effect of producing a gush of desperation in the tender heart of Nunaga, which amounted, almost, to courage. With a lively shriek she shut her eyes, rushed in on the bear, and gave it a dab in the side, which actually sent her weapon into the flesh about an inch deep, and there it stuck fast.

Feeling this new sting, the bear turned on her with a gasp of rage. She looked up. The great paws were extended over her head. The dreadful jaws were open. Letting go her weapon, Nunaga cast up her arms, shut her eyes again, and sank shuddering on the ice. Down came the bear, but at that critical moment an irresistible force effected what the united party had failed to accomplish. The butt of Nunaga's spear chanced to enter a crack in the ice, where it stuck fast, and the weight of the descending animal sent the point through flesh, ribs, and heart, and out at his backbone. The spear broke of course, but in breaking it turned the monster on one side, and saved the poor girl from being smothered. At the same moment Ujarak had made another desperate thrust, which, unlike the former, entered deep, but being misdirected, did not touch a vital part. In the violence of his effort the man fell, and the dying bear rolled upon him, rendering him also insensible.

When poor little Nunaga, recovering from her state of semi-consciousness, opened her eyes, and sat up, her first impression was that the bear, the wizard, and Kabelaw lay around her dead.

Bad as the state of matters was, however, it was not quite so bad as that. The poor girl's first act was to burst into a hysterical fit of laughter—so wonderfully constituted are some female minds—and she followed that up with an equally hysterical fit of weeping. But to do her justice, the fits did not last above half a minute. Then she suddenly stopped, dried her eyes, jumped up, and, pursing her lips and knitting her brows, ran to her friend, whom she found just returning to a state of consciousness.

"What has happened?" asked Kabelaw, in a dazed manner, as she looked at the blood which flowed from her wound.

Nunaga did not answer, but ran to the bear, which was quite dead, and began to drag it off Ujarak. With great difficulty, and by first hauling at its neck and then at its tail, she managed to move it just enough to set the man's head and chest free. The wizard, thus partially relieved, soon began to show signs of returning life. In a few minutes he was able to sit up and drag his right leg from under the bear, but he was much exhausted, and only got it free after great exertion.

"Are you hurt?" asked Nunaga, in a tone of commiseration.

"Not much, I think. I—I am not sure. I feel as if I had been much shaken, and my leg is painful. I hope," he added, feeling the limb with both hands, "that it is not—"

He finished the sentence with a deep groan. But it was not a groan of pain so much as of despair, for his leg, he found, was broken just above the ankle.

It may perhaps require a little thought on the part of those who dwell in civilised lands to understand fully all that this implied to the Eskimo. If it did not absolutely mean death by exposure and starvation, it at all events meant life under extremely uncomfortable conditions of helplessness and pain; it meant being completely at the mercy of two women whom he had grievously wronged; and it meant that, at the best, he could not avoid ultimately falling into the hands of his angry and outraged kinsmen. All this the wizard perceived at a glance—hence his groan.

Now it may not be out of place to remark here that the qualities of mercy, pity, forgiveness, etcetera, are not by any means confined to the people of Christian lands. We believe that, as our Saviour "died for the sins of the whole world," so the Spirit of Jesus is to be found working righteousness among individuals of even the worst and most savage nations of the earth. The extreme helplessness and pain to which her enemy was reduced, instead of gratifying revenge in Nunaga, aroused in her gentle breast feelings of the tenderest pity; and she not only showed her sympathy in her looks and tones, but by her actions, for she at once set to work to bind up the broken limb to the best of her ability.

In this operation she was gleefully assisted by little Tumbler and Pussi, who, having recovered from their horror when the bear fell dead, seemed to think that all succeeding acts were part of a play got up for their special amusement.

When the surgical work was done, Nunaga again turned her attention to Kabelaw. She had indeed felt a little surprised that her friend seemed to take no interest in the work in which she was engaged, and was still more surprised when, on going up to her, she found her sitting in the same position in which she had left her, and wearing the same stupid half-stunned look on her face. A few words sufficed to reveal the truth, and, to Nunaga's consternation, she found that her friend was suffering from what is known among the civilised as concussion of the brain.

When the full significance of her condition at last forced itself upon the poor girl, when she came to see clearly that she was, as it were, cast away in the Arctic wilderness, with the whole care of a helpless man and woman and two equally helpless children, besides a sledge and team of dogs, devolving on her she proved herself to be a true heroine by rising nobly to the occasion.

Her first act was to return, with characteristic humility, and ask Ujarak what she must do.

"You must take the dogs and sledge and the children," he answered in a low voice, "and save yourselves."

"What! and leave you here?"

"Yes; I am bad. It is well that I should die."

"But Kabelaw?" said the girl, with a glance at her friend. "She has got the head-sickness and cannot help herself."

"Leave her to die also," said the wizard carelessly; "she is not worth much."

"Never!" cried Nunaga, with emphasis. "I will save her, I will save you all. Did you not tell me that the village of the Kablunets is only two suns from here?"

"That is so, Nunaga."

"Can you creep to the sledge?" asked the girl quickly.

"I think I can."

"Try, then."

The wizard tried, and found that he could creep on his hands and one knee, dragging the wounded limb on the ice. It gave him excruciating pain, but he was too much of a man to mind that. In a few minutes he was lying at full length on the sledge.

"Now, Tumbler and Pussi," said Nunaga, "cover him well up with skins, while I go and fetch Kabelaw, but *don't touch his leg.*"

She found that Kabelaw could walk slowly, with support, and after much exertion succeeded in getting her also laid out upon the sledge alongside of the wizard. Then Nunaga tied them both firmly down with long walrus-lines. She also attached the children to the sledge with lines round their waists, to prevent their being jolted off. Having thus made things secure, and having cut off some choice portions of the bear for food, she harnessed the dogs, grasped the whip, mounted to the driver's place, brought the heavy lash down with wonderful effect on the backs of the whole team, and set off at full gallop towards the land where Kablunets were said to dwell.

Fortunately, the ice was smooth most of the way, for jolting was not only injurious to poor Kabelaw, but gave the wizard great additional pain. It also had the effect of bumping Tumbler and Pussi against each other, and sometimes strained their lashings almost to the breaking point.

At night Nunaga selected as comfortable a spot as she could find under the shelter of the Greenland cliffs, and there— after detaching the children, re-dressing Ujarak's leg, arranging the couch of the semi-conscious Kabelaw, and feeding the hungry dogs—she set up her lamp, and cooked savoury seal and bear cutlets for the whole party. And, not withstanding the prejudices with which fastidious people may receive the information, it is an unquestionable fact that the frying of seal and bear cutlets sends a most delicious influence up the nose, though perhaps it may require intense hunger and an Eskimo's digestion to enable one to appreciate to the full the value of such food.

These labours ended, Nunaga put the little ones to bed, made the wizard and Kabelaw as comfortable as possible for the night, fastened up the dogs, and, spreading her own couch in the most convenient spot beside them, commenced her well-earned night's repose. The first night her bed was a flat rock; the second, a patch of sand; but on both occasions the cheery little woman softened the place with a thick bear-skin, and, curling up, covered herself with the soft skin of a reindeer.

And what were the thoughts of the wicked Ujarak as he lay

there, helpless and suffering, silently watching Nunaga? We can tell, for he afterwards made a partial confession of them.

"She is very pretty," he thought, "and very kind. I always knew that, but now I see that she is much more. She is forgiving. I took her from her home by force, and would have made her my wife against her will—yet she is good to me. I have been harsh, unkind, cruel, sulky to her ever since we left home—yet she is good to me. I have torn her from all those whom she loves, with the intention that she should never see them again—yet she is good to me. She might have left me to die, and might easily have gone home by herself, and it would have served me right, but—but she is good to me. I am not a man. I am a beast—a bear—a fox—a walrus—"

As the wizard thought thus, a couple of tears overflowed their boundaries, and rolled down the hitherto untried channel of his cheeks.

Do you think, reader, that this line of thought and emotion, even in a savage, was unnatural? Is not the same principle set forth in Scripture in reference to far higher things? Need we remind you that it is "the *goodness* of God which leadeth thee, (or any one else), to repentance?"

As it is in the spiritual world, so is it in the natural. At the time of which we write the same grand principle was powerfully at work in Nature. "Thick-ribbed ice," which the united forces of humanity could not have disrupted, was being silently yet rapidly dissolved by the genial influence of the sun, insomuch that on the evening of the day after Nunaga had been compelled by circumstances to assume command of the expedition, several sheets of open water appeared where ice had been expected, and the anxious charioteer was more than once obliged to risk the lives of the whole party by driving out to sea on the floes—that being better than the alternative of remaining where they were, to die of starvation.

But by that time they were not far distant from the Kablunet settlements.

R. M. Ballantyne

CHAPTER NINETEEN

SPRING RETURNS—KAYAK EVOLUTIONS—
ANGUT IS PUZZLED

Why some people should wink and blink as well as smirk when they are comfortable is a question which might possibly be answered by cats if they could speak, but which we do not profess to understand. Nevertheless we are bound to record the fact that on the very day when Nunaga and her invalids drew near to the first Moravian settlements in Greenland, Ippegoo slowly mounted a hillside which overlooked the icy sea, flung himself down on a moss-clad bank, and began to wink and blink and smirk in a way that surpassed the most comfortable cat that ever revelled on rug or slumbered in sunshine.

Ippegoo was supremely happy, and his felicity, like that of most simple folk, reposed on a simple basis. It was merely this—that Spring had returned to the Arctic regions.

Spring! Ha! who among the dwellers in our favoured land has the faintest idea of—of—pooh!—words are wanting. The British poets, alive and dead, have sung of Spring, and doubtless have fancied that they understood it. They had no more idea of what they were singing about than—than the man in the moon, if we may venture to use a rather hackneyed comparison. Listen, reader, humbly, as becometh the ignorant.

Imagine yourself an Eskimo. Don't overdo it. You need not in imagination adopt the hairy garments, or smear yourself with oil, or eat raw blubber. For our purpose it will suffice to transport yourself into the Arctic regions, and invest yourself with the average intelligence of an ordinary human being who has not been debased by the artificial evils that surround modern civilisation, or demoralised by strong drink. In this condition of happy simplicity you draw near to the end of an Arctic winter.

During eight months or so you have been more or less shrivelled-up, petrified, mummified, by frost of the most intense and well-nigh intolerable description. Your whole body has frequently been pierced by winds, the constituents of which seemed to be needles and fire. Shelter has been one of your chief subjects of meditation every day—ofttimes all day; unwillingness to quit that shelter and eagerness to return to it being your dominant characteristic. Darkness palpable has been around you for many weeks, followed by a twilight of gloom so prolonged that you *feel* as if light were a long-past memory. Your eyes have become so accustomed to ice and snow that white, or rather whitey-grey, has long since usurped and exclusively held the place of colour in your imagination, so that even black—a black cliff or a black rock cropping up out of the snow—becomes a mitigated joy. Your ears have been so attuned to the howling blast with interludes of dead calm and variations of rending icebergs and bellowing walrus accompaniments, that melodious harmonies have fled affrighted from your brain. As for your nose—*esprit de marrow fat*, extract of singed hide, essence of lamp-smoke, *eau de cuisine*, and de-oxygenised atmosphere of snow-hut, have often inclined you to dash into the open air, regardless of frost and snow, for purposes of

R. M. Ballantyne

revivification. Imagine all these things intensified to the uttermost, and prolonged to nigh the limits of endurance, so that genial ideas and softening influences seem to have become things of the long-forgotten past, and *then* try to imagine a change, compared to which all the transformation scenes of all the pantomimes that ever blazed are as a tomtit's chirp to a lion's roar, or a—a—Words fail again! No matter.

But don't give in yet. Try, now, to imagine this sudden transformation wrought, perhaps, in a few days to the slow music of southern zephyrs, bearing on their wings light, and heat, and sunshine. Your ear is surprised—absolutely startled—by the sound of trickling water. Old memories that you thought were dead come back in the trumpet of the wild-goose, the whistling wing of the duck, the plaintive cry of the plover. Your nose—ah! your nose cocks up and snuffs a smell—pardon!—a scent. It is the scent of the great orb on which you stand, saturated *at last* with life-giving water, and beginning to vivify all the green things that have so long been hidden in her capacious bosom.

But it is to your eye, perhaps, that the strongest appeal is made, for while you throw off one by one the garments which have protected you for so many months, and open up body and soul to the loved, long-absent, influences of warmth, and sound, and odour, your eye drinks up the mighty draughts of light—light not only blazing in the blue above, but reflected from the blue below—for the solid ice-fields are now split into fragments; the swell of old Ocean sends a musical ripple to the shore; great icebergs are being shed from their parent glaciers, and are seen floating away in solemn procession to the south, lifting their pinnacles towards their grandparent clouds, until finally reduced to the melting mood, and merged in their great-grandparent the sea. Imagine such visions and sensations coming suddenly, almost as a surprise, at the end of the stern Arctic winter, and then, perchance, you will have some idea of the bounding joy that fills the soul on the advent of Spring, inducing it to feel, if not to say, "Let every thing that hath breath praise the Lord."

This is Spring! The Eskimos understand it, and so do the dwellers in Rupert's Land; perchance, also, the poor exiles of Siberia—but the poets—pooh!

Far down below the perch occupied by Ippegoo lay a little sandy bay, around which were scattered a number of Eskimo huts—rude and temporary buildings, meant to afford shelter for a time and then be forsaken. This was the bay which Angut, Okiok, Simek, Red Rooney, and the others had reached in their pursuit of the wizard when the ice broke up and effectually stopped them.

As it was utterly impossible to advance farther with dog and sledge, they were compelled to restrain their impatience as best they could, and await open water, when they might resume their journey in kayaks. Meanwhile, as there was a lead of open water to the northward as far as they could see, the youth Arbalik had been despatched with a small sledge and four of the strongest dogs along the strip of land-ice, or "ice-foot," which clung to the shore. His mission was to reach the village, and fetch Nuna, Pussimek, Kunelik, Sigokow, and his own mother, in one of the oomiaks or women's boats when open water should permit.

It was while our Eskimos were thus idly waiting for their wives, that the before-mentioned southern Eskimos arrived, and met them with every demonstration of friendliness and good-will.

These men, who had been forced to make a long, difficult detour inland after the ice gave way, were not a little pleased to find that the ice-foot to the northward was still practicable, and that the Eskimo village was so near. Of course they told of their meeting with Ujarak's sledge, which rendered inaction on the part of the pursuers still more unbearable. But they were all men who could accept the inevitable with a good grace, and as they knew it was impossible to advance without kayaks and oomiaks, they awaited the return of Arbalik as patiently as possible. Meanwhile they made themselves agreeable to the new arrivals, whose hearts they gladdened by telling them that their friends in the north had plenty of narwhal horns and bones and walrus tusks and sinews to exchange for their wood and iron.

But to return to Ippegoo on his distant and elevated outlook.

While he gazed at the busy groups below, our weak-minded youth observed two of the party step into kayaks which lay on the beach, push off into the bay, and commence what may be styled "kayak exercise." As Ippegoo greatly enjoyed witnessing such exercises, he threw off his lethargy, and, leaping up, quickly descended to the shore. The kayaks were old ones which had been found by the party on arriving at the deserted village. They had probably been left as useless by previous visitors, but Okiok's boys, Norrak and Ermigit, being energetic and ingenious fellows, had set to work with fish-bone-needles and sinew-threads, and repaired them with sealskin patches. They were now about to test their workmanship and practise their drill.

"Do they leak?" shouted Okiok, as the lads pushed off.

"Not more than I can soak up," replied Norrak, looking back with a laugh.

"Only a little," cried Ermigit, "and hoh! the water is still very cold."

"Paddle hard, and you'll soon warm it," cried Rooney.

When they had got fairly off, a spirit of emulation seized the brothers, and, without a direct challenge, they paddled side by side, gradually increasing their efforts, until they were putting forth their utmost exertions, and going through the water at racing speed.

"Well done, Norrak!" shouted the father, in rising excitement.

"Not so fast, Ermigit; not so fast," roared Simek.

Heedless of the advice, the brothers pushed on until they were brought up by the pack-ice at the mouth of the bay. Here they turned as quickly as possible, and raced back with such equal speed that they came in close together—so close that it was impossible for those on shore to judge which was winning as they approached.

As in all similar cases—whether on the Thames or on the Greenland seas—excitement became intense as the competitors neared the goal. They were still a hundred yards or so from land, when Ermigit missed a stroke of his paddle. The consequence was that the kayak overturned, and Ermigit disappeared.

A kayak, as is generally known, is a very long and narrow canoe, made of a light wooden frame, and covered all over with sealskin with the exception of a single hole, in what may be called the deck, which is just big enough to admit one man. This hole is surrounded by a strip of wood, which prevents water washing into the canoe, and serves as a ledge over which the Eskimo fastens his sealskin coat. As canoe and coat are waterproof, the paddler is kept dry, even in rough weather, and these cockle-shell craft will ride on a sea that would swamp an open boat. But the kayak is easily

R. M. Ballantyne

overturned, and if the paddler is not expert in the use of his paddle, he runs a chance of being drowned, for it is not easy to disengage himself from his craft. Constant practice, however, makes most natives as expert and fearless as tight-rope dancers, and quite as safe.

No sooner, therefore, did Ermigit find himself in the water, head downwards, than, with a rapid and peculiar action of the paddle, he sent himself quite round and up on the other side into the right position—dripping, however, like a seal emerging from the sea. He lost the race, as a matter of course. Norrak, after touching the beach, returned to Ermigit, laughing at his mishap.

"You laugh," said his brother somewhat sharply, "but you cannot do that as quickly as I did it."

Without a word of reply, Norrak threw himself on one side, vanished in the water, and came up on the other side in a decidedly shorter time.

"Well done!" cried Ermigit, who was, in truth, a good-natured fellow; "come, let us practise."

"Agreed," responded Norrak; and both brothers pushed a little nearer to land, so that their father and the others might observe and criticise their evolutions. As the exercises which they went through are practised by Eskimos in order to fit them to cope with the accidents and emergencies of actual life, we will briefly describe them.

First Norrak leaned over on one side, of course carrying the kayak with him, until his body lay on the water, in which position he maintained himself and prevented a total overset by manipulating his paddle, and then, with a downward dash of the blade and a vigorous jerk of his body, he regained his position, amid expressions of approval from the shore. Having performed the same feat on the other side, he nodded to Ermigit, and said—

"Now you go to work."

Ermigit went to work so well, that even a critical judge could not have pronounced him better or worse than his brother. After that they both repeated the complete overturn and recovery already described. In this effort, however, the lads had the free use of their paddles; but as in actual service the paddle may easily get entangled with straps and fishing cordage, a special exercise is arranged to prepare the hunter against such misfortunes.

Accordingly Norrak pushed one blade of his paddle among the straps and cordage, overset the kayak, and worked himself up again with a quick motion of the other blade. Of course this was not done either easily or quickly. Nevertheless, it was accomplished by both lads to the entire satisfaction of their critics.

Next, they performed the same feat of upsetting and recovering position with the paddle held fast behind their backs, and then with it held across the nape of the neck—and in several other positions, all of which represented cases of possible entanglement.

Sometimes, however, the paddle may be lost in an upset. This is the most serious misfortune that can befall a hunter. To prepare for it, therefore, the Eskimo boys and youths have a special drill, which Norrak now proceeded to go through. Overturning his kayak as before, he purposely let go the oar in the act, so that it floated on the water, and then, while thus inverted, he made an upward grasp, caught the paddle, pulled it down, and with it recovered his position.

R. M. Ballantyne

There would have been great danger in this if he had been alone, for in the event of his failing to catch the paddle he would probably have been drowned, but with Ermigit at hand to help, there was no danger.

Other exercises there are which the sons of Okiok were not able to practise at that time because of the weather being unsuitable. One of these consists in threading their way among sunken rocks and dashing surges; another, in breasting the billows of a tempest. It must not be supposed that all Eskimos become efficient in rough work of this kind. Many do become exceedingly expert, others moderately so; but some there are who, although very fair seal-hunters, never become experts in the management of the kayak, and who, in cases of great difficulty, are apt to be lost during the seasons of seal-fishing.

Now, it chanced while the youths were thus training themselves for future work, that a solitary seal put up its head, as if to have a look at the state of things in general above water. It also chanced that the Eskimos were to leeward of him, and a blaze of sunshine was at their backs, so that the seal when looking towards its human foes had its eyes dazzled. Ermigit had no weapons at the time, but by good-fortune a harpoon, line, and bladder were attached to Norrak's vessel.

As the cat pounces on the unwary mouse, so Norrak, crouching low, dipped his paddle twice with noiseless vigour, and shot his craft like an arrow towards the seal. It happened to be a stupid attarsoak, and it raised its bullet head with a look that said plainly, "What, in all the ocean, is that queer thing in the sunshine?"

Half a minute brought that queer thing in the sunshine within ten yards of him. Norrak grasped the light harpoon, and sent it whistling to its mark. Truer than the needle to the pole the weapon went, carrying its line with it, and sank deep into the shoulder of the seal.

Ermigit, meanwhile, had made for the shore, got a lance thrown to him by the excited Okiok, received an encouraging nod from Rooney with an English recommendation to "go it," and was off again to render aid. And not a moment too soon did that aid come, for, contrary to usual experience, that seal—instead of diving, and giving them an hour's hot pursuit—made a furious assault on Norrak. Probably the spear had touched it in a tender spot. At all events the creature's ire was roused to such an extent that when it reached him it seized the kayak and tore a large hole in it. Down went the bow, as a matter of course, and up went the stern. Norrak hastily disengaged himself, so as to be ready to spring clear of the sinking wreck, and was on the point of jumping out when his brother's kayak shot past him, and Ermigit sent a spear deep into the vitals of the seal—so deep, indeed, that it turned over and died without a groan.

By that time Norrak was in the water, but he made a vigorous grasp at his brother's kayak with one hand, while with the other he clutched the line of the harpoon—for well did he know that dead seals sink, and that if it went down it would perhaps carry the bladder along with it, and so be lost.

"Give me the line, brother," said Ermigit, extending a hand.

"No. I can hold it. You make for shore—quick." Ermigit plied his paddle with a will, and in a few minutes reached the shore with Norrak, bladder, line, and seal like a huge tail behind him.

Need we say that they were received by their friends, as well as by the strange Eskimos, with enthusiasm? We think not.

Neither is it necessary to comment on the enjoyment they found that night in a supper of fresh meat, and in fighting the battle, as well as a good many other battles, over again. But in the midst of it all there was a cloud on the brows of Angut, Simek, and Okiok, for their anxiety about the fate of Nunaga, Pussi, and Tumbler was intense.

Angut was particularly restless during the night, and got up several times to take a look at the weather, as Rooney expressed it.

On one of these occasions he found the Kablunet standing by the shore of the calm sea.

"I don't like the look o' things," said Rooney, giving a sailor-like glance at the horizon and the sky. "It seems to me as if we were goin' to have dirty weather."

Instead of replying to this remark, the Eskimo looked earnestly at his friend, and asked—

"Can Ridroonee tell me why the Great Spirit allows men to do evil?"

"No, Angut, no. That is beyond my knowledge. Indeed I remember puttin' the same question, or somethin' like it, to a learned man in my country, and he said it is beyond the knowledge of the wisest men that have ever lived—so it's no wonder that it's beyond you and me."

"But the Great Spirit is good," said Angut, rather as if he were soliloquising than addressing his friend.

"Yes; He is good—*must* be good," returned the sailor; "it cannot be otherwise."

"Then why does evil exist?" asked Angut quickly. "Why did He make evil? You have told me He made everything."

"So He did, but evil is not a *thing*. It is a state of being, so to speak."

"It is a great mystery," said Angut.

"It would be a greater mystery," returned the seaman, "if the Great Spirit was *not* mysterious."

"He has allowed Ujarak to carry off Nunaga, though she loves not Ujarak, and Ujarak does not love her, else he could not have treated her so badly. Why did the Great Spirit allow that?" demanded the Eskimo, with some bitterness of tone.

"I know not, Angut, yet I know it is for good, because the Great Spirit is our Great Father, and if human fathers know how to treat their children well, does the Great Father of all not know?"

The Eskimo gravely bowed his head in assent to this proposition, and the seaman continued—

"I have spoken to you more than once, Angut, about the men in our land called surgeons—that you call knife-men,—how they will cut and carve your body, and tie you down sometimes, and give you terrible and prolonged suffering for the purpose of curing you and relieving your pain."

"True," replied Angut, who at once saw the drift of his friend's remark; "but then you *know* that the knife-man's object is good. It is to cure, to relieve."

"But suppose," argued Rooney, "that you did *not* know that his object was good—that you looked on him as a cruel,

R. M. Ballantyne

bloody, heartless monster, who cared not for your cries of pain—would your ignorance change his character?"

"No, no; he would remain good, whatever you might think," said Angut quickly; "I see. I see. I will try to think as you think—the Great Father is good, *must* be good. And He will prove it some day. Don't you think so, Ridroonee?"

"Ay, truly, I think so; I am sure of it. But listen! Do you not hear sounds?"

They both listened intently, and gazed towards the northern headland of the bay, which at the time was bathed in brilliant moonlight. Presently two black specks, one larger than the other, were seen to round the point, and the chattering of women's voices was heard.

It was Arbalik in a kayak, preceding an oomiak propelled by several women. In her impatience to join her lord, Madame Okiok had insisted on a forced march. A few minutes more, and the women landed amid noisy demonstrations of satisfaction. Ere long the united party were busy round the unfailing lamps, enjoying social intercourse over an intermediate meal which, as it came between supper and breakfast, has not yet obtained a name.

CHAPTER TWENTY

THE CHASE CONTINUED
AND DISASTROUSLY INTERRUPTED

The day following that on which the wives of Simek and Okiok, and the mothers of Arbalik and Ippegoo with the spinster Sigokow arrived, the southern Eskimos resumed their route northward, and the pursuers continued their journey to the south—the former in their sledges over the still unmelted ice-foot along the shore; the latter, in kayaks, by a lead of open water, which extended as far as the eye could reach.

Angut, Okiok, and Simek led the way in kayaks, the kayak damaged by the seal having been repaired. The other men were forced to embark in the women's boat. Eskimo men deem this an undignified position, and will not usually condescend to work in oomiaks, which are invariably paddled by the women, but Rooney, being influenced by no such feelings, quietly took the steering paddle, and ultimately shamed Arbalik and Ippegoo as well as the sons of Okiok into lending a hand.

During the first part of the voyage all went well, but next day the lead of open water was found to trend off the land, and run out into the pack, where numerous great glaciers were seen—some aground, others surging slowly southward with the Polar current.

"I don't like the look of it," remarked Angut, when the other leaders of the party ranged alongside of him for a brief consultation.

"Neither do I," said Simek. "The season is far advanced, and if there should be a general break-up of the ice while we are out among the floes, we should be lost."

"But it is impossible for us to travel by land," said Okiok. "No man knows the land here. The sea runs so far in that we might spend many moons in going round the bays without advancing far on our journey."

"So there is nothing left for us but to go on by water," said Angut, with decision. "Nunaga must be rescued."

"And so must Tumbler," said Okiok.

"And so must Pussi," said Simek.

"What are you fellows consulting about?" shouted Red Rooney, coming up at that moment with the others in the oomiak.

"We are talking of the danger of the ice breaking up," answered Angut. "But there is no other way to travel than by the open lead, so we have decided to go on."

"Of course you have," returned Rooney; "what else can we do? We *must* risk something to save Nunaga, Pussi, and Tumbler, to say nothing of Kabelaw. Get along, my hearties!"

How Rooney translated the last phrase into Eskimo is a point on which we can throw no light,—but no matter.

In a short time the party reached the neighbourhood of one of the largest bergs, one of those gigantic masses of ice which resemble moderately-sized mountains, the peaks of which rose several hundred feet above the sea-level, while its base was more than a mile in diameter. There were little valleys extending into its interior, through which flowed rivulets, whose winding courses were broken here and there by cascades. In short, the berg resembled a veritable island made of white sugar, the glittering sun-lit slopes of which contrasted finely with its green-grey shadows and the dark-blue depths of its wide rifts and profound caverns.

The lead or lane of water ran to within fifty yards of this ice-island, so that Rooney had a splendid view of it, and, being of a romantic turn of mind, amused himself as the oomiak glided past by peopling the white cliffs and valleys with snow-white inhabitants. While he was thus employed, there occurred a sudden crashing and rending in the surrounding pack which filled him with consternation. It produced indeed the same effect on the Eskimos, as well it might, for the very catastrophe which they all dreaded was now taking place.

A slight swell on the sea appeared to be the originating cause, but, whatever it was, the whole surface was soon broken up, and the disintegrated masses began to grind against each other in confusion. At the same time the lead which the voyagers had been following grew narrower, and that so rapidly, that they had barely time to jump upon a mass of ice when the opening closed and crushed the oomiak and Okiok's kayak to pieces.

Angut and Simek had time to lift their kayaks on to the ice, but that, as it turned out, was of no advantage.

"Make for the berg," shouted Angut to the women, at the same time seizing the hand of Kunelik, who chanced to be nearest to him, and assisting her to leap from one heaving mass to another. Rooney performed the same act of gallantry for old Kannoa, who, to his surprise, went over the ice like an antique squirrel. Okiok took his own wife in hand. As for Pussimek, she did not wait for assistance, but being of a lively and active, as well as a stout and cheery disposition, she set off at a pace which caused her tail to fly straight out behind her, and made it difficult for Simek to keep up with her. Ippegoo and Arbalik, with the sons of Okiok, tried their best to save the two kayaks, for well they knew the danger of being left on the ice without the means of escaping; but the suddenness of the disruption, the width of the various channels they had to leap, and the instability of the masses, compelled them, after much delay, to drop their burdens and save themselves. They only managed to reach the berg with extreme difficulty.

"Thank God, all safe!—but we have had a close shave," exclaimed Rooney, as he held out his hand to assist Ippegoo, who was the last of the party to clamber up the rugged side of the berg from the broken floe-pieces which were grinding against it.

"I wish we could say with truth 'All safe,'" was Okiok's gloomy response, as he surveyed the ice-laden sea; "we have escaped being crushed or drowned, but only to be starved to death."

"A living man may hope," returned Angut gravely.

"Ay, and where there is life," added Rooney, "there ought to be thankfulness."

"I would be more thankful," said Ippegoo, with a woe-begone

expression, "if we had saved even a spear; but what can we do without food or weapons?"

"Do? my son," said Kunelik; "can we not at least keep up heart? Who ever heard of any good coming of groaning and looking miserable?"

"Right you are, old girl," cried Rooney, giving the mother of Ippegoo a hearty pat on the shoulder. "There is no use in despairing at the very beginning of our troubles; besides, is there not the Great Spirit who takes care of us, although we cannot see or hear Him? I believe in God, my friends, and I'll ask Him to help us now."

So saying, to the surprise of the Eskimos, the seaman uncovered his head, and looking upwards, uttered a few words of earnest prayer in the name of Jesus.

At first the unsophisticated natives looked about as if they expected some visible and immediate answer to the petition, but Rooney explained that the Great Spirit did not always answer at once or in the way that man might expect.

"God works by means of us and through us," he said. "We have committed the care of ourselves to Him. What we have now to do is to go to work, and do the best we can, and see what things He will throw in our way, or enable us to do, in answer to our prayer. Now, the first thing that occurs to me is to get away from where we stand, because that overhanging cliff beside us may fall at any moment and crush us. Next, we should go and search out some safe cavern in which we may spend the night, for we sha'n't be able to find such a place easily in the dark, and though it will be but a cold shelter, still, cold shelter is better than none—so come along."

R. M. Ballantyne

These remarks of the sailor, though so familiar—perhaps commonplace—to us, seemed so just and full of wisdom to the unsophisticated natives, and were uttered in such an off-hand cheery tone, that a powerful effect was created, and the whole party at once followed the seaman, who, by this display of coolness, firmness, and trustfulness in a higher power, established a complete ascendancy over his friends. From that time they regarded him as their leader, even although in regard to the details of Eskimo life he was of course immeasurably their inferior.

They soon found a small cave, not far from the spot where they had landed—if we may use that expression—and there made preparation to spend the night, which by that time was drawing on.

Although their craft had been thus suddenly destroyed and lost, they were not left absolutely destitute, for each one, with that prompt mental activity which is usually found in people whose lives are passed in the midst of danger, had seized the bear-skin, deerskin, or fur bag on which he or she happened to be sitting, and had flung it on to the floes before leaping thereon; and Ippegoo, with that regard for internal sustenance which was one of his chief characteristics, had grasped a huge lump of seal's flesh, and carried it along with him. Thus the whole party possessed bedding, and food for at least one meal.

Of course the meal was eaten not only cold but raw. In the circumstances, however, they were only too thankful, to care much about the style of it. Before it was finished daylight fled, the stars came out, and the aurora borealis was shooting brilliantly athwart the sky. Gradually the various members of the party spread their skins on the most level spot discoverable, and, with lumps of ice covered with bits of hide for pillows, went to sleep with what resembled free-and-easy indifference.

Two of the party, however, could not thus easily drop into happy oblivion. Red Rooney felt ill at ease. His knowledge of those Arctic seas had taught him that their position was most critical, and that escape would be almost miraculous, for they were eight or ten miles at least off the land, on a perishable iceberg, with an ice-encumbered sea around, and no means of going afloat, even if the water had been free. A feeling of gloom which he had not felt before, and which he could not banish, rendered sleep impossible; he therefore rose, and sauntered out of the cave.

Outside he found Angut, standing motionless near the edge of an ice-cliff, gazing up into the glorious constellations overhead.

"I can't sleep, Angut," said the seaman; "I suppose you are much in the same way?"

"I do not know. I did not try," returned the Eskimo in a low voice; "I wish to think, not to sleep. Why cannot the Kablunet sleep?"

"Well, it's hard to tell. I suppose thinking too much has something to do with it. The fact is, Angut, that we've got into what I call a fix, and I can't for the life of me see how we are to get out of it. Indeed I greatly fear that we shall never get out of it."

"If the Great Spirit wills that our end should be *now*," said Angut, "is the Kablunet afraid to die?"

The question puzzled Rooney not a little.

"Well," he replied, "I can't say that I'm afraid, but—but—I

don't exactly *want* to die just yet, you see. The fact is, my friend, that I've got a wife and children and a dear old grandmother at home, and I don't quite relish the idea of never seein' them again."

"Have you not told me," said Angut, with a look of solemn surprise, "that all who love the Great Spirit shall meet again up there?" He pointed to the sky as he spoke.

"Ay, truly, I said that, and I believe that. But a man sometimes wants to see his wife and children again in *this* life—and, to my thinkin', that's not likely with me, as things go at present. Have *you* much hope that we shall escape?"

"Yes, I have hope," answered the Eskimo, with a touch of enthusiasm in his tone. "I know not why. I know not how. Perhaps the Great Spirit who made me put it into me. I cannot tell. All around and within me is beyond my understanding—but—the Great Spirit is all-wise, all-powerful, and—good. Did you not say so?"

"Yes, I said so; and that's a trustworthy foundation, anyhow," returned the sailor meditatively; "wise, powerful, and good— a safe anchorage. But now, tell me, what chances, think you, have we of deliverance?"

"I can think of only one," said Angut. "If the pack sets fast again, we may walk over it to the land. Once there, we could manage to live—though not to continue our pursuit of Ujarak. *That* is at an end."

In spite of himself, the poor fellow said the last words in a tone which showed how deeply he was affected by the destruction of his hope to rescue Nunaga.

"Now my friend seems to me inconsistent," said Rooney.

"He trusts the Great Spirit for deliverance from danger. Is, then, the rescue of Nunaga too hard for Him?"

"I know not," returned Angut, who was, how ever, cheered a little by his friend's tone and manner. "Everything is mystery. I look up, I look around, I look within; all is dark, mysterious. Only on this is my mind clear—the Great Spirit is good. He cannot be otherwise. I will trust Him. One day, perhaps, He will explain all. What I understood not as a little boy, I understand now as a man. Why should there not be more light when I am an older man? If things go on in the mind as they have been going ever since I can remember, perfect light may perhaps come at last."

"You don't think like most of your countrymen," said Rooney, regarding the grave earnest face of his friend with increased interest.

There was a touch of sadness in the tone of the Eskimo as he replied—

"No; I sometimes wonder—for their minds seem to remain in the childish condition; though Okiok and Simek do seem at times as if they were struggling into more light. I often wonder that they think so little, and think so foolishly; but I do not speak much about it; it only makes them fear that I am growing mad."

"I have never asked you, Angut—do your tribes in the north here hold the same wild notions about the earth and heavens as the southern Eskimos do?"

"I believe they do," replied Angut; "but I know not all they think in the south. In this land they think,"—here a smile of good-natured pity flickered for a moment on the man's face—"that the earth rests on pillars, which are now mouldering away by age, so that they frequently crack. These pillars would have fallen long ago if they had not been kept in repair by the angekoks, who try to prove the truth of what they say by bringing home bits of them—rotten pieces of wood. And the strange thing is, that the people believe them!"

"Why don't you believe them, Angut?"

"I know not why."

"And what do your kinsmen think about heaven?" asked Rooney.

"They think it is supported on the peak of a lofty mountain in the north, on which it revolves. The stars are supposed to be ancient Greenlanders, or animals which have managed in some mysterious way to mount up there, and who shine with varied brightness, according to the nature of their food. The streaming lights of winter are the souls of the dead dancing and playing ball in the sky."

"These are strange ideas," observed Rooney; "what have you to say about them?"

"I think they are childish thoughts," replied the Eskimo.

"What, then, are your thoughts about these stars and streaming lights?" persisted the seaman, who was anxious to understand more of the mind of his philosophical companion.

"I know not what I think. When I try to think on these things my mind gets confused. Only this am I sure of—that they are, they must be, the wonderful works of the Good Spirit."

"But how do you know that?" asked Rooney.

Angut looked at his questioner very earnestly for a few moments.

"How does Ridroonee know that he is alive?" he asked abruptly.

"Oh, as to that, you know, everything tells me that I am alive. I look around, and I see. I listen, and I hear. I think, and I understand—leastwise to some extent,—and I *feel* in mind and heart."

"Now will I answer," said Angut. "Everything tells me that the Great Spirit is good, and the Maker of all things. I look, and I see Him in the things that exist. I listen, and I hear Him in the whispering wind, in the running water, in the voice of man and beast. I think, and I understand Him to some extent, and I *feel* Him both in mind and heart."

"I believe you are right, Angut, and your words bring strongly to my remembrance many of the words of the Great Spirit that my mother used to teach me when I was a little boy."

From this point in the conversation Angut became the questioner, being anxious to know all that the Kablunet had to tell about the mysterious Book, of which he had spoken to him more than once, and the teachings of his mother.

It was long past midnight when the descending moon warned them to turn their steps towards the ice-cave where they had left their slumbering companions.

"The frost is sharp to-night," remarked Rooney as they were about to enter.

Angut turned round, and cast a parting glance on sea and sky.

R. M. Ballantyne

"If it holds on like this," continued the sailor, "the ice will be firm enough to carry us to land in the morning."

"It will not hold on like this," said Angut. "The Innuit are very ignorant, but they know many things about the weather, for they are always watching it. To-morrow will be warm. We cannot escape. It will be safest and wisest to remain where we are."

"Remaining means starving," said the sailor in a desponding tone.

"It may be so; we cannot tell," returned the Eskimo.

With these uncomfortable reflections, the two men entered the cavern quietly, so as not to disturb their comrades. Spreading their bearskins on the ice-floor, they laid heads on ice-pillows, and soon fell into that dreamless, restful slumber which is the usual accompaniment of youth, health, and vigour.

CHAPTER TWENTY ONE

SHOWS A GLOOMY PROSPECT—STARVATION THREATENED, AND WONDERFULLY AVERTED

Angut was a true prophet. When Rooney awoke next morning, his ears told him that the rushing of ice-cold rivulets through ice-valleys, and the roar of ice-born cataracts had increased considerably during the hours of darkness.

The warmth which caused this did not, indeed, at first strike him, for the air of the cavern and the character of his bed had chilled him so much that he was shivering with cold. On glancing at his still sleeping comrades in misfortune, he observed that these tough creatures slept with the peaceful aspect of infants, whom, being both fat and rotund, they resembled in nearly everything except size.

Rising and going quietly out, he beat his arms vigorously across his chest until circulation was fully restored. Then he mounted a neighbouring ice-ledge, and saw at a glance that their case had become desperate.

"Angut was right," he murmured bitterly, and then stood for a long time contemplating the scene in silence.

Considered apart from their circumstances, the scene was

indeed glorious. Not only had the warmth of the air begun to swell the rivulets which leaped and brawled down the pale-green slopes around him, but the pack had opened out, so as to completely change the aspect of the sea. Instead of being clothed with ice, showing only a lane of water here and there, it was now an open sea crowded with innumerable ice-islets of every fantastic shape and size.

It added something to the bitterness of the poor man's feelings that this state of things would, he knew, have been the very best for their escape in kayaks and oomiaks, for a profound calm prevailed, and the sea, where clear of ice, glittered in the rising sun like a shield of polished gold.

He was roused from his meditations by the sound of footsteps behind him. Turning quickly, he beheld Ippegoo holding his jaws with both hands and with an expression of unutterable woe on his face.

"Halo, Ippe, what's wrong with you?"

A groan was the reply, and Rooney, although somewhat anxious, found it difficult to restrain a laugh.

"I've got—oh! oh! oh! oh!—a mad tooth," gasped the poor youth.

"A mad tooth! Poor fellow!—we call that *toothache* where I come from."

"What care I whether you call it mad tooth or *tootik*?" cried Ippegoo petulantly. "It is horrible! dreadful! awful!—like fire and fury in the heart."

The sufferer used one or two more Eskimo expressions, suggestive of excruciating agony, which are not translatable into English.

"If I only had a pair of pincers, but—look, Ippe, look," said Rooney, pointing to the sea, in the hope of distracting his mind from present pain by referring to threatening danger; "look—our kayaks being lost, we have no hope of escaping, so we must starve."

His little device, well-meant though it was, failed. A groan and glance of indifference was the Eskimo's reply, for starvation and danger were familiar and prospective evils, whereas toothache was a present horror.

We fear it must be told of Ippegoo that he was not celebrated for endurance of pain, and that, being fond of sympathy, he was apt to give full vent to his feelings—the result, perhaps, of having an over-indulgent mother. Toothache—one of the diseases to which Greenlanders are peculiarly liable—invariably drew forth Ippegoo's tenderest feelings for himself, accompanied by touching lamentations.

"Come, Ippe, be more of a man. Even your mother would scold you for groaning like that."

"But it is so shriekingly bad!" returned the afflicted youth, with increasing petulance.

"Of course it is. I know that; poor fellow! But come, I will try to cure you," said Rooney, who, under the impression that violent physical exertion coupled with distraction of mind would produce good effect, had suddenly conceived a simple ruse. "Do you see yon jutting ice-cliff that runs down to a point near the edge of the berg?"

"Yes, I see," whimpered Ippegoo.

"Well, it will require you to run at your top speed to get there while you count fifteen twenties. Now, if you run there within that time—at your very top speed, mind—" Rooney paused, and looked serious.

"Yes; well?" said Ippegoo, whose curiosity had already begun to check the groans.

"If you run there," continued the seaman, with a look and tone of deep solemnity, "at the very toppest speed that you can do, and look round that ice-point, you will see—"

"What?" gasped Ippegoo excitedly—for he was easily excited.

"*Something*," returned Rooney mysteriously. "I cannot tell exactly what you will see, because I am not an angekok, and have no torngak to tell me; but I am quite sure that you will see *something*! Only, the benefit of seeing it will depend on your running as fast as you can. Now, are you ready?"

"Yes, quite ready," exclaimed the youth, tightening his girdle of sealskin eagerly.

"Well then—*away*!" shouted Rooney.

Off went Ippegoo at a pace which was obviously the best that he was capable of putting forth. Rooney counted as he ran, and in a much shorter time than had been specified he reached the point, for the level track, or what we may style sea-shore, of the berg was not a bad race-course. Suddenly, however, he came to an abrupt halt, and threw up his arms as if in amazement. Then he turned round and ran back at a pace that was even greater than he had achieved on the outward run. Rooney was himself greatly surprised at this, for, as the youth drew nearer, the expression of his face showed that he had indeed seen "something" which had not been in the seaman's calculations. He spluttered and gasped as he came near, in his effort to speak.

"What is it?—take time, lad," said Rooney quietly.

"A b-bear! a bear!" cried Ippegoo.

"What! did it run at you?" asked Rooney, becoming slightly excited in his turn, and keeping his eye on the ice-point.

"N-no; no. It was sitting on—on its tail—l-looking at the—the s-sea."

"And we've no weapon bigger than an Eskimo knife," exclaimed the sailor, with a frown of discontent—"not even a bit of stick to tie the knife to. What a chance lost! He would have kept us in food for some weeks. Well, well, this *is* bad luck. Come, Ippe, we'll go back to the cave, and consult about this."

On returning to the cheerless retreat, they found the rest of the party just awakening. The men were yawning and rubbing their eyes, while the women, with characteristic activity and self-denial, were gathering together the few scraps of food that remained from the previous night's supper.

"There is a bear just round the point—so Ippe says—what's to be done?" asked Rooney on entering.

Up jumped the four men and two boys as if they had been made of indiarubber.

"Attack it," cried Arbalik.

"Kill it," exclaimed Norrak.

"And eat it," said Ermigit.

"What will you attack it with?" asked Simek in a slightly contemptuous tone—"with your fingernails? If so, you had better send Sigokow to do battle, for she could beat the three of you."

The youths stood abashed.

"We have no spears," said Simek, "and knives are useless. Bad luck follows us."

"It is my opinion," said Okiok, "that whatever we do, or try to do, we had better eat something before doing it. Bring the victuals, Nuna."

"Okiok is right," said Angut; "and Arbalik had better go out and watch while we consult, so as to give us timely warning if the bear comes this way."

Without a word, Arbalik caught up a piece of blubber, and went out of the cave to enjoy his frugal breakfast while acting sentinel. The others, sitting down on their respective bearskins, ate and consulted hastily. The consultation was of little use, for they were utterly helpless, and the breakfast was not much more profitable, for there was far too little of it. Still, as Rooney truly remarked when the last morsel was consumed, it was better than nothing.

"Well now, my friends," said Angut at last, "since our food is done, and all our talk has come to nothing, I propose that we go out in a body to see this bear. As we cannot kill him, we must get rid of him by driving him away, for if we let him remain on the berg, he will come upon us when we are asleep, perhaps, and kill us."

"Yes, that is best," said Okiok. "If we separate, so as to distract him, and then make a united rush from all points, shrieking, that will drive him into the sea."

"Let us put Ippe in front," suggested Simek, with a twinkling eye; "he yells better than any of us."

"'Specially when he's got the toothache," added Rooney.

The object of this touch of pleasantry smiled in a good-humouredly imbecile manner. It was clear that his malady had been cured, at least for the time.

"But we must be very cautious," remarked Rooney, becoming serious, as they rose to proceed on their adventure. "It would not do to let any of our party get hurt. To my thinking, the women should take to the ice-cliffs before we begin, and get upon pinnacles, up which the bear could not climb."

While he was speaking, Arbalik came running in with the information that the bear was approaching.

"Has it seen you?" asked Angut, as they all ran out.

"I think not. From the way it walks, I think it has no suspicion of any one being on the berg."

In a few seconds they reached the point of the promontory or cliff in which their cave lay, and each member of the party peeped round with excessive caution, and there, sure enough, they beheld a white Polar bear of truly formidable size. But it had changed its course after Arbalik saw it, for by that time it had turned up one of the ice-valleys before-mentioned and begun to ascend into the interior of the berg. The slow, heavy gait of the unwieldy animal suggested to Rooney the idea that an active man could easily get out of its way, but the cat-like activity with which it bounded over one or two rivulets that came in its way quickly dissipated that idea.

"The farther he goes up that valley," whispered Simek, "the more trouble we shall have in driving him into the sea."

"He does not seem to know his own mind," remarked Okiok, as the bear again changed his course, and entered one of the small gorges that opened into the larger valley.

"He knows it well enough," said Ermigit. "Don't you see he is making for the ice-top, where these gulls are sitting? The fool expects to catch them asleep."

Ermigit seemed to have guessed rightly, for after clambering up the ice-gorge referred to until he gained a high ledge or plateau, he began regularly to stalk the birds with the sly patience of a cat.

There was much in the bear's favour, for the recent fall of a pinnacle had covered the ledge with shattered blocks of all shapes and sizes, in the shelter of which it could creep towards its prey. Our Eskimos watched the proceeding open-mouthed, with profound interest. To within twenty yards or so of its game did that white-robed Arctic hunter approach. Then it crouched for a rush at the unconscious birds, for no other lump of ice lay between them and their foe.

The charge was vigorously made, almost too vigorously, for when the birds flew lightly off the ledge, and descended to a narrower one a little farther down, it was all the bear could do to check itself on the very edge of the precipice. If it had gone over, the consequences would have been dire, for the precipice was, not sheer, but still a very steep slope of ice, several hundred feet deep, which terminated in those rugged masses on the berg-shore that had fallen from the cliffs above. There was only one break in the vast slope, namely, the narrow ledge half-way down on which the birds had taken refuge.

Going to the extreme edge of the precipice, the bear sat down on his haunches, and hungrily contemplated the birds, which were now beyond his reach, twittering noisily as if to tantalise him.

"I would that I had a spear," growled Okiok.

"I would venture at him even with a big stick," said Simek.

"My friends," said Rooney, with sudden animation, "listen to me. If you will promise me to keep very quiet, and not to follow me whatever may happen, I will show you how Kablunets overcome difficulties."

Of course the Eskimos were ready to make any promises that might be required of them, and looked at their friend with surprise as he threw off his sealskin coat and tightened the belt round his waist. But they were still more surprised, when, without another word, he set off, in only shirt and trousers, to climb the valley of ice, and make for the spot where the bear sat in melancholy meditation.

While ascending, Rooney took care to avail himself of the rugged nature of the ice, so as to conceal himself entirely from the bear—though this was scarcely needful, for the animal's back was turned towards the Kablunet, and his whole attention was concentrated on the gulls. As Rooney wore Eskimo boots—the soles of which are soft,—he made little or no noise in walking, and thus managed to gain the

R. M. Ballantyne

platform unperceived by the bear, though visible all the time to the Eskimos, to whom he looked little bigger than a crow on the height. Their delight, however, began to be tempered with anxiety when they saw the reckless man creep to within twenty yards of the monster, making use of the ice-blocks as it had done before him.

The intentions of the Kablunet were incomprehensible to his friends. Could it be that, ignorant of the strength of the beast and its tenacity of life, the foolish man hoped to stab it to death with a small knife? Impossible! And yet he was evidently preparing for action of some sort.

But Red Rooney was not quite so foolish as they supposed him to be. Having gained the nearest possible point to his victim, he made a sudden and tremendous rush at it. He knew that life and death were in the balance at any rate; but he also knew that to remain inactive on that iceberg would remove life out of the balance altogether. He therefore threw all his energy of soul and body into that rush, and launched himself against the broad back of the bear. It was an awful shock. Rooney was swift as well as heavy, so that his weight, multiplied into his velocity, sufficed to dislodge the wonder-stricken animal. One wild spasmodic effort it made to recover itself, and in doing so gave Rooney what may be called a backhander on the head, that sent him reeling on the ice.

Curiously enough, it was this that saved the daring man, for if he had not received that blow, the impetus of his attack would have certainly sent himself as well as the bear over the cliff.

As it was, the monster went over headlong, with a sort of compound shriek and howl that made the very ice-cliffs ring. Then, down he went—not head or feet first, or sideways, or any way, but every way by turns, and no way long. Indeed, he spun and, as it were, spurted down that mighty face of ice. Each instant intensified the velocity; each whirl increased the complex nature of the force. The ledge half-way down, from which the affrighted gulls fled shrieking, did not even check the descent, but with bursting violence shunted the victim out into space, through which he hurled till re-met by the terrific slope farther down, which let him glissade like a shooting star into indescribable ruin!

Enough of that bear was left, however, to render it worth while picking up the fragments. Shouting with laughter and yelling with glee, the Eskimos made for the spot where the mangled carcass lay. Soon after they were joined by the hero of the day.

"Food enough now for a moon, or more," said Rooney, as he came up.

"Yes; and no need to beat the meat to make it tender," responded Okiok, lifting and letting fall one of the limp legs of the creature, whose every bone seemed to have been smashed to pieces in the tremendous descent.

It was no doubt a considerable reduction of their satisfaction at supper that evening that they had to eat their bear-chops raw, not having the means of making fire; but they were not disposed to find fault with their good-fortune on that account. If they had only possessed two small pieces of wood with which to create the necessary friction, they could easily have made a lamp out of one of the bear's shoulder-blades, and found oil enough in his own fat, while a tag of sealskin, or some other portion of clothing might have supplied a wick; but not a scrap of wood was to be obtained on that verdureless island. Okiok did indeed suggest that Norrak and Ippegoo, being both possessed of hard and prominent noses, might rub these organs together till they caught fire; but Norrak turned up his nose at the suggestion, and Ippegoo shook his head doubtfully.

In the circumstances, therefore, they obtained light at least for the purposes of vision by commencing supper long before sunset, and most of them continued it long after dark. Thus the second night was passed on the berg.

On the third day, the weather being still warm and calm, Angut, Simek, Okiok, and Rooney ascended, after their bear-breakfast, to the break-neck height from which that breakfast had been precipitated, for the purpose of taking a meteorological observation.

"It is quite plain to me," said Rooney—who, being in some sort at sea, was, as it were, more at home than his companions—"it is quite plain to me that we have got fairly into the great Polar current, and are travelling in a sou'-sou'-west direction down Davis Straits."

No doubt Rooney gave "sou'-sou'-west" in some sort of Eskimo jargon with which we are not acquainted. His lingual powers were indeed marvellous, and when simple words failed him he took refuge in compound phraseology.

"But," asked Okiok, "how can you tell that we are going south? The mist is thick; we cannot see land."

"Do you not see the small pieces of ice?" replied Rooney, pointing to the sea.

"Yes," said the Eskimo; "they are going north faster than we are; that is all."

"Why do they go north faster than we do?" asked Rooney.

"That I know not."

"I will tell you, Okiok. It is because there is a surface current here flowing northward, and the small pieces of ice go with it because they are not deep. But this berg is very deep. There is far more of it below water than what we see above. Its bottom goes deep down into the under-current which flows south, and so it is being carried south—not north at all,—*against* the variable surface-currents, and it would go even against the wind if there was any. Do you understand?"

"Huk!" exclaimed the Eskimo, though he still looked perplexed.

"I have seen these bergs breaking from the great land-ice since I was a little boy," said Angut, with earnest gravity, "and I have seen them float away and away till they vanished in the far-off. Can Ridroonee tell where they go to?"

"Truly I can. They are carried by currents out into the great sea—we call it the Atlantic,—and there they melt and disappear."

"Then shall we disappear with this berg, if we don't escape from it?" said Okiok, with a look so serious that it was almost humorous.

"That is the pleasant prospect in store for us, as you say," returned Rooney; "but cheer up, lad. We intend to escape from it; so don't let your heart sink, else your body won't be able to swim."

On the strength of this consolatory remark, the four men returned to the cave to recruit their energies and hopes on a fresh supply of the raw bear.

CHAPTER TWENTY TWO

A BRIEF BUT SINGULAR VOYAGE WINDS UP
WITH A GREAT SURPRISE

The calm which had fortunately prevailed since Angut and his friends found refuge on the iceberg was not destined to continue.

A smart breeze at last sprang up from the northward, which soon freshened into a gale, accompanied with heavy showers of snow, driving the party into the cave, where the cold was so severe that they were forced to take refuge in its deepest recesses, and to sit wrapped in their bearskins, and huddled together for warmth, as monkeys are sometimes seen on a cold day in a menagerie.

Being from the north, the wind not only intensified the cold, and brought back for a time all the worst conditions of winter, but assisted the great ocean current to carry the berg southward at a high rate of speed. Their progress, however, was not very apparent to the eyes of our voyagers, because all the surrounding bergs travelled in the same direction and at nearly the same speed. The blinding snow effectually hid the land from their view, and the only point of which they were quite sure was that their berg must be the nearest to the Greenland coast because all the others lay on their right hand.

Towards noon of the following day it was observed that the pack-ice thickened around them, and was seen in large fields here and there, through some of which the great berg ploughed its way with resistless momentum. Before the afternoon the pack had closed entirely around them, as if it had been one mass of solid, rugged ice—not a drop of water being visible. Even through this mass the berg ploughed its way slowly, but with great noise.

"There is something very awful to me in the sight of such tremendous force," said Red Rooney to Angut, as they stood contemplating the havoc their strange ship was making.

"Does it not make you think," returned the Eskimo, "how powerful must be the Great Spirit who made all things, when a little part of His work is so tremendous?"

Rooney did not reply, for at that moment the berg grounded, with a shock that sent all its spires and pinnacles tumbling. Fortunately, the Eskimos were near their cavern, into which they rushed, and escaped the terrible shower. But the cave could no longer be regarded as a place of safety. It did indeed shelter them from the immediate shower of masses, even the smaller of which were heavy enough to have killed a walrus; but at that advanced period of spring the bergs were becoming, so to speak, rotten, and liable at any moment to fall to pieces and float away in the form of pack-ice. If such an event had occurred when our Eskimos were in the cave, the destruction of all would of course have been inevitable.

"We dare not remain here," said Angut, when the icy shower had ceased.

"No; we must take to the floes," said Simek.

"Another shake like that," remarked Okiok, "might bring the whole berg down on our heads."

"Let us go, then, at once," said Rooney; "the sky clears a little, so we'll know how to steer."

No one replied, for all were already engaged with the utmost activity making bundles of their bear-skins and as much of the bear-meat as the men could carry—each of the women taking a smaller piece, according to her strength or her prudence. The sailor followed their example in silence, and in a very few minutes they issued from the cavern, and made for the shore of the berg.

Some difficulty was experienced in scrambling over the chaotic masses which had been thrown up in front of them by the ploughing process before referred to. When they stood fairly on the floes, however, they found that, although very rough, these were sufficiently level to admit of slow travelling. They were in the act of arranging the order of march, when the berg slid off into deep water, and, wheeling round as if annoyed at the slight detention, rejoined its stately comrades in their solemn procession to their doom in more southerly seas.

"Just in time," said Rooney, as they watched the berg floating slowly away, nodding its shattered head as if bidding them farewell. "Now then, ho! for the Greenland shore! Come, old Kannoa, I'll take you under my special care."

He took the old woman's bundle from her as he spoke, and, putting his left hand under her right arm, began to help her over the frozen sea.

But poor old thing though she certainly was, that antiquated creature became a griggy old thing immediately, and was so tickled with the idea of the stoutest and handsomest man of the party devoting himself entirely to her, when all the younger women were allowed to look after themselves, that she could scarcely walk during the first few minutes for laughing. But it must be said in justification of the Eskimo men, that their young women were quite capable of looking after themselves, and would, indeed, have been incommoded as well as surprised by offers of assistance.

Rooney had spoken cheerily, though his feelings were anything but cheerful, for he knew well the extreme danger of their position, but he felt it a duty to do his best to encourage his friends. The Eskimos were equally well, if not better, aware of their danger, and took to the floes with resolute purpose and in profound silence—for true men in such circumstances are not garrulous.

A gleam of sunshine from a rift in the dark clouds seemed sent as a heavenly messenger to guide them. By it the Eskimos as well as the sailor were enabled to judge of the position of land, and to steer, accordingly, in what western hunters would call "a bee-line." The great danger, of course, lay in the risk of the pack breaking up before they could reach the shore. There was also the possibility of the pack being a limited strip of floe-ice unconnected with the shore, which, if it had been so, would have decided their fate. In these circumstances they all pushed on at their best speed. At first the women seemed to get along as well as the men, but after a while the former showed evident symptoms of exhaustion, and towards dusk old Kannoa, despite Rooney's powerful aid, fairly broke down and refused to walk another step. The seaman overcame the difficulty by raising her in his arms and carrying her. As he had not at that time quite recovered his full strength, and was himself pretty well fatigued, he was constrained to think pretty steadily of the old woman's resemblance to his grandmother to enable him to hold out!

After another mile or so the mother of Arbalik succumbed, whereupon her son put his arm round her waist and helped her on. Then the pleasant little mother of Ippegoo broke down with a pitiful wail; but her son was unable to help her, for he was already undulating about like a piece of tape, as if he had no backbone to speak of. Okiok therefore came to her aid. As for the hardy spinster Sikogow, she seemed inexhaustible, and scorned assistance. Nuna was also vigorous, but her sons Norrak and Ermigit, being amiable, came on each side of her, and took her in tow before the breaking-down point was reached.

Thus they continued to advance until the darkness became so profound as to render further travelling impossible. The danger of delay they knew was extreme, but men must perforce bow to the inevitable. To advance without light over rugged ice, in which were cracks and fissures and hummocks innumerable, being out of the question, Rooney called a halt.

"Rest and food, friends," he said, "are essential to life."

"Huk!" was the brief reply.

Without wasting breath on another word, they untied their bundles, spread their bearskins in the lee of a hummock, fed hastily but heartily, rolled themselves in their simple bedding, and went to sleep.

During the night there occurred one of those sudden changes which are common in Arctic lands at that season of the year. Snow ceased to fall, the sky cleared, and the temperature rose until the air became quite balmy. The ice of the floes eased off, narrow openings grew into lanes and leads and wide pools, until water predominated, and the ice finally resolved itself into innumerable islets. When Rooney was at last awakened by a blaze of sunshine in his face, he found that the party occupied a small cake of ice in the midst of a grand crystal archipelago. Not a zephyr ruffled the sea, and the hills of Greenland were visible, not more than six or eight miles distant, on their left hand. What particular part of Greenland it was, of course they had no means of knowing.

The sight was indeed such as might have filled human hearts with admiration and joy, but neither joy nor admiration touched the hearts of Red Rooney and his companions. So far from land, on a bit of ice scarce large enough to sustain them, and melting rapidly away, exposed to the vicissitudes of a changeful and stormy climate, without the means of escape—the case seemed very desperate.

"The Great Spirit has forsaken us," said Angut gloomily, as he surveyed the scene.

"That He has *not*," returned the sailor, "whatever may befall."

An exclamation from Arbalik drew attention to a particular part of the horizon.

"A flat island," said Okiok, after a long earnest gaze; "but we cannot reach it," he added in a low voice.

"You know not," said Angut. "The current sets that way, I think."

"A few minutes will show," said Rooney.

With almost trembling eagerness they watched the islet, and, as Rooney had said, it soon became evident that the current was indeed carrying their ice-raft slowly towards the spot.

R. M. Ballantyne

"We can scarcely expect to drift right on to it," said Rooney, "and it is apparently our last chance, so we shall have to take to the water when near it. Can we all swim—eh?"

To this question some answered Yes and some No, while others shook their heads as if uncertain on the point. But the seaman was wrong. Straight as an arrow to a bull's eye the raft went at that islet and struck on its upper end with such force as to send a tongue of ice high on the shore, so that the whole party actually landed dryshod. Even old Kannoa got on shore without assistance.

The joy of the party at this piece of unlooked-for good-fortune was unbounded, although, after all, the improvement in their circumstances did not seem to be great, for the islet was not more than a hundred yards in diameter, and appeared to be quite barren, with only a clump of willows in its centre. Still, their recent danger had been so imminent that the spot seemed quite a secure refuge by contrast.

The men of the party, after landing, were only just beginning to comment on their prospects, when they saw the willows in the centre of the islet part asunder, and a man of strange aspect and costume stood before them.

The stranger who had burst thus unexpectedly upon them like a visitant from another world, bereaving them for a few minutes of speech and motion, was evidently not a native of the land. His pale and somewhat melancholy face, as well as parts of his costume, betokened him one who had come from civilised lands; and Rooney's first thought was that he must be a shipwrecked sailor like himself; but a second glance caused him to reject the idea. The calm dignity of his carriage, the intellectuality of his expression, and, withal, the look of gentle humility in his manner, were not the usual characteristics of seamen in those days. He also looked very haggard and worn, as if from severe fatigue or illness.

A slight smile played for a moment on his lips as he observed the blank amazement which his appearance had produced. Hastening forward he held out his hand to Rooney whom he at once recognised as a man of civilised lands.

"Let me congratulate you, friends, on your escape, for I can see that you must have been in great jeopardy from which the Lord has delivered you."

The stranger spoke in the Danish language, which was of course utterly incomprehensible to the natives. Not so, however, to Red Rooney, who in his seafaring life had frequently visited Copenhagen, Bergen, and Christiania, and other Scandinavian ports, and had learned to speak Danish at least fluently, if not very correctly. He at once replied, at the same time returning the warm grasp of the stranger's hand—

"We have indeed just escaped from great danger, through the mercy of God. But who are *you*, and how come you to be in such a lonely place, and, if I do not greatly mistake, in a starving condition?"

"I am a missionary to the Eskimos," replied the stranger, "and have been forced to take refuge here by stress of weather. But I am not absolutely alone, as you seem to think. There are five natives with me, and we have an oomiak up there in the bushes. They are now asleep under it. For five days we have been detained here almost without food, by the recent storm and the pack-ice. Now, thanks to my Father in heaven, we shall be able to launch our little boat, and get away. In fact, being the first of my party to awake this morning, I rose very quietly so as not to disturb the poor people, who stand much in need of rest, and I had come to look at the state of the ice when I unexpectedly discovered

R. M. Ballantyne

you on the shore."

"Stay now, sir; not another word till you have broken your fast," said Rooney, with kindly violence, as he hastily cut a large slice from his piece of bear's meat. "Sit down on that stone, and eat it at once. A fasting man should not talk."

"But my companions need food to the full as much as I do," objected the missionary.

"Do as I bid ye, sir," returned Rooney, with decision. "You say they are asleep. Well, sleep is as needful as food and sleeping men cannot eat. When you have eaten we will go up and awake and feed them."

Thus urged, the poor man began to eat the raw meat with as much relish as if it had been the finest venison cooked to a turn. Before commencing, however, he clasped his hands, closed his eyes, and audibly thanked God for the supply.

While he was thus engaged Red Rooney did not speak, but sat looking at his new friend with profound interest. Perchance his interest would have deepened had he known that the man was none other than the famous Norwegian clergyman Hans Egede, the originator of the Danish mission to Greenland, who founded the colony of Godhaab in the year 1721, about twelve years before the commencement of the missions of the Moravian Brethren to that land.

The surprise which our voyagers had received by the unexpected appearance of the missionary was, however, as nothing, compared with the surprise that was yet in store for them on that eventful day.

CHAPTER TWENTY THREE

DESCRIBES A MOST AMAZING SURPRISE, AND TREATS OF HANS EGEDE

When the starving missionary had taken the edge off his appetite, he closed the clasp-knife with which he had been eating.

"Now, my friend," he said, looking at Rooney, "I have eaten quite enough to do me good in my present condition,—perhaps more than enough. You know it is not safe for starving men to eat heartily. Besides, I am anxious to give some food to the poor fellows who are with me. One of them has met with a severe accident and is dying I fear. He does not belong to my party, I found him on the mainland and brought him here just before the storm burst on us, intending to take him on to Godhaab. He stands more in need of food than sleep, I think."

"Come, then, we will go to him at once," said Rooney, tying up the remains of Egede's breakfast. "How did he come by his accident?" continued the sailor, as the party walked up towards the bushes.

"The girl who takes care of him—his daughter, I think—says he was injured by a bear."

"If it is a case of broken bones, perhaps I may be of use to him," said Rooney, "for I've had some experience in that way."

Egede shook his head, "I fear it is too late," he replied. "Besides, his mind seems to give him more trouble even than his wasted frame. He has come, he says, from the far north, and would certainly have perished after his accident if it had not been for the care and kindness of the women who are with him—especially the younger woman. See, there she comes. Her father must have awakened, for she rests near him at night and never leaves him in the morning till he wakes up."

The missionary was startled at that moment by a loud shout from his companion. Next instant Angut rushed past him, and, catching the girl in his arms, gave her a most fervent and lover-like embrace, to which she seemed in no ways averse.

It soon became obvious to the missionary that a most unexpected and pleasant meeting of friends was taking place; but the surprise expressed on his grave visage had barely given place to a benignant smile of sympathy, when a female shriek was heard, and Sigokow was seen running towards her sister Kabelaw. These two did not leap into each other's arms. The feelings of Eskimo females do not usually find vent in that way; but they waltzed round each other, and grinned, and smoothed each other's hair, and when Kabelaw observed that her sister had a huge black eye and a yet unhealed cut across the bridge of her rather flat nose, she clapped her hands, and went into fits of laughter, which helped her somewhat to relieve her feelings.

The surprise and pleasure of this meeting was still at its height when two shrill cries were heard. These were instantly followed by the bursting of Pussi and Tumbler on the scene, the former of whom rushed into the ready arms of Pussimek, while the latter plunged into the bosom of Nuna. Ippegoo, unable to contain himself for joy, began an impromptu and original waltz round his own mother.

Of course it was some time before the party calmed down sufficiently to give or receive explanations. When this state, however, was arrived at, a feeling of sadness was cast over, them all by the re-announcement of the fact that Ujarak was certainly dying. He had been carried out of the hole in the snow in which Egede and his party had taken refuge from the storm, and laid on a dry spot among the bushes where he could enjoy the sunshine, so that he became visible to his former friends the instant they entered the cleared space where he lay.

Any feelings of revenge that may have lingered in the breast of Angut were dissipated like a summer cloud when he saw the thin worn frame, and the pale haggard countenance, of the poor wizard. He went forward at once, and, kneeling beside him, took hold of one of his hands.

"You—you—forgive me, I *see*?" said Ujarak, anxiously.

"Yes, I forgive you," replied Angut, with fervour, for his heart was touched at the sight of the once strong and self-reliant man, who in so short a time had been reduced to such utter helplessness.

"I am glad—glad," continued Ujarak, "that you have come before I die. I thank God for sending you. I have prayed for this."

"You thank God! you have prayed!" exclaimed Angut in surprise. "Is it the Kablunets' God you thank and pray to?"

R. M. Ballantyne

"Yes; Jesus—not only the Kablunets' God, but the God and Saviour of the Innuit also—the Saviour of the whole world. I have found Him—or rather, He has found *me*, the wicked angekok, since I came here."

The dying man turned a grateful look on Egede as he spoke.

"It is true," said the missionary, coming forward. "I believe that God, who brings about all good things, sent me here, and sent this man here, so that we should meet for the purpose of bringing about his salvation. The Almighty is confined to no such plans, yet it pleases Him to work by means, and often with poor tools."

Egede spoke now in the language of the Eskimos, having long before that time learned to speak it sufficiently well to be understood.

"Angut," said Ujarak, after a few moments, "listen to me. I cannot live long. Before I go, let me tell you that Nunaga is good—good—good! She is true to you, and she has been very, very good to *me*. She forgives me, though I meant to take her from you and from her home for ever. But for her, I should have been left to die on the ice. She must have had the Spirit of Jesus in her before she heard His name. Take care of her, Angut. She will serve you well. Listen to her, and she will teach you to be wise—"

He ceased abruptly. The energy with which he spoke proved to be the last flare of the mysterious lamp of life. Next moment only the worn-out tenement of the angekok lay before his people, for his spirit had "returned to God who gave it."

The joy which had been so suddenly created by this unexpected union of friends and kindred was damped, not only by the sad though happy death of the wizard, but by the recurrence of the storm which had already proved almost fatal to them all. The recent clearing up of the weather was only a lull in the gale. Soon the sky overclouded again, snow began to fall so thickly that they could not see more than a few yards in any direction, and the wind drove them back into the hole or cave in the snow out of which the short-lived sunshine had drawn them.

The body of Ujarak was buried under a heap of stones, for they had no implements with which to dig a grave. Then Okiok and his party hastily constructed a rude snow-hut to protect them from the storm. Here for two more days and nights they were imprisoned, and much of that time they passed in listening to the pleasant discourse of Hans Egede, as he told the northern natives the wonderful story of redemption through Jesus Christ, or recounted some of his own difficulties in getting out to Greenland.

Few missionaries, we should imagine, have experienced or overcome greater difficulties in getting to their field of labour than this same earnest Norwegian, Hans Egede, though doubtless many may have equalled him in their experience of dangers and difficulties after the fight began.

Even after having made up his mind to go to Greenland out of pure desire for the salvation of souls—for his knowledge of that inhospitable land precluded the possibility of his having been *tempted* to go to it from any other motive—he had to spend over ten years of his life in overcoming objections and obstructions to his starting.

At first his friends gave him credit for being mad, for people are somewhat slow to believe in disinterested self-sacrifice; and the idea of a clergyman with a comfortable living in Norway, who had, besides, a wife and four small children,

R. M. Ballantyne

voluntarily resolving to go to a region in which men could be barely said to live, merely for the purpose of preaching Christ to uncivilised savages, seemed to them absurd. They little knew the power of the missionary spirit, or rather, the power of the Holy Spirit, by which some great men are actuated! But, after all, if in the world's experience many men are found ready to take their lives in their hands, and cheerfully go to the coldest, hottest, and wildest regions of earth at the call of duty, or "glory," or gold, is it strange that some men should be found willing to do the same thing for the love of God and the souls of men?

Be this as it may, it is certain that the soul of good Hans Egede became inflamed with a burning desire to go as a missionary to Greenland, and from the time that the desire arose, he never ceased to pray and strive towards the accomplishment of his purpose. His thoughts were first turned in that direction by reading of Christian men from his own country, who, centuries before, had gone to Greenland, established colonies, been decimated by sickness, and then almost exterminated by the natives—at least so it was thought, but all knowledge of them had long been lost. A friend in Bergen who had made several voyages to Greenland aroused Egede's pity for his lost countrymen, some of whom, it was supposed, had sunk back into paganism for want of teachers. His thoughts and his desires grew, and the first difficulty presented itself in the form of a doubt as to whether it was allowable to forsake his congregation. Besides, several near relations as well as wife and children were dependent on him for sustenance, which increased the initial difficulty.

But "where there's a will there's a way" is a proverb, the truth of which Hans Egede very soon began to exemplify. Not least among this good man's difficulties seemed to be his modesty, for he was troubled with "extreme diffidence and the fear of being charged with presumption."

At last, in the year 1710, he determined to make a humble proposal to Bishop Randulph of Bergen, and to Bishop Krog of Drontheim, entreating them to support at court his plans for the conversion of the Greenlanders. Both bishops replied favourably; but when his friends saw that he was in earnest, they set up vehement opposition to what they styled his preposterous enterprise. Even his wife and family were at first among his foes, so that the poor man was greatly perplexed, and well-nigh gave up in despair. Happily, his wife at the time became involved in a series of troubles and persecutions, which so affected her that she left the enemy, and ever afterwards supported her husband loyally, heart and soul.

That Egede regarded his wife's opposition as more formidable than that of all the rest of his kith and kin put together, may be gathered from the fact that he says, on her coming over, that his "joy was complete," and that he "believed every obstacle to have been vanquished." In the strength of these feelings he immediately drew up a memorial to the worthy College of Missions, and again entreated the help of the bishops of Bergen and Drontheim. But bishops then, as now, were not to be unduly hurried. They recommended patience till more favourable and peaceful times!

Thus Egede's plans were postponed from year to year, for peaceful times seemed very far off. Moreover, he was assailed with all kinds of reproaches and misunderstandings as to motives, so that in the year 1715 he thought it necessary to draw up a vindication of his conduct entitled, "A Scriptural and Rational Solution and Explanation of the Difficulties and Objections raised against the Design of converting the Heathen Greenlanders."

Then people tried to divert Egede from his purpose by picturing to him the dangers of his enterprise; the miseries he must endure; the cruelty of endangering the lives of his wife and children; and lastly, by pointing out the madness of relinquishing a certain for an uncertain livelihood. They even went so far as to insinuate that, under a cloak of religious motive, he wished to "aggrandise his reputation;" but Egede was heroically firm—some folk would say obstinate.

Wearied with delays, and having reason to believe that his memorial was not properly supported, he resolved at last to go himself to the fountain-head. Resigning his office in 1718, he went to Bergen, from which port there had been in time past considerable trade with Greenland. Here he received little or no encouragement, but the sudden death at this time of King Charles the Twelfth, giving hopes of the speedy restoration of peace, Egede thought it advisable to go to Copenhagen and personally present his memorial to the College of Missions. He did so, and received the encouraging answer that the King would "consider his matter."

Kings have a wonderful capacity for taking time to "consider matters"—sometimes to the extent of passing out of time altogether, and leaving the consideration to successors. But the King on this occasion was true to his word. He gave Egede a private audience, and in 1719 sent orders to the magistrates of Bergen to collect all the opinions and information that could be gathered in regard to the trade with Greenland and the propriety of establishing a colony there, with a statement of the privileges that might be desired by adventurers wishing to settle in the new land. But, alas! no adventurers wished to settle there; the royal efforts failed, and poor Egede was left to fall back on his own exertions and private enterprise.

For another year this indefatigable man vainly importuned

the King and the College of Missions. At last he prevailed on a number of sympathisers to hold a conference. These, under his persuasive powers, subscribed forty pounds a-piece towards a mission fund. Egede set a good example by giving sixty pounds. Then, by begging from the bishop and people of Bergen, he raised the fund to about two thousand pounds. With this sum he bought a ship, and called it the *Hope*. Two other vessels were chartered and freighted—one for the whale fishery, the other to take home news of the colony. The King, although unable to start the enterprise, appointed Egede missionary to the colony with a salary of sixty pounds a year, besides a present of a hundred pounds for immediate expenses, and finally, on the 12th May 1721, the indomitable Hans, with his heroic wife and four children, set sail for "Greenland's icy mountains," after an unprecedented ten years' conflict.

Dangers and partial disasters greeted them on their arrival, in July, at Baal's River, latitude 64 degrees, where they established the colony of Godhaab.

It would require a volume to tell of Hans Egede's difficulties, doings, and sufferings in the new land. Suffice it to say that they were *tremendous*, and that he acted as the pioneer to the interesting missions of the Moravian Brethren to the same neighbourhood.

Hans Egede had been several years at his post when the meeting already described took place between him and the northern Eskimos.

R. M. Ballantyne

CHAPTER TWENTY FOUR

ESCAPE FROM PRESENT DANGER, AND A CURIOUS INSTANCE OF THE EFFECTS OF GIN

Although Nunaga, Kabelaw, and the children were now happily re-united to friends and kindred, their dangers were by no means over, for a wide space of ice-blocked sea separated the small island from the shores of Greenland, and their supply of meat was not sufficient, even with economy, to maintain the whole party for more than a couple of days.

In these circumstances they were much comforted, after the storm had blown itself out, to find that the pack had been considerably loosened, and that several lanes of open water extended through it in the direction of the shore.

"There is a temporary settlement of natives not far from here, on the mainland," said Egede, when he and some of the men were assembled on the beach discussing their plans. "Although not very friendly, they would nevertheless help us, I think, in this hour of need. They have been demoralised by traders, and drawn away from the mission at Godhaab. But how we are to get to the mainland it is difficult to see, unless God mercifully clears away the ice."

"Why don't you ask your God to clear it away?" demanded

Simek. "Have you not told us that He answers prayer offered in the name of Jesus?"

Egede looked at his questioner in some surprise, mingled with pleasure, for his experience had taught him that too many of the natives either assented without thought to whatever he said, or listened with absolute indifference, if not aversion—especially when he attempted to bring truth home, or apply it personally.

"I am glad you ask the question, Simek," he replied, "because it gives me the opportunity of telling you that I *have* asked God, in the name of Jesus, to bring us out of our present trouble, and also of explaining that I never pray without adding the words 'if it be Thy will'—for God does not always answer prayer exactly in accordance with our request, but according to His own wisdom; so that, if He were hereafter to say, 'Now, is not that better than you asked?' we would be obliged to reply, 'Yes, Lord, it is better.'"

As the expression on Simek's face showed that he was not quite convinced, Egede added—

"Listen, Simek. I and my people were starving here. I prayed to God, in Jesus' name, to send us deliverance. Did He not answer my prayer by sending you and your party with food!"

"True," assented Simek.

"Listen again, Simek. Were you not in great danger when your oomiak and kayaks were crushed in the ice?"

"Yes."

"Were you not in very great danger when you were imprisoned on the iceberg—in danger of starvation, in danger of being crushed by its disruption?"

"Yes."

"Well, now, if you had believed in the great and good Spirit at that time, what would you have asked Him to do for you?"

"I would have asked Him to clear the sea of ice," replied the Eskimo promptly, "and send us kayaks and oomiaks to take us on shore."

"And if He had answered you according to your prayer, you would have said, no doubt, 'That is well.'"

"Yes," answered Simek emphatically, and with a smile.

"But suppose," continued Egede, "that God had answered you by delivering you in *another* way—by keeping you on the berg; by making that berg, as it were, into a great oomiak, and causing it to voyage as no oomiak ever voyaged—causing it to plough through pack-ice as no ship made by man ever ploughed; to go straight to an island to which no human power could have brought you; and to have done it all in time to save your own dear Pussi and all the rest of us from starvation—would you not have said that God had answered your prayer in a way that was far better?"

While the missionary was speaking, profound gravity took the place of the puzzled expression on the countenance of Simek and of the others who were listening, for their intelligence was quite quick enough to perceive the drift of his argument before it was finished.

"But," said Simek earnestly, "I did *not* pray for this, yet I got it."

"True, the Good Spirit guided you, even though you did not pray," returned Egede. "Is not this a proof of His love? If He is so good to thankless and careless children, what sure ground have we for trusting that He will be good to those who love Him! What our Great Father wants is that we should love and trust Him."

There was one man of the group whose lips were parted, and whose eyes seemed to glitter as he listened. This was Angut. Much and deeply had that intelligent Eskimo thought about the Great Spirit and the mysteries around and within himself, but never till that moment did the curtain seem to rise so decidedly from before his spiritual vision. Egede observed the keen gaze, though he judged it wise to take no notice of it at the time, but he did not fail to pray mentally that the good seed might take root.

The attention of the party was called off the subject of discourse just then by a further movement of the pack-ice.

"See, the lanes of open water widen," exclaimed Okiok eagerly, pointing seaward.

"Perhaps," said Egede, "God intends to deliver us."

"Have you prayed to be delivered?" asked Angut quickly.

"Yes, I have."

"Suppose," continued the inquisitive Eskimo, "that God does *not* deliver you, but leaves you here to die. Would *that* be answering your prayer?"

"Yes; for instead of granting my request in the way I wished, namely, that I might be permitted to live and preach about the Great Spirit to your countrymen for many years, He would have answered my prayer for deliverance by taking me away from *all* evil, to be with Jesus, *which is far better*."

To the surprise of the missionary, a look of disappointment settled on the face of Angut.

"What ails you?" he asked.

"From what you say," returned the Eskimo, somewhat coldly, "I see that, with you, *whatever* happens is best; *nothing* can be wrong. There is something which tells me here,"—he placed his hand on his breast—"that that is not true."

"You misunderstand me, friend," said Egede; "I did not say that nothing can be wrong. What I do say is that whatever God does is and must be right. But God has given to man a free will, and with his free will *man* does wrong. It is just to save man from this wrong-doing that Jesus came to earth."

"Free will?" murmured the Eskimo, with a recurrence of the perplexed look. And well might that look recur, for his untrained yet philosophical mind had been brought for the first time face to face with the great insoluble problem of the ages.

"Yes," said Egede, "you have got hold of a thought which no man has ever yet been able to fathom. Free will is a great mystery, nevertheless every child knows that it is a great *fact*."

From this point Angut seemed to commune only with his own spirit, for he put no more questions. At the same time the opening up of the pack rendered the less philosophical among the Eskimos anxious to make some practical efforts for their deliverance.

At Rooney's suggestion it was arranged that the boldest of the men should take the missionary's boat—a very small one that could not carry above a third of the party,—and examine the leads of open water, until they should ascertain whether they seemed safe or practicable; then return at once, and, if the report should be favourable, begin by taking off the women and children. This plan was carried out. A favourable report was brought back, the women were immediately embarked, and before evening closed the whole party was landed on the mainland in safety.

Being too late to proceed further that day, the Eskimos ran up a rude shelter of stones, moss, and sticks, the women being accommodated under the upturned boat. Next day they found that the pack had continued to ease off during the night, so that there was a lead of open water between it and the shore.

"You have been praying during the night," said Okiok to Egede in an abrupt manner, almost as if he were accusing him of taking an unfair advantage of circumstances.

"Truly I have," answered the missionary, with an amused look, "but I did not presume to ask the Great Spirit to help us in this particular way. I left that to His wisdom and love. I have been taught to trust Him."

"And if you had not got an answer at all," returned Okiok, wrinkling his brows in perplexity, "you would still have said that all was right?"

"Just so. If I get an answer it is well. If I get no answer it is still well, for then I know that He sees delay to be best for me and I feel sure that the answer will come at last, in the right way, and in good time, for in the Book of the Great Spirit I am told that 'all things work together for good to

R. M. Ballantyne

them that love God.'"

"What!" exclaimed Angut, who had listened to the conversation with intense interest; "would it be good for you if I killed you?"

"Of course it would, if God allowed it. Thousands of men and women in time past have chosen to be killed rather than offend God by sinning."

"This is very strange teaching," said Angut, glancing at his friend Okiok.

"It is the teaching of Jesus, the Son of God. I am only His servant," said the missionary, "and I hope to tell you much more that will seem very strange before long; but at present we must arrange what is now to be done, for it is the duty of all men to take advantage of opportunities as they are presented to them."

The truth of this was so obvious that the Eskimos at once dropped into the region of the practical by advising that the women should all get into the boat and advance by water, while the men should walk by the shore.

This being agreed to, the boat was launched. Although not an Eskimo oomiak, the little craft, which was made of wood, and resembled a punt, was propelled by oomiak paddles, so that Madame Okiok, who was appointed steerswoman, felt herself quite at home when seated in her place. Sigokow, being a powerful creature, physically as well as mentally, was put in charge of the bow-paddle. The other women were ranged along the sides, each with a paddle except old Kannoa who was allowed to sit in the bottom of the craft as a passenger, and guardian of Pussi and Tumbler.

As these last were prone to jump about under violent impulses of joyous hilarity, and had an irresistible desire to lean over the sides for the purpose of dipping their hands in the sea, the duty of the old woman, although connected with children's play, was by no mean's child's play.

Three miles an hour being the average speed at which the boat went, the walkers easily kept up with it. Only once did a difficulty occur when they came to a narrow bay which, although not more than a mile or so across from point to point, ran so far inland that the walkers could not have gone round it without great loss of time.

"We must be ferried across here," said Egede; "but as it is past noon, I think we had better call a halt, and dine before making the traverse."

"That is my opinion, too, sir," said Rooney, throwing down the bundle he had been carrying.

As the invitation to feed seldom comes amiss to a healthy Eskimo, Egede's proposal was at once agreed to, and in a few minutes they were all busily engaged.

It was a pretty spot, that on which they dined. Bushes just beginning to bud surrounded them; brilliant sunshine drew forth delicious scents from the long, long frozen earth and the reviving herbage on which they sat. It also drew forth gushing rivulets from the patches of snow and heavy drifts, which here and there by their depth and solidity seemed to bid defiance to the sweet influences of spring. The ice-laden sea sent gentle wavelets to the pebbly shore. A group of large willows formed a background to their lordly hall, and behind them, in receding and grand perspective, uprose the great shoulders of Greenland's mountains.

R. M. Ballantyne

On all those natural objects of interest and beauty, however, the travellers did not at first bestow more than a passing glance. They were too much engrossed with "metal more attractive," in the shape of bear blubber; but when appetite began to fail conversation began to flow. At that point it occurred to Pussi and Tumbler that they would go and have some fun.

Child-nature is much the same all the world over and curiously enough, it bears strong resemblance to adult nature. Having fed to satiety, these chips of Simek and Okiok lifted up their eyes, and beheld the surrounding shrubs. At once the idea arose—"Let us explore." The very same impulse that sent Mungo Park and Livingstone to Africa; Ross, Parry, Franklin, Kane, and all the rest of them toward the Pole, led our little hero and heroine into that thicket, and curiosity urged them to explore as far as possible. They did so, and, as a natural consequence, lost themselves. But what cared they for that? With youth, and health, and strength, they were as easy in their minds as Lieutenant Greely was with sextant, chart, and compass. As to food, were they not already victualled for, not a three years', but a three hours', expedition?

And their parents were not disturbed on their account. Eskimo fathers and mothers are not, as a rule, nervous or anxious about their offspring.

In a remarkably short space of time Pussi and Tumbler, walking hand in hand, put more than a mile of "bush" between them and their feeding-place.

"Oh! wha's dat?" exclaimed Pussi, stopping short, and gazing into the thicket in front of her.

We pause to remind the reader that our little ones lisped in

Eskimo, and that, in order to delineate faithfully, our only resource is to translate into lisping English.

"It's a man," exclaimed Tumbler.

"I tink him's a funny man," murmured the little girl, as the man approached.

Pussi was right. But it was not his dress, so much as his gait and expression, that were funny. For the stranger was obviously an Eskimo, being flat and fat-visaged, black-and-straight haired, and seal-skinnily clad.

The singular point about him was his walk. To all appearance it was a recently acquired power, for the man frowned almost fiercely at the ground as he advanced, and took each step with an amount of forethought and deliberation which to the children seemed quite unaccountable. Nay, after having taken a step, he would seem suddenly to repent, and draw back, putting a foot behind him again, or even to one side or the other—anywhere, in short, rather than in front. Coming up to the children at last by this painful process, he became suddenly aware of their presence, and opened his eyes to an extent that could only be accounted for on the wild supposition that he had never seen a child in all his life before.

Having stared for a minute or so with all the intensity of the most solemn surprise, he blinked like a sleepy owl, his mouth expanded, and his whole countenance beamed with good-will; but suddenly he changed back, as if by magic, to the solemn-surprise condition.

This was too much for the children, who simultaneously burst into a hilarious fit of laughter.

The fit seemed catching, for the man joined them with a loud roar of delight, swaying to and fro with closed eyes as he did so.

The roar brought up Red Rooney, who had followed the children's steps and happened to be close to them at the time of the explosion. He looked at the man for a moment, and then his muttered remark, "Drunk as a fiddler!" cleared up the mystery.

When the man opened his eyes, having finished his laugh, and beheld a tall Kablunet gazing sternly at him, all the fire of his ancestors blazed up in his breast, and came out at his eyes. Drawing his knife, he sprang at our seaman with the murderous weapon uplifted.

Rooney caught his wrist, put a foot behind his leg, gave him a sort of twirl, and laid him flat on his back. The fall caused the knife to spin into the air, and the poor Eskimo found himself at the mercy of the Kablunet.

Instead of taking the man's life, Rooney bade him sit up. The man did so with a solemn look, not unmixed with perplexity.

There is a phase of that terrible vice drunkenness which is comic, and it is not of the slightest use to ignore that fact. There were probably few men who detested strong drink and grieved over its dire effects more than Red Rooney. He had been led, at a time when total abstinence was almost unknown, to hate the very name of drink and to become a total abstainer. Yet he could not for the life of him resist a hearty laugh when the befuddled Eskimo blinked up in his face with an imbecile smile, and said—"Wh-whash 'e matter, y-you st-stupid ole' K-K-Kablunet?"

The difficulty and faulty nature of his pronunciation was such that slipshod English serves admirably to indicate his state of mind, although neither English nor Eskimo, Arabic nor Hebrew, will suffice to describe in adequate terms the tremendous solemnity of his gaze after the imbecile smile had passed away.

"You disreputable old seal," said Rooney, "where did you get the drink?"

Words are wanting to express the dignified look of injured innocence with which the man replied—"I—I've had *no* d-drink. Nosh a d-drop!"

"Yes, truly you *are* a man and a brother," muttered Rooney, as he noted this "touch of nature," and felt that he was in the company of "kin." "What's your name, you walrus?"

"K-Kazho," answered the man indignantly.

"What!"

"K-Ka-zho," he repeated, with emphasis.

"I suppose you mean Kajo, you unnatural jellyfish."

Kajo did not condescend to say what he meant, but continued to eye the Kablunet with lofty disdain, though the effect of his expression was marred by his attention being distracted by Pussi and Tumbler, whose faces were fiery red, owing to fits of suppressed laughter.

"Get up now, you old rascal," said Rooney. "Come along with me, and I'll show you to my friends."

At first the Eskimo showed a disposition to resist, but when the powerful seaman lifted him up by the neck of his coat, as if he had been a little dog, and set him on his legs, he thought better of it, smiled benignly, and moved on.

Hans Egede at once recognised this fellow as one of the most troublesome of his flock.

"I have done my best to keep strong drink from that man," he explained to Rooney, "but, as you must be aware from your long residence among them, the traders *will* supply the poor creatures with rum, and Kajo's naturally sanguine temperament is unable to withstand its influence. Over and over again he has promised me—with tears of, I believe, true repentance in his eyes—to give it up; but as surely as the traders offer it to him, and prevail on him to take one drop, so surely does he give way to a regular debauch."

While he spoke to Rooney in the Danish tongue, the subject of conversation stood with bowed head, conscience-smitten, before him, for, although he did not understand the language, he guessed correctly that the talk was about his own misdeeds.

"Come with me," said the missionary, taking the poor man by the arm, leading him aside to some distance, and evidently entering into serious remonstrance—while Kajo, as evidently, commenced energetic protestations.

On returning, Egede said that the Eskimo told him his tribe had moved along the coast to a better hunting-ground, and were at that moment located in an old deserted village, just beyond the point for which they were making, on the other side of the bay. He therefore advised that they should start off at once, so as to reach the camp early in the evening.

"Kajo tells me," added Egede, "that his kayak lies hid in the bushes at no great distance; so he can go with us. He is not too drunk, I think, to manage his light craft."

But Egede was wrong, for even while he was speaking Kajo had slipped quietly behind a bush. There, after a cautious look round to see that no one observed him, he drew a curious little flat earthenware bottle from some place of concealment about his dress, applied it to his lips, and took what Rooney would have styled "a long, hearty pull."

That draught was the turning-point. The comic and humorous were put to flight, and nothing but fierce, furious savagery remained behind. Many men in their cups become lachrymose, others silly, and some combative. The fiery liquor had the latter effect on Kajo. Issuing from his place of retirement with a fiendish yell and glaring eyes, he made an insane attack on Angut. That Eskimo, having no desire to hurt the man, merely stepped lightly out of his way and let him pass. Fortunately his knife had been left on the ground where Rooney first met him, for he stumbled and fell upon Kabelaw, into whom he would certainly have plunged the weapon had it still been in his hand.

Jumping up, he looked round with the glaring eyes of a tiger, while his fingers clutched nervously at the place where he was wont to carry the lost knife.

Seeing his condition, Arbalik sprang towards him, but, stooping quickly, Kajo darted out of his way. At the same moment he snatched up a knife that had been left lying on the ground. The first effect of the last draught seemed for the time to have increased the man's powers of action, for, rushing round the circle, he came suddenly upon poor old Kannoa, who chanced to be seated a little apart from the others. Seizing her thin hair, Kajo brandished the knife in front of her throat, and, glaring at the men, gave vent to a wild laugh of triumph.

It was evident that he was for the time quite mad and

R. M. Ballantyne

unaccountable for his actions—though by no means unaccountable for taking the accursed drink that reduced him to that state of temporary insanity. Red Rooney, aghast with horror at the impending fate of the dear old remembrancer of his grandmother, sprang forward with the agility of a wild cat, but his energy, intensified though it was by rage, could not have prevented the catastrophe if Ippegoo had not come to the rescue.

Yes, that mild youth was the instrument chosen to avert the blow. He chanced to be standing beside a mass of turf which Okiok had cut from the ground for the purpose of making a dry seat for Nuna. Seizing this, Ippegoo hurled it at the head of the drunken Eskimo. Never before did the feeble youth make such a good shot. Full on the flat face of the drunkard it went, like the wad of a siege-gun, scattering earth and *debris* all round—and down went the Eskimo. Unable to check himself, down also went Rooney on the top of him.

Next moment the luckless Kajo was secured with a piece of walrus-line, and flung on one side, while the indignant party held a noisy consultation as to what was to be done with him.

CHAPTER TWENTY FIVE

THE ESKIMO ENCAMPMENT—
A MURDER AND ITS CONSEQUENCES

With Hans Egede, Red Rooney, and Angut as chief councillors, it may be easily understood that the punishment awarded to Kajo was not severe. He was merely condemned, in the meantime, to be taken to his own people as a prisoner, and then let go free with a rebuke.

"But how are we to carry him there?" asked Egede. "He cannot walk, and we must not delay."

"That's true," said Rooney; "and it will never do to burden the women's boat with him. It is too full already."

"Did he not say that he had his kayak with him?" asked Angut.

"He did," cried Okiok, with the sudden animation of one who has conceived an idea. "Run, Arbalik, Ippegoo, Ermigit, Norrak, and seek for the kayak."

The youths named ran off to obey, with the alacrity of well-trained children, and in half an hour returned in triumph with the kayak on their shoulders. Meanwhile Kajo had recovered slightly, and was allowed to sit up, though his hands were still bound.

"Now we'll try him. Launch the boat, boys," said Okiok, "and be ready to paddle."

The young men did as they were bid, and Okiok, unloosening Kajo's bonds, asked him if he could manage his kayak.

"O-of—c-course I can," replied the man, somewhat indignantly.

"Come, then, embark an' do it," returned Okiok, seizing his arm, and giving it a squeeze to convince him that he was in the hands of a strong man.

Kajo staggered towards his little vessel, and, lifting it with difficulty, went down to the beach. He would certainly have fallen and damaged it if Okiok had not stood on one side and Angut on the other to prevent a fall. When the kayak was launched, he attempted to step into the little oval opening in it, but with so little success that Okiok, losing patience, lifted, him in, and crammed him down. Then he sent him afloat with a vigorous push.

Feeling all right, with the familiar paddle in his hands, Kajo tried to rouse himself, bethought him of flight, gave a hiccoughing cheer, and went skimming away like a sword-fish.

"After him now, boys, and keep alongside," cried Okiok.

Responsive to the order, the boat shot after the kayak, but they had barely got under weigh when Kajo made a false stroke with the paddle, lost his balance, and disappeared.

"I expected that," remarked Okiok, with a laugh.

"But the poor man will drown," said Egede anxiously; "he is too drunk to recover himself."

This was obvious, for the overturned craft seemed to quiver like a dying whale, while its owner made wild but fruitless efforts to recover his proper position; and it is certain that the poor man would then and there have paid the penalty of his intemperance with his life, if the boat had not ranged alongside, and rescued him.

"So then," said Angut to Egede, as they were bringing Kajo ashore, "this is the effect of the mad waters that I have often heard of, but never seen till now."

"Yes, Angut, you see the effect of them—at least on one man; but their effects vary according to the nature of those who drink. Some men they make violent, like Kajo; others become silly; while not a few become heavy, stupid, and brutal. In my country most if not all of the murders that take place are committed under the influence of strong drink. The Red Indians, who dwell far to the south-west of your lands, call strong drink 'fire-water.' Your own name 'mad waters' is better, I think."

Kajo was led forward at this moment, looking very much dejected, and greatly sobered. He made no further attempt to resist, but, as a precaution, his hands were again tied, and then he was left to dry in the sun, and to his meditations, while the party made the traverse of the bay.

This was accomplished in three trips. As the last party was about to start, Okiok and Kajo alone remained on the shore.

"You had better think twice," said Rooney, as he was about

to push off the boat. "He may give you some trouble."

"Fear not," returned Okiok, with a grin, in which there were mingled fun and contempt. "I have thought twice—three—four—ten times," and he extended the fingers of both hands.

"Very good; we'll keep an eye on you," said Rooney, with a laugh.

"He runs no risk," remarked Egede, taking up one of the paddles to share in the work. "His plan is one which Eskimos frequently adopt when one of their kayaks has been destroyed by rocks or walruses."

The plan referred to consisted in making the man whose kayak has been lost lie out on what may be called the deck of a friend's kayak. The well-known little craft named the "Rob Roy Canoe" bears much resemblance to the Eskimo kayak—the chief difference being that the former is made of thin, light wood, the latter of a light framework covered with sealskin. Both are long and narrow; decked entirely over, with the exception of a hole in the centre; can hold only one person, and are propelled with one double paddle having a blade at each end. The only way, therefore, of helping a friend in distress with such craft is to lay him out flat at full length on the deck, and require him to keep perfectly still while you paddle to a place of safety.

Okiok intended to take the helpless drunkard across the bay in this fashion, but for the sake of safety, resolved to do it in an unfriendly manner.

When the boat had shot away, he pushed the kayak into the water until it was afloat in the fore-part, arranged the spears which formed its armament, made fast the various lines, and laid the paddle across the opening. Then he went up to Kajo, who had been watching his movements with much curiosity, not quite unmingled with discomfort.

"Go," he said, pointing to the kayak, "and lay yourself out in front, on your face."

Kajo looked earnestly at the speaker. There was much less of the heroic in his gaze by that time, and therefore more of manly determination; but Okiok said "go" again. And Kajo went.

When he was laid flat on his face in front of the opening, with his feet on either side, and his head towards the bow, Okiok proceeded to tie him down there.

"You need not fear," he said; "I will not move." Okiok did not cease his work, but he said—

"I will make sure that you do not move. Any man with the sense of a puffin might be trusted to lie still for his own sake, but I have learned this day that a man full of mad water is a fool—not to be trusted at all."

Having expressed himself thus, and finished the lashing, he got softly into his place, pushed off, and paddled gently over the sea.

He had not advanced far when Kajo, feeling uncomfortable, tried slightly to alter his position, whereupon Okiok took up a spear that lay handy, and gave him a slight prick by way of reminding him of his duty. The rest of the voyage was accomplished in peace and safety.

In the evening the party arrived at the temporary abode of the tribe to which Kajo belonged. By that time the Eskimo was thoroughly sober, but the same could not be said of all his

R. M. Ballantyne

people—of whom there were upwards of a hundred men, besides women and children. It was found that a chance trader to Godhaab had brought a considerable quantity of rum, and the families of which we now speak had secured several kegs.

All of these Eskimos were well acquainted with Egede, and a few of them were friendly towards him; but many were the reverse. There was great excitement among them at the time the party arrived—excitement that could scarcely be accounted for either by the rum or by the unexpected arrival.

Egede soon found out what it was. A terrible murder had been committed the night before by one of the Eskimos, who was considered not only the best hunter of the band to which he belonged, but one of the best husbands and fathers. His name was Mangek. He was one of those who had been well disposed towards the missionary, and in regard to whom much hope had been entertained. But he had been treated to rum by the traders, and having conceived an ardent desire for more, had managed to obtain a keg of the mad water. Although kind and amiable by nature, his temperament was sanguine and his nerves sensitively strung. A very little of the rum excited him to extravagant exuberance of spirit, and a large dose made him temporarily insane.

It was during one of these fits of insanity that Mangek had on the previous night struck his wife, when she was trying to soothe him. The blow would not in itself have killed her, but as she fell her head struck on a stone, her skull was fractured, and she died in a few minutes.

Indifferent to—indeed, ignorant of—what he had done, the Eskimo sat beside the corpse all that night drinking. No one dared to go near him, until he fell back helplessly drunk. Then they removed the body of his wife.

It was bad enough to see this hitherto respected man mad with drink, but it was ten times worse to see him next day mad with horror at what he had done. For it was not merely that his wife was dead, but that, although he had loved that wife with all his heart and soul, he had killed her with his own hand. The wretched man had rushed about the place shrieking all the morning, sometimes with horror and sometimes with fury, until he was physically exhausted. Every one had kept carefully out of his way. When our travellers arrived he was lying in his hut groaning heavily; but no one knew what state he was in, for they still feared to disturb him.

No such fear affected Hans Egede. Knowing that he could point to the only remedy for sin and broken hearts, he went straight into the poor man's hut. Shortly afterwards the groaning ceased, and the natives listened with awe to what they knew was the voice of prayer. As they could not, however, distinguish the words, they gradually drew off, and circled round the strangers who had so unexpectedly arrived.

Great was their surprise when they found that their comrade Kajo had been brought home as a prisoner; and still greater was their surprise when they found that a bottle of rum which had been stolen from one of their hunters, and carried off the day before, was found on the person of Kajo—for Kajo had been, like Mangek, a respectable man up to that date, and no one believed it possible that he would condescend to steal.

One of those who was himself under the influence of rum at the time looked sternly at Kajo, and began to abuse him as a hypocrite and deceiver.

"Now, look here," cried Red Rooney, stepping forward; "listen to me."

Having regard to his commanding look and tone, the natives considered him the leader of the party, and listened with respect.

"What right have *you*," he continued, turning sharply on the last speaker, "to look with contempt on Kajo? You have been drinking mad water yourself. I smell it in your breath. If you were to take a little more, you would be quite ready to commit murder."

"No, I would not," replied the Eskimo stoutly.

"Yes, you would," said the sailor, still more stoutly. "Even my good-natured friend Okiok here would be ready to murder his wife Nuna if he was full of mad water."

This unexpected statement took our kindly Eskimo so much by surprise that for a moment or two he could not speak. Then he thundered forth—

"Never! What! kill Nuna? If I was stuffed with mad water from the toes to the eyelids, I *could* not kill Nuna."

At that moment an aged Eskimo pressed to the front. Tears were on his wrinkled cheeks, as he said, in a quavering voice—

"Yes, you *could*, my son. The wife of Mangek was my dear child. No man ever loved his wife better than Mangek loved my child. He would have killed himself sooner than he would have killed her. But Mangek did not kill her. It was the mad water that killed her. He did not know what the mad water would do when he drank it. How could he? It is the first time he has drunk it; he will *never* drink it again. But that will not bring back my child."

The old man tried to say more, but his lip trembled and his voice failed. His head drooped, and, turning abruptly round, he mingled with the crowd.

It was evident that the people were deeply moved by this speech. Probably they had never before given the mad water much of their thoughts, but now, after what had been said, and especially after the awful event of the previous night, opinion on the subject was beginning to form.

Red Rooney noted the fact, and was quick to take advantage of the opportunity.

"My friends," he said, and the natives listened all the more eagerly that he spoke their language so well, "when a cruel enemy comes to your shore, and begins to kill, how do you act?"

"We drive him into the sea; kill—destroy him," shouted the men promptly.

"Is not mad water a cruel enemy? Has he not already begun his deadly work? Has he not killed one of your best women, and broken the heart of one of your best men?"

"Huk! huk! Yes, that is true."

"Then who will fight him?" shouted Rooney.

There was a chorus of "I wills," and many of the men, running up to their huts, returned, some with bottles, and some with kegs. Foremost among them was the old father of the murdered woman. He stumbled, fell, and his keg rolled to Rooney's feet.

Catching it up, the sailor raised it high above his head and

R. M. Ballantyne

dashed it to splinters on the stones. With a shout of enthusiasm the Eskimos followed his example with bottle and keg, and in another moment quite a cataract of the vile spirit was flowing into the sea.

"That is well done," said Hans Egede, coming up at the moment. "You know how to take the tide at the flood, Rooney."

"Nay, sir," returned the sailor; "God brought about all the circumstances that raised the tide, and gave me power to see and act when the tide was up. I claim to be naught but an instrument."

"I will not quarrel with you on that point," rejoined Egede; "nevertheless, as an instrument, you did it well, and for that I thank God who has granted to you what I have prayed and toiled for, without success, for many a day. It is another illustration of prayer being answered in a different and better way from what I had asked or expected."

In this strange manner was originated, on the spur of the moment, an effectual and comprehensive total abstinence movement. We are bound of course to recognise the fact that it began in impulse, and was continued from necessity—no more drink being obtainable there at that time. Still, Egede and Rooney, as well as the better-disposed among the Eskimos, rejoiced in the event, for it was an unquestionable blessing so far as it went.

As the Eskimos had settled down on that spot for some weeks for the purpose of hunting—which was their only method of procuring the necessaries of life,—and as there was no pressing necessity for the missionary or his friends proceeding just then to Godhaab, it was resolved that they should all make a short stay at the place, to assist the

Eskimos in their work, as well as to recruit the health and strength of those who had been enfeebled by recent hardship and starvation.

CHAPTER TWENTY SIX

TELLS OF MEN WHOSE ACTIONS END IN SMOKE, AND OF OTHERS WHOSE PLOTS END IN DEEDS OF DARKNESS

This is a world of surprises. However long we may live, and however much we may learn, the possibility of being surprised remains with us, and our capacity for blazing astonishment is as great as when first, with staggering gait, we escaped from the nursery into space and stood irresolute, with the world before us where to choose.

These thoughts arise from the remembrance of Okiok as he stood one morning open-mouthed, open-eyed, open-souled, and, figuratively, petrified, gazing at something over a ledge of rock.

What that something was we must learn from Okiok himself, after he had cautiously retired from the scene, and run breathlessly back towards the Eskimo village, where the first man he met was Red Rooney.

"I—I've seen it," gasped the Eskimo, gripping the seaman's arm convulsively.

"Seen what?"

"Seen a man—on fire; and he seems not to mind it!"

"On fire! A man! Surely not. You must be mistaken."

"No, I am quite sure," returned Okiok, with intense earnestness. "I saw him with my two eyes, and smoke was coming out of him."

Rooney half-suspected what the Eskimo had seen, but there was just enough of uncertainty to induce him to say, "Come, take me to him."

"Is the man alone?" he asked, as they hurried along.

"No; Ippegoo is with him, staring at him." They soon reached the ledge of rock where Okiok had seen the "something," and, looking cautiously over it, Rooney beheld his friend Kajo smoking a long clay pipe such as Dutchmen are supposed to love. Ippegoo was watching him in a state of ecstatic absorption.

Rooney drew back and indulged in a fit of stifled laughter for a minute, but his companion was too much surprised even to smile.

"Is he doing that curious thing," asked Okiok in a low voice, "which you once told me about—smookin' tibooko?"

"Yes; that's it," replied Rooney with a broad grin, "only you had better say 'smokin' tobacco' next time."

"'Smokkin' tibucco,'" repeated the Eskimo; "well, that *is* funny. But why does he spit it out? Does he not like it?"

"Of course he likes it. At least I suppose he does, by the expression of his face."

There could be little doubt that Rooney was right. Kajo had evidently got over the preliminary stages of incapacity and repugnance long ago, and had acquired the power of enjoying that mild and partial stupefaction—sometimes called "soothing influence"—which tobacco smoke affords. His eyes blinked happily, like those of a cat in the sunshine; his thickish lips protruded poutingly as they gripped the stem; and the smoke was expelled slowly at each puff, as if he grudged losing a single whiff of the full flavour.

Scarcely less interesting was the entranced gaze of Ippegoo. Self-oblivion had been effectively achieved in that youth. A compound of feelings—interest, surprise, philosophical inquiry, eager expectancy, and mild alarm—played hide-and-seek with each other in his bosom, and kept him observant and still.

"Why," asked Okiok, after gazing in silent admiration for a few minutes over the ledge, "why does he not swallow it, if he likes it, and keep it down?"

"It's hard to say," answered Rooney. "Perhaps he'd blow up or catch fire if he were to try. It might be dangerous!"

"See," exclaimed Okiok, in an eager whisper; "he is going to let Ippegoo taste it."

Rooney looked on with increased interest, for at that moment Kajo, having had enough, offered the pipe to his friend, who accepted it with the air of a man who half expected it to bite and put the end in his mouth with diffidence. He was not successful with the first draw, for instead of taking the smoke merely into his mouth he drew it straight down his throat, and spent nearly five minutes thereafter in violent coughing with tears running down his cheeks.

Kajo spent the same period in laughing, and then gravely and carefully explained how the thing should be done.

Ippegoo was an apt scholar. Almost immediately he learned to puff, and in a very short time was rolling thick white clouds from him like a turret-gun in action. Evidently he was proud of his rapid attainments.

"Humph! That won't last long," murmured Rooney to his companion.

"Isn't it good?" said Kajo to Ippegoo.

"Ye-es. O yes. It's good; a-at least, I suppose it is," replied the youth, with modesty.

A peculiar tinge of pallor overspread his face at that moment.

"What's wrong, Ippegoo?"

"I—I—feel f-funny."

"Never mind that," said Kajo. "It's always the way at first. When I first tried it I—"

He was cut short by Ippegoo suddenly rising, dropping the pipe, clapping one hand on his breast, the other on his mouth, and rushing into the bushes where he disappeared like one of his own puffs of smoke. At the same moment Rooney and Okiok appeared on the scene, laughing heartily.

"You rascal!" said Rooney to Kajo, on recovering his gravity; "you have learned to drink, and you have learned to smoke, and, not satisfied with that extent of depravity, you try to teach Ippegoo. You pitiful creature! Are you not ashamed of yourself?"

Kajo looked sheepish, and admitted that he had some sensations of that sort, but wasn't sure.

"Tell me," continued the seaman sternly, "before you tasted strong drink or tobacco, did you want them?"

"No," replied Kajo.

"Are you in better health now that you've got them?"

"I—I *feel* the better for them," replied Kajo.

"I did not ask what you *feel*," returned Rooney. "*Are* you better now than you were before? That's the question."

But Rooney never got a satisfactory answer to that question, and Kajo continued to drink and smoke until, happily for himself, he had to quit the settlements and proceed to the lands of thick-ribbed ice, where nothing stronger than train oil and lamp-smoke were procurable.

As for poor Ippegoo, he did not show himself to his friends during the remainder of that day. Being half an idiot, no one could prevail on him thereafter to touch another pipe.

Now, while the Eskimos and our friends were engaged in hunting, and holding an unwonted amount both of religious and philosophical intercourse, a band of desperadoes was descending the valleys of the interior of Greenland, with a view to plunder the Eskimos of the coast.

Hitherto we have written about comparatively well-behaved and genial natives, but it must not be supposed that there were no villains of an out-and-out character among those denizens of the north. It is true there were not many—for the sparseness of the population, the superabundance of game on land and sea, as well as the wealth of unoccupied hunting-grounds, and the rigour of the climate, rendered robbery and war quite unnecessary, as well as disagreeable. Still, there were a few spirits of evil even there, to whom a quiet life seemed an abomination, and for whom the violent acquisition of other men's goods possessed a charm far transcending the practice of the peaceful industries of life.

The band referred to was not remarkably strong in numbers—about thirty or so; but these were sturdy and daring villains, led by a chief who must have had some of the old Norse blood in his veins, he was so tall, fair of complexion, and strong.

Descending first on the little settlement of Godhaab at night, this robber band found that a Dutch trading-vessel had just arrived, the crew of which, added to the settlers attracted from their hunting-grounds to the village, formed a force which they dared not venture to attack openly. Grimlek, the robber chief, therefore resolved to wait for a better opportunity. Meanwhile, passing himself and band off as hunters, he purchased a few things from the traders and then proceeded along the coast, intending to hunt, as well as to wait till the vessel should depart.

While the robbers were thus engaged, they came unexpectedly on another trading-ship—a Dutchman—part of the crew of which had landed for some purpose or other in their boat. On seeing the Eskimos, the Dutchmen got quickly into their boat, and pushed off; but the robbers made signs of peace to them, and, carrying their bows, arrows, and spears up to the woods, left them there, returning to the shore as if unarmed, though in reality they had retained their knives. Again they made signs, as if they wished to trade with the Dutchmen.

R. M. Ballantyne

Deceived by appearances, the sailors once more drew in to the shore. While they were approaching, Grimlek called his men round him and gave a few hasty directions. When the sailors had landed, the Eskimos mingled with them, and began to offer sealskins for trade—each selecting a particular man with whom to transact business. At a given signal they drew their knives from under their coats, and each robber stabbed his man to the heart. The men left in the ship, seeing what had occurred, and that it was too late to attempt rescue, instantly filled her sails, and went off to sea.

The villains having thus easily slain their victims, carried off the booty found in the boat, and hid it in the bushes, to be taken away at a convenient opportunity.

But this deed of darkness was not done unwitnessed. Early in the morning of that day, various hunting parties had dispersed in different directions—some to the hills, others to the sea. Among the latter was an oomiak full of women who went along-shore to fish, and with whom were old Kannoa, Nunaga, and others. They went in a northerly direction. Rooney, Angut, and Okiok proceeded along the coast to the southward.

The direction taken by these last brought them near to the spot where the Dutch sailors had landed, at the critical moment when the robbers were mingling with their unsuspecting victims.

Although only three to thirty, it is certain that our heroes would have sprung to the aid of the sailors if they had suspected what was about to happen, but the deed was done so promptly that there was no time for action. Fortunately Rooney and his companions had not shown themselves. They were therefore able to draw back into the shelter of the bushes, where they held a hasty council of war.

"We must run back to camp," said Rooney, "tell what we have seen, and return with a band of men to punish the murderers."

"Agreed," said Okiok; "but how are we to do it? The shore is open. We cannot take a step that way without being seen, and chased. We might outrun them, though I don't feel quite as supple as I used to; but we should barely arrive before them in time to warn the camp, and should then be almost unfit to fight."

To this Angut replied that they could go inland over the hills, and so come down on the camp in rear. It might not, he thought, add much to the distance. This plan was quickly adopted and put in practice.

But there are few things more deceptive than formation and distance in mountain lands. What seemed to the trio easy, proved to be tremendously difficult; and the distance they had to travel in order to avoid precipices and surmount ridges, gradually increased to many miles, so that it was late, and twilight was deepening into night, before they reached the camp.

Meanwhile the robbers were not idle. Although ignorant of the fact that their bloody work had been observed, they were not long ignorant of the near neighbourhood of the Eskimo camp. Early in the morning they had sent two of their swiftest young men to spy out the land ahead. These had discovered the camp, entered it, professing to be wandering hunters, and had then returned to their friends with the news that many of the men had gone away hunting, and would probably remain out all night; also that an oomiak full of women had gone off to the southward to fish.

The runners, happening to descend to the coast on the

opposite side of a ridge from Rooney and his companions, just missed meeting them, and returned to their comrades shortly after the massacre. Grimlek knew that whatever course he should pursue must be prompt and decisive. He at once divided his men into two bands, one of which he sent to pursue and capture the women who had gone to fish; with the other, which he led in person, he resolved either to storm the camp or take it by surprise, as circumstances might point out.

By the straight way of the shore the distance was not great. In fact, the camp might have been seen from the spot where the massacre had been perpetrated, but for a high promontory which concealed it. On rounding this promontory, the party detailed to pursue the women glided into the bushes and disappeared. Grimlek, with the remaining men, advanced straight and openly towards the camp. He saw, however, on drawing near, that the number of men in it were more than a match for his small party, and therefore approached with friendly demonstrations.

They were hospitably received by Hans Egede.

"My friends," he said, "you have arrived just as we are assembling to talk about the things that concern our souls, the future life, and the Good Spirit. Will you and your men sit down and listen?"

For a few moments Grimlek did not reply. Then he said, "You are not an Eskimo?"

"No, I am a Kablunet," replied Egede; "I have been sent to tell the Eskimos about the true God."

Again the robber chief was silent. Then he said that he would consult with his men, and retired with them a short distance to do so.

"Nothing better could have happened," he said in a low tone. "The Kablunet is going to talk to them about his God. All we have to do is to mingle with them. Let each of you choose his man and sit down beside him. When I give the signal, strike at once, and let no second blow be needed."

A murmur of assent was all that the band returned to this speech, and Grimlek, returning to the missionary, said that he and his men were ready to hear.

In a few minutes each of the assassins was seated on the ground beside his chosen victim.

R. M. Ballantyne

CHAPTER TWENTY SEVEN

A STRANGE MEETING
STRANGELY INTERRUPTED

The meeting which had been thus strangely invaded was no ordinary prayer or missionary meeting. It had been assembled by Egede for the express purpose of affording some unbelievers among the Eskimos an opportunity of stating their difficulties and objections in regard to the new religion.

Interesting though its proceedings were, as showing the similarity of the workings of the civilised and savage minds, we cannot afford space to enter much into detail, yet some account of the matter seems necessary in order to show what it was that induced the robber chief to delay, though not to alter, his fell purpose.

After prayer offered by the missionary, that the Holy Spirit might descend on and bless the discussion, a hymn was sung. It had been translated into Eskimo, and taught to his converts by Egede. Then the missionary made a brief but complete statement of the leading facts of the good news of salvation to sinful man in Jesus Christ,—this, not only to clear the way for what was to come, but for the purpose of teaching the newcomers, so as to render them somewhat intelligent listeners.

Then an old grey-haired man arose.

"I do not object to the new religion," he said, "but I am puzzled. You tell me that God is everywhere and knows everything; why, then, did he not go to our first mother, Eve, and warn her of her danger when the Evil One tempted her in the form of a serpent?"

"My friend, the question you ask cannot be fully answered," said Egede. "I can explain, however, that our first parents were put into the world to be tried or tested in that way. To have warned Eve would have rendered the test useless. Enough for us to know that she was told what to do. Her duty was to obey. But let me ask *you* a question: is not sin—is not murder—hateful?"

Grimlek imagined that Egede looked him straight in the face as he asked the question, and felt uneasy, but was by no means softened.

"Yes," answered the old man; "murder—sin—is hateful."

"Yet it certainly exists," continued Egede; "you cannot help believing that?"

"Yes, I must admit that."

"Then why did God permit sin?"

Of course the old man could not reply, and the missionary pointed out that some things were incomprehensible, and that that was one of them.

"But," he continued, "that is no reason why we should not talk of things that *are* comprehensible. Let us turn to these."

R. M. Ballantyne

At this point a middle-aged man with a burly frame and resolute expression started up, and said in an excited yet somewhat reckless manner—

"I don't believe a word that you say. Everything exists as it was from the beginning until now, and will continue the same to the end."

"Who told you that?" asked Egede, in a prompt yet quiet manner.

The man was silenced. He resumed his seat without answering.

"You have talked of the 'end,' my friend," continued the missionary, in the same quiet tone. "When is the end? and what will come after it? I wait for enlightenment."

Still the man remained dumb. He had evidently exhausted himself in one grand explosion, and was unable for more. There was a disposition to quiet laughter on the part of the audience, but the missionary checked this by pointing to another man in the crowd and remarking—

"I think, friend, that you have something to say."

Thus invited, the man spoke at once, and with unexpected vigour. He was a stupid-looking, heavy-faced man, but when roused, as he then was, his face lighted up amazingly.

"We do not understand you," he said sternly. "Show us the God you describe; then we will believe in Him and obey Him. You make Him too high and incomprehensible. How can we know Him? Will He trouble Himself about the like of us? Some of us have prayed to Him when we were faint and hungry, but we got no answer. What you say of Him cannot be true, or, if you know Him better than we do, why don't you pray for us and procure for us plenty of food, good health, and a dry house? That is all we want. As for our souls, they are healthy enough already. You are of a different race from us. People in your country may have diseased souls. Very likely they have. From the specimens we have seen of them we are quite ready to believe that. For them a doctor of souls may be necessary. Your heaven and your spiritual joys may be good enough for you, but they would be very dull for us. We must have seals, and fishes, and birds. Our souls can no more live without these than our bodies. You say we shall not find any of these in your heaven; well then, we do not want to go there; we will leave it to you and to the worthless part of our own countrymen, but as for us, we prefer to go to Torngarsuk, where we shall find more than we require of all things, and enjoy them without trouble."

[See Note.]

With an energetic "humph!" or some such exclamation, this self-satisfied philosopher sat down, and many of his countrymen expressed their sympathy with his views by a decided "Huk!" but others remained silent and puzzled.

And well they might, for in these few sentences the Eskimo had opened up a number of the problems on which man, both civilised and savage, has been exercising his brain unsuccessfully from the days of Adam and Eve until now. No wonder that poor Hans Egede paused thoughtfully—and no doubt prayerfully—for a few minutes ere he ventured a reply. He was about to open his lips, when, to his astonishment, a tall strong man who had been sitting near the outside circle of the audience close to the robber chief Grimlek started to his feet, and, in a tone that had in it more of a demand than a request, asked permission to speak.

It was our friend Angut.

Before listening to his remarks, however, it behoves us to account for his sudden appearance.

Having been led, as we have said, far out of their way by the detour they were compelled to take, Red Rooney and his friends did not reach the camp till some time after the meeting above described had begun. As it was growing dusk at the time, they easily approached without being observed—all the more that during the whole time of the meeting men and women kept coming and going, according as they felt more or less interested in the proceedings.

Great was the surprise of the three friends on arriving to find the band of robbers sitting peacefully among the audience; but still greater would have been their surprise had they known the murderous purpose these had in view. Rooney, however, having had knowledge of men in many savage lands, half guessed the true state of matters, and, touching his two friends on the shoulders, beckoned to them to withdraw.

"Things look peaceful," he whispered when beyond the circle, "but there is no peace in the hearts of cold-blooded murderers. What they have done they will do again. 'Quick' is the word. Let us gather a dozen strong young men."

They had no difficulty in doing this. From among the youths who were indifferent to the proceedings at the meeting they soon gathered twelve of the strongest.

"Now, lads," said Rooney, after having briefly told them of the recent massacre, "fifteen of these murderers are seated in that meeting. You cannot fail to know them from our own people, for they are all strangers. Let each one here creep into the meeting with a short spear, choose his man, sit down beside him, and be ready when the signal is given by Angut or me. But do not kill. You are young and strong. Throw each man on his back, but do not kill unless he seems likely to get the better of you. Hold them down, and wait for orders."

No more was said. Rooney felt that delay might be fatal. With the promptitude of men accustomed to be led, the youths crept into the circle of listeners, and seated themselves as desired. Rooney and Okiok selected their men, like the rest. Angut chanced to place himself beside Grimlek.

The chief cast a quick, suspicious glance on him as he sat down, but as Angut immediately became intent on the discussion that was going on, and as the robber himself had become interested in spite of himself, the suspicion was allayed as quickly as roused.

These quiet proceedings took place just before the heavy-faced Eskimo began the speech which we have detailed. Notwithstanding the serious—it might be bloody—work which was presently to engage all his physical energies, the spirit of Angut was deeply stirred by the string of objections which the man had flung out so easily. Most of the points touched on had often engaged his thoughtful mind, and he felt—as many reasoning men have felt before and since—how easy it is for a fool to state a string of objections in a few minutes, which it might take a learned man several hours fully to answer and refute.

Oppressed, and, as it were, boiling over, with this feeling, Angut, as we have said, started to his feet, to the no small alarm of the guilty man at his side. But the chief's fears were dissipated when Angut spoke.

"Foolish fellow!" he said, turning with a blazing gaze to the

R. M. Ballantyne

heavy-faced man. "You talk like a child of what you do not understand. You ask to see God, else you won't believe. You believe in your life, don't you? Yet you have never seen it. You stab a bear, and let its life out. You know when the life is there. You have let it out. You know when it is gone. But you have not *seen* it. Then why do you believe in it? You do not see a sound, yet you believe in it. Do not lift your stupid face; I know what you would say: you *hear* the sound, therefore it exists. A deaf man does not hear the sound. Does it therefore not exist? That which produces the sound is there, though the deaf man neither sees nor hears, nor feels nor tastes, nor smells it. My friend, the man of God, says he thinks the cause of sound is motion in the air passing from particle to particle, till the last particle next my ear is moved, and then—I hear. Is there, then, no motion in the air to cause sound because the deaf man does not hear?

"O stupid-face! You say that God does not answer prayer, because you have asked and have not received. What would you think of your little boy if he should say, 'I asked a dead poisonous fish from my father the other day, and he did not give it to me; therefore my father *never* gives me what I want.' Would that be true? Every morning you awake hungry, and you *wish* for food; then you get up, and you find it. Is not your wish a silent prayer? And is it not answered every day? Who sends the seals, and fishes, and birds, even when we do *not* ask with our lips? Did these animals make themselves? Stupid-face! you say your soul is healthy. Sometimes you are angry, sometimes discontented, sometimes jealous, sometimes greedy. Is an angry, discontented, jealous, greedy soul healthy? You know it is not. It is diseased, and the disease of the soul is *sin*. This disease takes the bad forms I have mentioned, and many other bad forms—one of which is *murder*."

Angut emphasised the last word and paused, but did not look

at the robber beside him, for he knew that the arrow would reach its mark. Then he resumed—

"The Kablunet has brought to us the better knowledge of God. He tells us that God's great purpose from the beginning of time has been to cure our soul-disease. We deserve punishment for our sins: God sent His Son and Equal, Jesus Christ, to bear our sins. We need deliverance from the power of sin: God sent His Equal—the Spirit of Jesus—to cure us. I believe it. I have felt that Great Spirit in my breast long before I saw the Kablunets, and have asked the Great Spirit to send more light. He has answered my prayer. I *have* more light, and am satisfied."

Again Angut paused, while the Eskimos gazed at him in breathless interest, and a strange thrill—almost of expectation—passed through the assembly, while he continued in a low and solemn tone—

"Jesus," he said, "saves *from* all sin. But,"—he turned his eyes here full on Grimlek—"He does not save *in* sin. Murder—foul and wicked murder—has been done!"

Grimlek grew pale, but did not otherwise betray himself. Reference to murder was no uncommon thing among his countrymen. He did not yet feel sure that Angut referred to the deed which he had so recently perpetrated.

"This day," continued Angut, "I saw a band of Kablunet sailors—"

He got no further than that, for Grimlek attempted to spring up. The heavy hand of Angut, however, crushed him back instantly, and a spear-point touched his throat.

"Down with the villains!" shouted Rooney, laying the grasp

of a vice on the neck of the man next to him, and hurling him to the ground.

In the twinkling of an eye the fifteen robbers were lying flat on their backs, with fingers grasping their throats, knees compressing their stomachs, and spear-points at their hearts; but no blood was shed. One or two of the fiercest, indeed, struggled at first, but without avail—for the intended victim of each robber was handy and ready to lend assistance at the capture, as if in righteous retribution.

It was of course a startling incident to those who were not in the secret. Every man sprang up and drew his knife, not knowing where a foe might appear, but Rooney's strong voice quieted them.

"We're all safe enough, Mr Egede," he cried, as he bound Grimlek's hands behind him with a cord. The Eskimos quickly performed the same office for their respective prisoners, and then, setting them up in a row, proceeded to talk over the massacre, and to discuss in their presence the best method of getting rid of the murderers.

"I propose," said Okiok, whose naturally kind heart had been deeply stirred by the cowardly massacre which he had witnessed, "I propose that we should drown them."

"No; drowning is far too good. Let us spear them," said Kajo, who had become sober by that time.

"That would not hurt them," cried a fierce Eskimo, smiting his knee with his clenched fist. "We must cut off their ears and noses, poke out their eyes, and then roast them alive—"

"Hush! hush!" cried Egede, stepping forward; "we must do nothing of the kind. We must not act like devils. Have we not been talking of the mercy of the Great Spirit? Let us be just, but let us temper justice with mercy. Angut has not yet spoken; let us hear what he will propose."

Considering the energy with which he had denounced the murders, and the vigour with which he had captured Grimlek, Angut's proposal was somewhat surprising.

"Kablunet," he said, turning to the missionary, "have you not told me that in your Book of God it is written that men should do to other men what they wish other men to do to them?"

"Truly, that is so," answered Egede.

"If I were very wicked," continued Angut, "and had done many evil deeds, I should like to be forgiven and set free; therefore, let us forgive these men, and set them free."

We know not with what feelings the robbers listened to the inhuman proposals that were at first made as to their fate, but certain it is that after Angut had spoken there was a visible improvement in the expression of their faces.

Considerable astonishment and dissatisfaction were expressed by the majority of the Eskimos. Even Egede, much though he delighted in the spirit which dictated it, could not quite see his way to so simple and direct an application of the golden rule in the case of men who had so recently been caught red-handed in a cold-blooded murder. While he was still hesitating as to his reply to this humane proposal, an event occurred which rendered all their discussion unnecessary.

We have said that fifteen robbers had been captured; but there were sixteen who had entered the camp and joined the meeting. One of these had, without particular motive, seated himself on the outskirt of the circle under the shadow of a bush, which shadow had grown darker as the twilight deepened. Thus it came to pass that he had been overlooked, and, when the melee took place, he quietly retreated into the brush-wood. He was a brave man, however, although a robber, and scorned to forsake his comrades in their distress. While the discussion above described was going on, he crept stealthily towards the place where the captives had been ranged.

This he did the more easily that they sat on the summit of a bank or mound which sloped behind them into the bushes. Thus he was able to pass in a serpentine fashion behind them all without being seen, and, as he did so, to cut the bonds of each. Their knives had been removed, else, being desperate villains, they might now have attacked their captors. As it was, when the cords of all had been cut, they rose up with a mingled yell of laughter and triumph and dashed into the bushes.

The hunters were not slow to follow, with brandished knives and spears, but their chief called them back with a Stentorian roar, for well he knew that his men might as well try to follow up a troop of squirrels as pursue a band of reckless men in the rapidly increasing darkness, and that there was nearly as much likelihood of their stabbing each other by mistake in the dark, as of killing or catching their foes.

When the hunters had again re-assembled in front of their chief man's house, they found new cause of anxiety which effectually put to flight their annoyance at having been outwitted by the robbers.

This was the fact that, although night was coming on, the oomiak with the women had not returned.

* * * * *

Note. This is no fanciful speech. It is the substance of an actual speech made by a Greenlander to the Moravian brethren in 1737.

R. M. Ballantyne

CHAPTER TWENTY EIGHT

A CAPTURE, FLIGHT, SURPRISE, AND RESCUE

If true love is, according to the proverb, more distinctly proved to be true by the extreme roughness of its course, then must the truth of the love of Angut and Nunaga be held as proved beyond all question, for its course was a very cataract from beginning to end.

Poor Nunaga, in the trusting simplicity of her nature, was strong in the belief that, having been found and saved by Angut, there was no further cause for anxiety. With an easy mind, therefore, she set herself to the present duty of spearing cat fish with a prong.

It was fine healthy work, giving strength to the muscles, grace and activity to the frame, at the same time that it stimulated the appetite which the catfish were soon to appease.

"It grows late," said Pussimek, "and will be dark before we get back to camp."

"Never mind; who cares?" said the independent Sigokow, who was fond of "sport."

"But the men will be angry," suggested the mother of Ippegoo.

"Let them be angry—bo-o-o!" returned the reckless Kabelaw.

"Nunaga," said Nuna, looking eagerly over the side, "there goes another—a big one; poke it."

Nunaga poked it, but missed, and only brought up a small flat-fish, speared by accident.

Old Kannoa, who also gazed into the clear depths, was here observed to smile benignantly, and wave one of her skinny arms, while with the other she pointed downwards.

The sisters Kabelaw and Sigokow, each wielding a pronged stick, responded to the signal, and were gazing down into the sea with uplifted weapons when Pussimek uttered an exclamation of surprise and pointed to the shore, where, on a bush, a small piece of what resembled scarlet ribbon or a strip of cloth was seen waving in the wind.

"A beast!" exclaimed Pussimek, who had never before seen or heard of scarlet ribbon.

"Saw you ever a beast so *very* red?" said the wife of Okiok doubtfully.

"It is no beast," remarked the mother of Ippegoo; "it is only a bit of sealskin dyed red."

"No sealskin ever fluttered like that," said the mother of Arbalik sternly. "It is something new and beautiful that some one has lost. We are lucky. Let us go and take it."

No one objecting to this, the oomiak was paddled towards the land. Nunaga observed that the sisters Kabelaw and Sigokow were each eager to spring ashore before the other and snatch the prize. Having a spice of mischievous fun in her she resolved to be beforehand, and, being active as a kitten, while the sisters were only what we may style lumberingly vigorous, she succeeded.

Before the boat quite touched the gravel, she had sprung on shore, and flew towards the coveted streamer. The sisters did not attempt to follow. Knowing that it would be useless, they sat still and the other women laughed.

At the success of his little device the robber-lieutenant of Grimlek chuckled quietly, as he crouched behind that bush. When Nunaga laid her hand on the gaudy bait he sprang up, grasped her round the waist, and bore her off into the bushes. At the same moment the rest of the band made a rush at the oomiak. With a yell in unison, the women shoved off—only just in time, for the leading robber dashed into the sea nearly up to the neck, and his outstretched hand was within a foot of the gunwale when he received a smart rap over the knuckles from Sigokow. Another moment, and the oomiak was beyond his reach.

Alas for old Kannoa! She had been seated on the gunwale of the craft, and the vigorous push that set the others free had toppled her over backwards into the sea. As this happened in shallow water, the poor old creature had no difficulty in creeping on to the beach. The incident would have tried the nerves of most old ladies, but Kannoa had no nerves; and in regard to being wet—well, she was naturally tough and accustomed to rough it.

The disappointed robber observed her, of course, on wading back to land, but passed her with contemptuous indifference, as if she had been merely an over-grown crab or lobster. But Kannoa determined not to be left to die on the shore. She rose, squeezed the water out of her garments and followed the robber, whom she soon found in the bushes with his companions eagerly discussing their future plans. Nunaga was seated on the ground with her face bowed on her knees. Kannoa went and sat down beside her, patted her on the shoulder and began to comfort her.

"We must not stay here," said the leader of the band, merely casting a look of indifference at the old creature. "The women who have escaped will tell the men, and in a very short time we shall have them howling on our track."

"Let us wait and fight them," said one of the men, fiercely.

"It would be great glory for a small band to fight a big one, no doubt," returned the leader in a sarcastic tone; "but it would be greater glory for one man to do that alone—so you had better stay here and fight them yourself."

A short laugh greeted this remark.

"It will be very dark to-night," said another man.

"Yes; too dark for our foes to follow us, but not too dark for us to advance steadily, though slowly, into the mountains," returned the leader. "When there, we shall be safe. Come, we will start at once."

"But what are we to do with the old woman?" asked one. "She cannot walk."

"Leave her," said another.

"No; she will bring evil on us if we leave her," cried the

R. M. Ballantyne

fierce man. "I am sure she is a witch. We must carry her with us, and when we come to a convenient cliff, toss her into the sea."

In pursuance of this plan, the fierce robber tied the old woman up in a bear-skin—made a bundle of her, in fact—and swung her on his back. Fortunately, being rather deaf, Kannoa had not heard what was in store for her; and as the position she occupied on the fierce man's broad back was not uncomfortable, all things considered, she submitted with characteristic patience. Poor, horrified Nunaga thought it best to let her companion remain in ignorance of what was proposed, and cast about in her mind the possibility of making her escape, and carrying the news of her danger to the camp. If she could only get there and see Angut, she was sure that all would go well, for Angut, she felt, could put everything right—somehow.

In a short time the robbers were far away from the scene of their consultation; and the darkness of the night, as predicted, became so intense that it was quite impossible to advance further over the rough ground without the risk of broken limbs, if not worse. A halt was therefore called for rest, food, and consultation.

The spot on which they stood was the top of a little mound, with thick shrubs on the land side, which clothed a steep, almost precipitous descent. Just within these shrubs, as it were under the brow of the hill, Nunaga observed a small natural rut or hollow. The other, or sea, side of the mound, was quite free from underwood, and also very steep. On the top there was a low ledge of rock, on which the fierce robber laid his bundle down, while the others stood round and began to discuss their circumstances. The leader, who had taken charge of Nunaga, and held one of her hands during the journey, set the girl close in front of him, to prevent the possibility of her attempting to escape, for he had noted her activity and strength, and knew how easily she might elude him if once free in the dark woods.

Although these woods were as black as Erebus, there was light enough to enable them to distinguish the glimmer of the sea not far off, and a tremendous cliff rising in solemn grandeur above it.

"Yonder is a good place to throw your witch over," remarked the leader carelessly.

The fierce robber looked at the place.

"Yes," he said, "that might do; and the way to it is open enough to be crossed, even at night, without much trouble."

At that moment a bright idea suddenly struck Nunaga.

Have you ever noticed, reader, how invariably "bright ideas" deal sudden blows? This one struck Nunaga, as the saying goes, "all of a heap."

She happened to observe that the leader of the band was standing with his heels close against the ledge of rock already mentioned. In an instant she plunged at the robber's chest like a female thunderbolt. Having no room to stagger back, of course the man was tripped up by the ledge, and, tumbling headlong over it, went down the steep slope on the other side with an indignant roar.

The rest of the robbers were taken by surprise, and so immensely tickled with the humour of the thing that they burst into hearty laughter as they watched the frantic efforts of their chief to arrest his career.

All at the same instant, however, seemed to recover their presence of mind, for they looked round simultaneously with sudden gravity—and found that Nunaga was gone!

With a wild shout, they sprang after her—down the slope, crashing through the underwood, scattering right and left, and, in more than one instance, tumbling head over heels. They were quickly joined by their now furious leader; but they crashed, and tumbled, and searched in vain. Nunaga had vanished as completely and almost as mysteriously as if she had been a spirit.

The explanation is simple. She had merely dropped into the rut or hollow under the brow of the hill; and there she lay, covered with grasses and branches, listening to the growlings of indignation and astonishment expressed by the men when they re-assembled on the top of the mound to bewail their bad fortune.

"We've got the old witch, anyhow," growled the fierce robber, with a scowl at the bundle which was lying perfectly still.

"Away, men," cried their leader, "and search the other side of the mound. The young witch may have doubled on us like a rabbit, while we were seeking towards the hills."

Obedient to the command, they all dispersed again—this time towards the sea.

What Nunaga's thought was at the time we cannot tell, but there is reason to believe it must have been equivalent to "Now or never," for she leaped out of her place of concealment and made for the hills at the top of her speed. Truth requires us to add that she was not much better on her legs than were the men, for darkness, haste, and rugged ground are a trying combination. But there is this to be said for the girl: being small, she fell lightly; being rotund, she fell softly; being india-rubbery, she rebounded; and, being young, she took it easily. In a very short time she felt quite safe from pursuit.

Then she addressed herself diligently to find out the direction of the Eskimo camp, being filled with desperate anxiety for her old friend Kannoa. Strong, almost, as a young Greenland fawn, and gifted, apparently, with some of that animal's power to find its way through the woods, she was not long of hitting the right direction, and gaining the coast, along which she ran at her utmost speed.

On arriving—breathless and thoroughly exhausted—she found to her dismay that Angut, Simek, Rooney, and Okiok had left. The news of her capture had already been brought in by the women with the oomiak, and these men, with as many others as could be spared, had started off instantly to the rescue.

"But they are not long gone," said Nunaga's mother, by way of comforting her child.

"What matters that?" cried Nunaga in despair; "dear old Kannoa will be lost, for they know nothing of her danger."

While the poor girl spoke, her brother Ermigit began to prepare himself hastily for action.

"Fear not, sister," he said; "I will run to the great cliff, for I know it well. They left me to help to guard the camp, but are there not enough to guard it without me?"

With these words, the youth caught up a spear, and darted out of the hut.

Well was it for old Kannoa that night that Ermigit was, when roused, one of the fleetest runners of his tribe. Down to the shore he sprang—partly tumbled—and then sped along like the Arctic wind, which, we may remark, is fully as swift as more southerly breezes. The beach near the sea was mostly smooth, so that the absence of light was not a serious drawback. In a remarkably short space of time the lad overtook the rescue party, not far beyond the spot where the women had been surprised and Nunaga captured. Great was their satisfaction on hearing of the girl's safe return.

"It's a pity you didn't arrive half an hour sooner, however," said Rooney, "for poor Angut has gone off with a party towards the hills, in a state of wild despair, to carry on the search in that direction. But you look anxious, boy; what more have you to tell?"

In a few rapidly-spoken words Ermigit told of Kannoa's danger. Instant action was of course taken. One of the natives, who was well acquainted with the whole land, and knew the mound where the robbers had halted, was despatched with a strong party to search in that direction, while Rooney, Okiok, and the rest set off at a sharp run in the direction of the great cliff which they soon reached, panting like race-horses.

Scrambling to the top, they found no one there. By that time the short night of spring had passed, and the faint light of the coming day enabled them to make an investigation of the ground, which tended to prove that no one had been there recently.

"We can do nothing now but wait," said Red Rooney, as he sat on a projecting cliff, wiping the perspiration from his brow.

"But we might send some of the young men to look round,

and bring us word if they see any of the robbers," said Simek.

"If we do that," replied Okiok, "they will get wind of us, and clear off. Then they would kill my great-mother before casting her away."

"That's true, Okiok. We must keep quiet," said Rooney. "Besides, they are pretty sure to bring her to the cliff, for that is a favourite mode among you of getting rid of witches."

"But what if they *don't* come here?" asked Ippegoo.

"Then we must hope that they have slept on the mound," returned Okiok; "and Angut will be sure to find them, and kill them all in their sleep."

"Too good to hope for," murmured Arbalik.

"We must hide, if we don't want to be seen," suggested Simek.

Feeling the propriety of this suggestion, the whole party went into a cave which they found close at hand and sat down to wait as patiently as might be. Rooney was the last to enter. Before doing so he crept on hands and knees to the extreme edge of the cliff and looked down. Nothing was visible, however; only a black, unfathomable abyss. But he could hear the sullen roar of ocean as the waves rushed in and out of the rocky caverns far below. Drawing back with a shudder, a feeling of mingled horror, rage, and tender pity oppressed him as he thought of Kannoa's poor old bones being shattered on the rocks, or swallowed by the waves at the foot of the cliff, while behind and through Kannoa there rose up the vision of that grandmother in the old country, whose image seemed to have acquired a fixed habit of

R. M. Ballantyne

beckoning him to come home, with a remonstrative shake of the head and a kindly smile.

They had not long to wait. They had been seated about ten minutes in the cavern when the man who had been left outside to watch came gliding in on tip-toe, stepping high, and with a blazing look about the eyes.

"They come," he said in a hoarse whisper.

"*Who* come, you walrus?" whispered Okiok.

"The man with the witch."

On hearing this, Rooney, Okiok, and Simek went to the entrance of the cave, followed by the rest, who, however, were instructed to keep under cover till required, if no more than three or four men should arrive.

A few seconds later, and the robber chief appeared on the flat space in front of them. He was closely followed by a squat comrade and the fierce man with the bundle on his back. As they passed the cave, the bundle gave a pitiful wail.

This was enough. With a silent rush, like three bull-dogs, our heroes shot forth. Rooney, having forgotten his weapon, used his fist instead, planted his knuckles on the bridge of the leader's nose, and ruined it, as a bridge, for evermore. The robber went down, turned a complete back-somersault, regained his feet, and fled. Okiok seized the fierce man by the throat almost before he was aware of the attack, causing him to drop his bundle which Rooney was just in time to catch and carry into the cave. There he set it down tenderly, cut the fastenings of the skin, and freed the poor old woman's head.

It was a beautiful sight to see the livid hue and gaze of horror change into a flush of loving benignity when Kannoa observed who it was that kneeled beside her.

"Poor old woman!" shouted Rooney in her ear. "Are you much hurt?"

"No; not hurt at all; only squeezed too much. But I'm afraid for Nunaga. I think she got away, but I was bundled, when I last heard her voice."

"Fear no more, then, for Nunaga is safe," said Rooney; but at that moment all the men rushed from the cave, and he heard sounds outside which induced him to follow them and leave the old woman to look after herself.

On issuing from the cave, he saw that the fierce robber was the only one captured, and that he was on the point of receiving summary justice, for Simek and Okiok had hold of his arms, while Arbalik and Ippegoo held his legs and bore him to the edge of the cliff.

"Now then!" cried Simek.

"Stop, stop!" shouted Rooney.

"*One—two—heave!*" cried Okiok.

And they did heave—vigorously and together, so that the fierce man went out from their grasp like a huge stone from a Roman catapult. There was a hideous yell, and, after a brief but suggestive pause, an awful splash!

They did not wait to ascertain whether that fierce man managed to swim ashore—but certain it is that no one answering to his description has attempted to hurl a witch from those cliffs from that day to this.

CHAPTER TWENTY NINE

CONCLUSION

Need we enlarge on the despair of Angut being turned into joy on his return, when he found Nunaga and Kannoa safe and sound? We think not.

A few days thereafter our adventurers arrived at the settlement of the Kablunets; and these northern Eskimos soon forgot their rough experiences under the influence of the kind, hospitable reception they met with from the Moravian Brethren.

The joy of the brethren at welcoming Hans Egede, too, was very great, for they had heard of his recent expedition, and had begun to fear that he was lost. Not the less welcome was he that he came accompanied by a band of Eskimos who seemed not only willing to listen to the Gospel but more than usually able to understand it. The interest of these devoted men was specially roused by Angut, whom they at once recognised as of greatly superior mental power to his companions.

"I cannot help thinking," said Egede, in commenting on his character to one of the brethren, "that he must be a descendant of those Norse settlers who inhabited this part of

Greenland long, long ago, who, we think, were massacred by the natives, and the remains of whose buildings are still to be seen."

"It may be so," returned the brother; "your Viking country-men were vastly superior in brain-power to the Eskimos. We are glad and thankful that our Father has sent Angut to us, for it is not improbable that he may one day become an evangelist to his brethren in the far north."

But of all those who were assembled at the station at that time, Red Rooney was the man who rejoiced most, for there he found an English vessel on the eve of starting for the "old country," the captain of which was not only willing but glad to get such an able seaman to strengthen his crew.

"Angut," said Rooney, as they walked one evening by the margin of the sea, "it grieves me to the heart to leave you; but the best of friends must part. Even for your sake, much though I love you, I cannot remain here, now that I have got the chance of returning to my dear wife and bairns and my native land."

"But we shall meet again," replied Angut earnestly. "Does not your great Book teach that the Father of all is bringing all people to Himself in Jesus Christ? In the spirit-land Angut and Nunaga, Okiok, Nuna, Simek, and all the Innuit friends, when washed in the blood of Jesus, will again see the face of Ridroonee, and rejoice."

This was the first time that Angut had distinctly declared his faith, and it afforded matter for profound satisfaction to Rooney, who grasped and warmly shook his friend's hand.

"Right—right you are, Angut," he said; "I do believe that we shall meet again in the Fatherland, and that hope takes away much o' the sadness of parting. But you have not yet told me about the wedding. Have you arranged it with the Brethren?"

"Yes; it is fixed for the day beyond to-morrow."

"Good; an' the next day we sail—so, my friend, I'll have the satisfaction of dancing at your wedding before I go."

"I know not as to dancing," said Angut, with a grave smile, "but we are to have kick-ball, and a feast."

"I'm game for both, or any other sort o' fun you like," returned the seaman heartily.

While they were speaking they observed a youth running towards them in great haste, and in a state of violent excitement. A whale, he said, had stranded itself in a shallow bay not far off, and he was running to let the people of the settlement know the good news.

The commotion occasioned by this event is indescribable. Every man and boy who could handle a kayak took to the water with harpoon and lance. Ippegoo, Arbalik, Okiok, Simek, Norrak, and Ermigit were among them, in borrowed kayaks, and mad as the maddest with glee. Even Kajo joined them. He was as drunk as the proverbial fiddler, having obtained rum from the sailors, and much more solemn than an owl.

While these hastened to the conflict, the women and children who could run or walk proceeded by land to view the battle.

And it was indeed a grand fight! The unlucky monster had got thoroughly embayed, and was evidently in a state of consternation, for in its efforts to regain deep water it rushed hither and thither, thrusting its blunt snout continually on some shoal, and wriggling off again with difficulty and enormous splutter. The shouts of men, shrieks of women, and yells of children co-mingled in stupendous discord.

Simek, the mighty hunter, was first to launch his harpoon. It went deep and was well aimed. Blood dyed the sea at once, and the efforts of the whale to escape were redoubled. There was also danger in this attack, for no one could tell, each time the creature got into water deep enough to float in, to what point of the shore its next rush would be.

"Look out!" cried Rooney in alarm, for, being close to Arbalik in a kayak, he saw that the whale was coming straight at them. It ran on a shoal when close to them, doubled round in terror and whirled its great tail aloft.

Right over Arbalik's head the fan-like mass quivered for one moment. The youth did not give it a chance. Over he went and shot down into the water like an eel, just as the tail came down like a thunder-clap on his kayak, and reduced it to a jumble of its shattered elements, while Rooney paddled out of danger. Arbalik swam ashore, and landed just in time to see the whale rise out of the water, lifting Ippegoo in his kayak on its shoulders. The electrified youth uttered a shriek of horror in which the tone of surprise was discernible, slid off, kayak and all, into the sea—and was none the worse!

By this time some dozens of harpoons had been fixed in the body of the whale, and the number of bladders attached to them interfered slightly with its movements, but did not render an approach to it by any means safer. At last Simek, losing patience, made a bold rush in his kayak, and drove his lance deep into the huge creature's side. The act was greeted with a cheer—or something like one,—which was repeated when Red Rooney followed suit successfully. Okiok and his two sons were not slow to repeat the process. Other Eskimos

R. M. Ballantyne

rushed in, hovered round, and acted their part, so that finally the whale was killed and hauled nearly out of the water by the united exertion of the entire population of the land.

Then succeeded the distribution of the prize.

Eskimos have peculiar and not unreasonable laws on such matters. If two hunters strike a seal at the same time, they divide it. The same holds in regard to wild-fowl or deer. If a dead seal is found with a harpoon sticking in it, the finder keeps the seal, but restores the harpoon to the owner. The harpooner of a walrus claims the head and tail, while any one may take away as much as he can carry of the carcass. But when a whale is captured, the harpooners have no special advantage. There is such a superabundance of wealth that all—even spectators—may cut and come again as often and as long as they please.

When, therefore, the whale whose capture we have described was dead, hundreds of men and boys mounted at once, knife in hand, on the carcass, and the scene of blood and confusion that ensued baffles description.

"Won't we stuff to-night!" remarked Kabelaw to her sister, as they went home bending under a weight of blubber.

"Ay—and to-morrow," replied Sigokow.

"And some days beyond to-morrow," observed old Kannoa, who staggered after them under a lighter load of the spoil.

But it was not the Eskimos alone who derived benefit from this unexpected prize. The captain of the English ship also got some barrels of oil and a large quantity of whalebone to fill up his cargo, and the bright shawls and real *iron* knives that were given in exchange soon graced the shoulders of the native women and the belts of the men.

It was indeed a time of immense jubilation—for every one was gratified more or less—from the chief of the Moravian Brethren down to Tumbler and Pussi, who absolutely wallowed in fun and unctuous food, while Angut and Nunaga were of course supremely happy.

The wedding ceremony, performed by Hans Egede, we need hardly say, was simple, and the festivities which followed were not complex. The game at kick-ball which preceded the wedding was admittedly one of the best that had ever been played at that station, partly, no doubt, because the captain and crew of the English ship, headed by Red Rooney, took part in it.

Strange to say, the only man who seemed to be at all cast down on that occasion was Ippegoo. He was found by his mother in the evening in a retired spot by the sea, sitting on the rocks with a very disconsolate countenance.

"My son, what is the matter?"

"Mother, my heart is heavy. I cannot forget Ujarak."

"But he treated you ill, my son."

"Sometimes—not always. Often he was kind—and—and I loved him. I cannot help it."

"Grieve not, Ippe," rejoined pleasant little Kunelik. "Do we not know now that we shall meet him again in the great Fatherland?"

The poor youth was comforted. He dried his eyes, and went home with his mother. Yet he did not cease to mourn for his departed wizard friend.

We will not harrow the reader's feelings by describing the leave-taking of the Eskimos from their friend the Kablunet. After he was gone those men of the North remained a considerable time at the settlement, listening to the missionaries as they revealed the love of God to man in Jesus Christ.

What resulted from this of course we cannot tell, but of this we are certain—that their "labour was not in vain in the Lord." When the time comes for the Creator to reveal His plans to man, surely it will be found that no word spoken, no cup of water given, by these Danish and Moravian Christians, shall lose its appropriate reward.

When at last the northern men and their families stood on the sea-shore, with their kayaks, oomiaks and families ready, Angut stood forth, and, grasping Hans Egede by the hand, said earnestly—

"Brother, farewell till we meet again. I go now to carry the Good News to my kindred who dwell where the ice-mountains cover the land and sea."

* * * * *

But what of the Kablunet? Shall we permit him to slip quietly through our fingers, and disappear? Nay, verily.

He reached England. He crossed over to Ireland. There, in a well-remembered cottage-home, he found a blooming "widow," who discovered to her inexpressible joy that she was still a wife! He found six children, who had grown so tremendously out of all remembrance that their faces seemed like a faint but familiar dream, which had to be dreamed over again a good deal and studied much, before the attainment by the seaman of a satisfactory state of mind. And, last, he found a little old woman with wrinkled brow and toothless gums, who looked at and listened to him with benignant wonder, and whose visage reminded him powerfully of another little old woman who dwelt in the land of ice and snow where he used to be known as the Kablunet.

This Kablunet—*alias* Ridroonee,—now regretfully makes his bow and exit from our little stage as RED ROONEY, THE LAST OF THE CREW.

THE END

R. M. Ballantyne

Choose from Thousands of 1stWorldLibrary Classics By

A. M. Barnard
Ada Leverson
Adolphus William Ward
Aesop
Agatha Christie
Alexander Aaronsohn
Alexander Kielland
Alexandre Dumas
Alfred Gatty
Alfred Ollivant
Alice Duer Miller
Alice Turner Curtis
Alice Dunbar
Allen Chapman
Alleyne Ireland
Ambrose Bierce
Amelia E. Barr
Amory H. Bradford
Andrew Lang
Andrew McFarland Davis
Andy Adams
Angela Brazil
Anna Alice Chapin
Anna Sewell
Annie Besant
Annie Hamilton Donnell
Annie Payson Call
Annie Roe Carr
Annonaymous
Anton Chekhov
Archibald Lee Fletcher
Arnold Bennett
Arthur C. Benson
Arthur Conan Doyle
Arthur M. Winfield
Arthur Ransome
Arthur Schnitzler
Arthur Train
Atticus
B.H. Baden-Powell
B. M. Bower
B. C. Chatterjee
Baroness Emmuska Orczy
Baroness Orczy
Basil King
Bayard Taylor
Ben Macomber
Bertha Muzzy Bower
Bjornstjerne Bjornson

Booth Tarkington
Boyd Cable
Bram Stoker
C. Collodi
C. E. Orr
C. M. Ingleby
Carolyn Wells
Catherine Parr Traill
Charles A. Eastman
Charles Amory Beach
Charles Dickens
Charles Dudley Warner
Charles Farrar Browne
Charles Ives
Charles Kingsley
Charles Klein
Charles Hanson Towne
Charles Lathrop Pack
Charles Romyn Dake
Charles Whibley
Charles Willing Beale
Charlotte M. Braeme
Charlotte M. Yonge
Charlotte Perkins Stetson
Clair W. Hayes
Clarence Day Jr.
Clarence E. Mulford
Clemence Housman
Confucius
Coningsby Dawson
Cornelis DeWitt Wilcox
Cyril Burleigh
D. H. Lawrence
Daniel Defoe
David Garnett
Dinah Craik
Don Carlos Janes
Donald Keyhoe
Dorothy Kilner
Dougan Clark
Douglas Fairbanks
E. Nesbit
E. P. Roe
E. Phillips Oppenheim
E. S. Brooks
Earl Barnes
Edgar Rice Burroughs
Edith Van Dyne
Edith Wharton

Edward Everett Hale
Edward J. O'Biren
Edward S. Ellis
Edwin L. Arnold
Eleanor Atkins
Eleanor Hallowell Abbott
Eliot Gregory
Elizabeth Gaskell
Elizabeth McCracken
Elizabeth Von Arnim
Ellem Key
Emerson Hough
Emilie F. Carlen
Emily Bronte
Emily Dickinson
Enid Bagnold
Enilor Macartney Lane
Erasmus W. Jones
Ernie Howard Pie
Ethel May Dell
Ethel Turner
Ethel Watts Mumford
Eugene Sue
Eugenie Foa
Eugene Wood
Eustace Hale Ball
Evelyn Everett-green
Everard Cotes
F. H. Cheley
F. J. Cross
F. Marion Crawford
Fannie E. Newberry
Federick Austin Ogg
Ferdinand Ossendowski
Fergus Hume
Florence A. Kilpatrick
Fremont B. Deering
Francis Bacon
Francis Darwin
Frances Hodgson Burnett
Frances Parkinson Keyes
Frank Gee Patchin
Frank Harris
Frank Jewett Mather
Frank L. Packard
Frank V. Webster
Frederic Stewart Isham
Frederick Trevor Hill
Frederick Winslow Taylor

Friedrich Kerst
Friedrich Nietzsche
Fyodor Dostoyevsky
G.A. Henty
G.K. Chesterton
Gabrielle E. Jackson
Garrett P. Serviss
Gaston Leroux
George A. Warren
George Ade
Geroge Bernard Shaw
George Cary Eggleston
George Durston
George Ebers
George Eliot
George Gissing
George MacDonald
George Meredith
George Orwell
George Sylvester Viereck
George Tucker
George W. Cable
George Wharton James
Gertrude Atherton
Gordon Casserly
Grace E. King
Grace Gallatin
Grace Greenwood
Grant Allen
Guillermo A. Sherwell
Gulielma Zollinger
Gustav Flaubert
H. A. Cody
H. B. Irving
H.C. Bailey
H. G. Wells
H. H. Munro
H. Irving Hancock
H. R. Naylor
H. Rider Haggard
H. W. C. Davis
Haldeman Julius
Hall Caine
Hamilton Wright Mabie
Hans Christian Andersen
Harold Avery
Harold McGrath
Harriet Beecher Stowe
Harry Castlemon
Harry Coghill
Harry Houidini

Hayden Carruth
Helent Hunt Jackson
Helen Nicolay
Hendrik Conscience
Hendy David Thoreau
Henri Barbusse
Henrik Ibsen
Henry Adams
Henry Ford
Henry Frost
Henry James
Henry Jones Ford
Henry Seton Merriman
Henry W Longfellow
Herbert A. Giles
Herbert Carter
Herbert N. Casson
Herman Hesse
Hildegard G. Frey
Homer
Honore De Balzac
Horace B. Day
Horace Walpole
Horatio Alger Jr.
Howard Pyle
Howard R. Garis
Hugh Lofting
Hugh Walpole
Humphry Ward
Ian Maclaren
Inez Haynes Gillmore
Irving Bacheller
Isabel Cecilia Williams
Isabel Hornibrook
Israel Abrahams
Ivan Turgenev
J.G.Austin
J. Henri Fabre
J. M. Barrie
J. M. Walsh
J. Macdonald Oxley
J. R. Miller
J. S. Fletcher
J. S. Knowles
J. Storer Clouston
J. W. Duffield
Jack London
Jacob Abbott
James Allen
James Andrews
James Baldwin

James Branch Cabell
James DeMille
James Joyce
James Lane Allen
James Lane Allen
James Oliver Curwood
James Oppenheim
James Otis
James R. Driscoll
Jane Abbott
Jane Austen
Jane L. Stewart
Janet Aldridge
Jens Peter Jacobsen
Jerome K. Jerome
Jessie Graham Flower
John Buchan
John Burroughs
John Cournos
John F. Kennedy
John Gay
John Glasworthy
John Habberton
John Joy Bell
John Kendrick Bangs
John Milton
John Philip Sousa
John Taintor Foote
Jonas Lauritz Idemil Lie
Jonathan Swift
Joseph A. Altsheler
Joseph Carey
Joseph Conrad
Joseph E. Badger Jr
Joseph Hergesheimer
Joseph Jacobs
Jules Vernes
Julian Hawthrone
Julie A Lippmann
Justin Huntly McCarthy
Kakuzo Okakura
Karle Wilson Baker
Kate Chopin
Kenneth Grahame
Kenneth McGaffey
Kate Langley Bosher
Kate Langley Bosher
Katherine Cecil Thurston
Katherine Stokes
L. A. Abbot
L. T. Meade

L. Frank Baum
Latta Griswold
Laura Dent Crane
Laura Lee Hope
Laurence Housman
Lawrence Beasley
Leo Tolstoy
Leonid Andreyev
Lewis Carroll
Lewis Sperry Chafer
Lilian Bell
Lloyd Osbourne
Louis Hughes
Louis Joseph Vance
Louis Tracy
Louisa May Alcott
Lucy Fitch Perkins
Lucy Maud Montgomery
Luther Benson
Lydia Miller Middleton
Lyndon Orr
M. Corvus
M. H. Adams
Margaret E. Sangster
Margret Howth
Margaret Vandercook
Margaret W. Hungerford
Margret Penrose
Maria Edgeworth
Maria Thompson Daviess
Mariano Azuela
Marion Polk Angellotti
Mark Overton
Mark Twain
Mary Austin
Mary Catherine Crowley
Mary Cole
Mary Hastings Bradley
Mary Roberts Rinehart
Mary Rowlandson
M. Wollstonecraft Shelley
Maud Lindsay
Max Beerbohm
Myra Kelly
Nathaniel Hawthrone
Nicolo Machiavelli
O. F. Walton
Oscar Wilde

Owen Johnson
P.G. Wodehouse
Paul and Mabel Thorne
Paul G. Tomlinson
Paul Severing
Percy Brebner
Percy Keese Fitzhugh
Peter B. Kyne
Plato
Quincy Allen
R. Derby Holmes
R. L. Stevenson
R. S. Ball
Rabindranath Tagore
Rahul Alvares
Ralph Bonehill
Ralph Henry Barbour
Ralph Victor
Ralph Waldo Emmerson
Rene Descartes
Ray Cummings
Rex Beach
Rex E. Beach
Richard Harding Davis
Richard Jefferies
Richard Le Gallienne
Robert Barr
Robert Frost
Robert Gordon Anderson
Robert L. Drake
Robert Lansing
Robert Lynd
Robert Michael Ballantyne
Robert W. Chambers
Rosa Nouchette Carey
Rudyard Kipling
Saint Augustine
Samuel B. Allison
Samuel Hopkins Adams
Sarah Bernhardt
Sarah C. Hallowell
Selma Lagerlof
Sherwood Anderson
Sigmund Freud
Standish O'Grady
Stanley Weyman
Stella Benson
Stella M. Francis

Stephen Crane
Stewart Edward White
Stijn Streuvels
Swami Abhedananda
Swami Parmananda
T. S. Ackland
T. S. Arthur
The Princess Der Ling
Thomas A. Janvier
Thomas A Kempis
Thomas Anderton
Thomas Bailey Aldrich
Thomas Bulfinch
Thomas De Quincey
Thomas Dixon
Thomas H. Huxley
Thomas Hardy
Thomas More
Thornton W. Burgess
U. S. Grant
Upton Sinclair
Valentine Williams
Various Authors
Vaughan Kester
Victor Appleton
Victor G. Durham
Victoria Cross
Virginia Woolf
Wadsworth Camp
Walter Camp
Walter Scott
Washington Irving
Wilbur Lawton
Wilkie Collins
Willa Cather
Willard F. Baker
William Dean Howells
William le Queux
W. Makepeace Thackeray
William W. Walter
William Shakespeare
Winston Churchill
Yei Theodora Ozaki
Yogi Ramacharaka
Young E. Allison
Zane Grey

www.ingramcontent.com/pod-product-compliance
Lightning Source LLC
Chambersburg PA
CBHW030239280626
47172CB00012B/81